OUT OF
THE DARK

OUT OF THE DARK

The Complete Guide to Beings From Beyond

BRAD STEIGER

KENSINGTON BOOKS
http://www.kensingtonbooks.com

Some of the names and dates have been changed to protect the privacy of the percipients.

KENSINGTON BOOKS are published by

Kensington Publishing Corp.
850 Third Avenue
New York, NY 10022

ISBN 1-57566-896-3

First Kensington Trade Paperback Printing: September 2001
10 9 8 7 6 5 4 3 2 1

Printed in the United States of America

Contents

Introduction

WHEN NIGHTMARES COME TO LIFE

When I began collecting data about sea monsters, hauntings, and strange, unidentified creatures as an eleven-year-old Iowa schoolboy back in 1947, I would have found it difficult to believe any elf or friendly ghost who would have predicted that one day I would travel to all fifty states, most of the Canadian provinces, and many foreign countries in search of the unknown and the mysterious entities that dwell in the shadows.

Certainly back then, perhaps even more than today, my interest in things that went bump in the dark was considered a most peculiar hobby. It was fashionable to discard all such accounts of monsters and ghosts as being due to psychological aberrations, intentional or unintentional hoaxes, or the misinterpretation of natural phenomena and/or perfectly natural animals. Such things as weird apelike creatures wandering about in the forests or sightings of flying saucers from other worlds just could not be real things—because they were just plain impossible.

Fifty-four years later, I am of the opinion that more impossible things are becoming possible every day. It seems as though each year the laws of our physical universe are being modified, adapted, amended, and restructured. Learned and respected physics professors speak almost casually of parallel universes, in-between universes, effects preceding causes, other dimensions of being, and alternate realities. Thoughts and concepts recited by the mad scientists in the science fiction movies of my youth have become an accepted part of everyday reality in my senior years.

Before I continue and let all the monsters in this present book out of their cages to charge on the unsuspecting reader, I must say that perhaps as many as 90 percent of all the reports that I have collected over the past half-century can quite likely be explained as the misinterpretation of natural phenomena, perfectly normal animals somehow misidentified, and the suggestibility of excited human minds. But then there is that 10 percent of the sightings wherein I completely believe that those witnesses who have claimed to have experienced monsters appearing from out of the dark have truly had genuine encounters with an unidentified *something* and have truthfully described whatever it was they saw as accurately as possible.

Over the past five decades, I have come to believe that the monster business is much more complex than some casual creature hunters might expect. For example, some creatures that inhabit the dark corners of our planet—Bigfoot, lake monsters, sea serpents—may truly be unidentified life-forms indigenous to Earth. But in other cases, Bigfoot, together with such monsters as werewolves and vampires, might be archetypal, quasireal entities that have been created by the human collective unconscious. In other instances, entities such as the elves, fairies, and alien-type beings might be members of a paraphysical tribe that have coexisted on this planet with us as a kind of companion species. Somehow, we participate with all these creatures according to some as yet unknown evolutionary design.

Some monsters may, quite frankly, be supernatural beings, frightening demons, such as those described in the scriptures of many world religions as the messengers and legions of a disruptive and evil Master.

Maybe all these creatures that we call monsters are really the inhabitants of another dimension. Entities that we consider werewolves, ghosts, and long-legged beasties might very well originate in an adjacent time-space continuum, which actually coexists on Earth with us—but because they exist on another vibrational level, we see them (and presumably they see us) only under extraordinary circumstances. From time to time, an opening, a doorway between dimensions, appears, and these citizens from another dimension—frightening and grotesque to our human eyes—walk among us for a brief time before wandering back into the shadow world from which they came.

But enough of the theorizing. Let us get on with our expedition into the unknown, into the darkness, where, indeed, monsters—whatever they may really be—do most certainly exist. And by the time you have finished reading this book, I suspect you will have decided that it is better to be an armchair adventurer when it comes to leaving the safety of your home to hunt those creatures who prefer the night and the darkness. For it is in the dark, when you are far from the security of your locked door, far from the comforting light that streams from your lamp, far from the cheer and warmth of other human voices, that nightmares truly come alive.

One

GHOSTS

The moment in June 1994 that David and Mary Jacobsen first saw the magnificent and ornate Victorian house that stood atop a forested hill, it had seemed like their dream home in the country. With its lofty, spired towers stretching toward the sky, the old manse seemed as if it were an armored sentinel that would guard them from the harsh realities and negativity of the outside world. To make the place even more appealing, the drive from the end of the lane to David's office in the city took less than an hour—and the picturesque scenery enroute would be certain to lift his spirits, regardless of whatever company crises awaited him.

If they hadn't been so excited over finding what they believed to be their perfect new home, David and Mary might have asked the real estate agent why it was that the house had sat empty and uninhabited for so many years. If they hadn't been so eager to move into the place, they might have taken more time to walk through the old house and sensed the dark and ominous presence that dwelt within its shadowy corridors.

David and Mary, both in their early forties, had grown up

in the same city in upstate New York and had lived and worked there all of their lives. Idealistically, they envisioned this sprawling house in the country as the perfect place to bring up their kids, eleven-year-old Mark and eight-year-old Alice. As two realists, however, they decided to take advantage of the fact that the place had sat empty for several years and make an offer to rent with an option to buy. After all, neither David nor Mary could be absolutely certain that either they or their children could adjust to country life. It would be unwise to invest all of their savings and their immediate financial future in a move that might not work out for them. Fortunately for the Jacobsens, the real estate agency did not hesitate to accept their offer to rent—for the house of their dreams would soon turn into a waking nightmare.

It was on that Sunday afternoon, just two days before the movers would arrive with their furniture, that the Jacobsens first experienced a strange, eerie presence in certain rooms.

Mary, an accomplished illustrator of children's books, was trying to decide whether one of the upstairs rooms that had especially good natural light would serve as her studio or be one of the children's bedrooms. Out of the corner of an eye, she thought she saw someone moving in the hallway. When she called out, she received no response—but a few minutes later, she felt a firm, solid hand on her left shoulder.

Expecting to turn around and face her husband, Mary could not suppress a startled scream when she saw that she was alone—and there was no one behind her. She was suddenly overwhelmed with a sensation of cold that chilled her to her bones.

At about the same time, David was experiencing a similar phenomenon as he was using a tape measure to mark off an area on a wall where he intended to place bookcases. He remembered seeing what he could only describe as a strange kind of shadow that seemed to be moving toward him from the hallway. Later, he said that the very sight of the dark presence made him feel as if he had been suddenly drenched with ice water.

Two sensible, modern individuals, who prided themselves on their lack of superstitious beliefs, Mary and David Jacobsen attributed their strange experiences to tricks of shadows and light, fatigue over working long hours packing their household belongings for the move to the country, and a general case of nerves over their big decision to move from the familiar environment of the city to the unfamiliar trappings of rustic living.

"I think we both knew that there was something strange going on in that old house," David wrote in his report of their experience with the supernatural for the *Steiger Questionnaire of Mystical, Paranormal, and UFO Experiences.* "But we had made such a major commitment in renting the place and packing up all of our stuff, that we stubbornly wanted to see it through. Although neither of us was the least bit superstitious, I think at that point we were willing to battle ghosts or monsters for the place."

However, it did not take very long after the Jacobsens had made their move to the grand old Victorian mansion that their resolve to fight against the unknown began quickly to weaken. Especially when whatever was in the house started to trouble their children.

"We had been in the place only two days," Mary said, "when we were awakened late one night by little Alice crying that someone was in her room. After we managed to calm her, she said that an ugly old witch had come out of her closet and stared at her."

By that time, Mark had left his own bedroom and had joined his parents in Alice's room. He told them that he had seen an old woman with a cane in the upstairs hallway on the first night they moved in. Unfamiliar with country living, the boy had assumed she was a nosy old neighbor come to check them out.

When he approached her and asked if he could help her with anything, she had stared at him and walked down the back stairs. Mark went on to say that he had seen her on two other occasions—once looking in at him from an outside window as he watched television, and another time, standing at the outside gate, looking up at his room.

"When we asked Mark why he hadn't said anything before," David said, "he shrugged and reminded us that we had lectured him about getting along with their new country neighbors. He had seen some television programs where it appeared that countryfolk just dropped in to visit one another without invitation. He assumed that the stern-looking old woman was just an eccentric neighbor lady who from time to time would wander into the house without being invited."

The next night, the "eccentric neighbor lady" got downright mean. Alice cried out in pain, shrieking that the "ugly old witch" had pulled her hair. Awakened by his sister's screams, Mark told his parents that he had had a nightmare in which the old woman had appeared in his room and had shaken her cane at him in a threatening manner.

"We tried so hard to convince the children—and ourselves— that they had simply had some bad dreams," Mary said, "but we remembered our eerie experience with the cold, chilling shadows before we moved into the old house."

Two days later, as David was standing on a ladder, stretching to hang a picture on a living room wall, he felt a sudden, stinging blow across his back, as if someone had swatted him smartly with a stick—or a cane. "I actually had a red welt across my back where the invisible object had struck me," he said.

That same evening, Mary went to her studio to find that her easel had been tipped over and the canvas on which she had been painting had been ripped. "I knew that neither of the children would do such a thing," she said. "They regarded my studio as sacrosanct, and they would not have been playing in there and accidentally knocked over the easel. They loved watching me paint—and they understood that this was Mommy's way of helping to pay the family's bills."

Later that night, as the Jacobsen family lay sleeping, they were awakened by the sounds of someone—or *something*—pounding on the walls of their bedrooms and the hallway. "The sharp, striking blows sounded for all the world like someone hitting the walls with a stick or a cane," David said. "When Mary and I rushed out to the hall to investigate, we clearly saw the image of an old woman with a cane staring malevolently at us. She was surrounded by an eerie, greenish glow, and we heard her tell us in a high-pitched shout to leave the house at once. It was her home, she screamed, and she did not tolerate interlopers."

According to the Jacobsens' report, they attempted to stick it out in the old house for another few weeks before they could no longer endure the psychic and emotional stresses caused by the ghost of the angry old woman. "Our kids were on the brink of hysteria and they would never be anywhere alone in the house," Mary said. "They insisted on sleeping with us, and they seldom left our sides."

When David and Mary were forced to accept the grim truth that they had encountered something beyond their previous beliefs and understanding about the boundaries of reality, they knew that they had to leave the place and return to the city. "We crowded into a two-bedroom apartment for nearly a year before we could afford a larger place," David said.

"Before we left the old house in the country," David said, "we learned from some of the neighbors that many years ago, around 1917, a young woman had inherited the place from her father. Although she had been engaged to be married at the time, her fiancé was killed in the trenches during World War I. Heartbroken, she had never married and had become an embittered woman, walking about with a cane after she had injured her legs in a fall down the back stairs. She had died in 1972, and the very next family to inhabit the house had soon moved out, insisting that it was haunted by the ghost of an old lady with a cane. Ever since that time, the house had only occasional short-term occupants, who always moved out after a few weeks, complaining that the place was haunted."

Although the Jacobsens sought legal redress, stating that the real estate agent had not informed them that the old house was haunted, they soon realized that proving the reality of a nasty ghost in a sterile courtroom environment would be very unproductive.

"We had to bite the bullet and accept the loss of our moving expenses and the first and last months' rental deposit," David said, "but the real estate agency did waive the remainder of the contract. Thank God we didn't buy the place, for in all conscience, we could never have sold it to anyone, and we probably could never have recovered from that financial drain. As it was, we just hope and pray that Alice and Mark will recover psychically and emotionally from the experience of sharing that old mansion with a very inhospitable ghost. And as far as that goes, Mary and I still wake up some nights thinking we hear that old lady hitting her cane against our bedroom wall."

GHOSTS, GHOSTS EVERYWHERE

Is it possible that the ghost of a previous owner still walked the shadowy corridors of the old Victorian house that David and Mary Jacobsen hoped would one day become their dream home? These two individuals, who swear that they are not superstitious and did not believe in ghosts prior to their experience in the sprawling mansion, vehemently reject any suggestion that they allowed their imaginations to run away with them or that they yielded to the power of suggestion after they moved into a house that some might consider a classic candidate for a haunting. The Jacobsens care not one whit if the skeptical have their own theories for what they might have encountered in those darkened hallways.

"The doubters and the skeptics weren't there," David Jacobsen said, responding firmly to those who question the true nature of the haunting. "We were! We know that we experienced something that we could not explain by any of our known scientific laws of physical reality."

Ghosts, unbound by the "known laws of physical reality," are materializing everywhere—even in prison cells.

On October 30, 1997, accused murderer Craig Rabinowitz told a shocked courtroom in Norristown, Pennsylvania, that the spirits of his dead wife, his dead father-in-law, and that of Rabinowitz's own deceased father materialized in his cell on the night before his trial was to begin for murder and 32 counts of felony fraud and told him to confess to the murder of his wife and the other crimes. Prosecutor Bruce L. Castor was ready to present evidence that Rabinowitz was $671,000 in debt from deceptive business practices and had planned to take $2.1 million from his wife Stefanie's life insurance policy, stock holdings, and the sale of their home and run away with an exotic dancer when Rabinowitz stunned the courtroom by confessing to all charges. As he sat sobbing on the witness stand, Rabinowitz said that Stefanie's ghost had told him that it was "time to do what was right."

Ghosts are everywhere—and we can never go far enough in any direction to escape them. When television executives were seeking a remote Australian location for the next installment of the popular "Survivor" series, they selected a spot near the Herbert River Gorge, nearly 1,200 miles from Sydney and almost 100 miles from the nearest town. Although the area is sparsely populated by living humans, local residents claim the place is heavily populated by the spirits of hundreds of Aborigines who were brutally massacred in the gorge a century ago. According to local ranchers and townsfolk, ghastly screams have been heard coming from the gorge when darkness falls, and the place is generally avoided for fear of disturbing the restless spirits of the slaughtered native people.

According to the "USA Snapshots" feature in the April 20, 1998 issue of *USA Today,* 52 percent of all adult Americans believe that such encounters with the dead are possible.

The December 1996 issue of *George,* a monthly magazine of political commentary, revealed, in their survey of what Americans believed, that 39 percent of those polled believed in ghosts and haunted houses.

In his 1994 analysis of a national sociological survey, Jeffrey S. Levin, an associate professor at Eastern Virginia Medical School, found that two-thirds of Americans claimed to have had at least one mystical experience. Of that remarkably high number of experiencers, 39.9 percent said that they had had an encounter with a ghost or had achieved contact with the spirit of a deceased person.

According to our own *Steiger Questionnaire of Mystical, Paranormal, and UFO Experiences,* a survey process that we began in 1967 and have since distributed to over 30,000 men and women, 48.9 percent are convinced that they have seen a ghost, 43 percent have perceived the spirit of a departed loved one, and 63 percent state that they have encountered spirit entities in haunted places.

STUDYING AND IDENTIFYING GHOSTS
AND RESTLESS SPIRITS

Although people have been reporting seeing ghosts and the spirits of the dead since our earliest historical records of human activity, the first organized effort to study such phenomena occurred in 1882, as the first major undertaking of the newly formed Society for Psychical Research (SPR) in London. By means of a circulated questionnaire, the SPR asked whether its recipients had ever, when they believed themselves to be completely awake, experienced some kind of visual or auditory phenomena. Of the 17,000 people who responded, 1,684 answered "yes." From this, the committee members who were conducting the survey estimated that nearly 10 percent of the population of London had undergone some kind of paranormal manifestation, and they sent forms requesting additional details to all those who had indicated such encounters. Subsequent investigation and interviews enabled the early psychical researchers to arrive at a number of basic premises regarding ghosts.

The committee was able to conclude that although ghosts are connected with other events besides death, they are more likely to be linked with death than with anything else. Visual sightings of ghosts were the most common, and of such cases reported, nearly one-quarter had been shared by more than one percipient. Those who answered the second form of the questionnaire requesting more information stated that they had not been ill when they had witnessed the paranormal visitations and they insisted that these manifestations were quite unlike the bizarre, nightmarish creatures which might appear during high fevers or high alcoholic consumption. Of those cases in which the percipients had experienced auditory phenomena, such as hearing voices, one-third were collective, that is, witnessed by more than one percipient at the same time.

After the findings of the research committee had been made public, the SPR began to be flooded by personal accounts of spontaneous cases of ghosts and spirits. In order to aid the committee in the handling of such an influx of information, the SPR worked out a series of questions that could be applied to each case that came in. Among the questions were the following:

Is the account firsthand? Has the principal witness been corroborated? Was the percipient awake at the time? Was the apparition recognized? Was the percipient anxious or in a state of expectancy? Could relevant details have been read back into the narrative after the event?

Today, almost 120 years after the British Society for Psychical Research began its earnest efforts to chart and categorize ghosts, what percentage of London's population believes in ghosts? According to a survey released on March 20, 2000, by television station GMTV in London, 42 percent believe in ghosts and almost half of this number said that they had seen or felt the presence of a ghost.

Since those early surveys and attempts to study and identify haunting phenomena, psychical researchers have long recognized four main categories of ghosts and apparitions:

1. Experimental cases, in which an individual has deliberately attempted to make his "apparition," his ghostly image, appear to a particular participant, as in efforts to project one's spiritual essence during out-of-body experience.

2. "Crisis apparitions," in which a recognized apparition is seen, heard, or felt when the actual individual represented by the ghostly image is undergoing a crisis, especially death.
3. "Postmortem apparitions," in which a recognized ghostly image is seen or heard long after the actual person represented by the apparition has died.
4. Ghosts or apparitions which habitually appear in a room, house, or locale.

As a result of more than forty years investigating a wide range of supernatural occurrences, I have compiled my own definitions of haunting phenomena. According to my research and my personal encounters with entities from out of the dark, the things that are going bump in the night may be:

Spirits of the Dead, in which the manifestations are caused by earthbound spirits of deceased humans who have been unable to quit their attachments to the people, places, or things of the material world and have not yet progressed into the Light of a higher spiritual dimension.

Spirit Residue, in which the ghost that is seen may actually be a kind of holographic image that has been somehow impressed into the environment by powerful human emotions such as hate, jealously, fear, and pain. Rather than an actual spirit entity, however, the "ghost" is the product of psychic residue and may be seen by a psychically sensitive percipient as if it were an animated photograph.

Poltergeists, in which the violent and disruptive outbursts of haunting phenomena may be caused by the psyche of a living human—most often an adolescent or someone undergoing severe psychological adjustment or psychic upheaval.

Phantoms, in which the same ghostly forms have been seen in the same locales over so many years by so many people that they may literally begin to assume independent existences of their own, thus becoming, in effect, psychic marionettes, responding to the fears and expectations of the percipients.

Animal Spirits, in which the spiritual essence of a beloved pet that was devoted to a person or a place or any other animal that became associated with a specific location may continue its attachments after physical death.

Nature Spirits, in which those entities who have made themselves known to humans for centuries as fairies, elves, or devas guard and defend areas held sacred by them and often produce very lively paranormal phenomena in the process.

Spirit Parasites, in which vulnerable and unaware humans have been possessed by grotesque entities and have committed acts of violence toward their families. These spirit beings, perhaps the traditional demons, accumulate in places where murders and other violent deeds have been perpetrated.

As we shall see, there can be overlapping of the above phenomena, such as when poltergeistic manifestations may be triggered by a haunting, thus blending to create a maddeningly chaotic carnival of terror for the percipients.

SPIRITS OF THE DEAD

Their Home Was Built Over a Burial Ground

When the Lawson family moved into a home that was only two years old and had been constructed on the outskirts of a picturesque village in Vermont, they certainly didn't expect it to be haunted. What they discovered after the manifestations began was that a portion of the house had been constructed over a mass grave that contained the bodies of nearly one hundred men, women, and children from a Native American tribe that had been deliberately infected with smallpox in the early 1800s. Since communicable diseases such as smallpox had been unknown in the Americas prior to the European invasion, it was a common ploy of inhumane whites who lusted for tribal lands to trade to the tribespeople blankets that had been used by those afflicted with smallpox . With no generational immunity to such diseases, entire villages would quickly fall prey to the epidemic and be annihilated without a shot having been fired. Such had been the case in the mass burial site that now lay beneath the recreation room of the Lawsons' new home.

"Let me say at the outset of this interview," Patricia Lawson told me, "my husband Cliff, myself, and our three daughters have learned how thin the line can be between the living and the dead—even if those unfortunate souls died well over 170 years ago."

Before the Lawsons had learned that a portion of their home had been constructed on sacred ground, their three daughters—Teri, 16; Christie, 13; and Kim, 10—had complained of strange things occurring in the family room. The overhead lights, as well as the television set, the CD player, and the computer would turn on and off without anyone being near any of the switches. The same was true of the faucets in the bathroom.

"The girls started complaining that the house was haunted," Patricia said, "but Cliff and I did the practical, rational things of checking the wiring, the switch boxes, and the plumbing. The trouble was, we found everything to be fine and in order."

About twelve days after they had moved in, Kim and Christie screamed that they had seen shadows moving across the walls of the recreation room. When Patricia went to investigate, she saw what appeared to be the shadows of two or three people moving in a repetitious pattern that she eventually decided was a dance of some kind.

"The next night, as if to accompany the dancing shadows,

we could hear, very faintly, but completely discernible, the sound of faraway flutes, drums, rattles, and singing or chanting," Patricia said. "We all saw and heard them. Cliff couldn't believe his senses, and at first the girls were really frightened."

Then a strange thing happened. According to Patricia, the girls began to move rhythmically and to mimic the movements of the shadow dancers. "Within a few minutes, their actions were so fluid and seemed to come so natural to them, that Cliff and I feared that they had become possessed by the spirits of the dancers."

When they attempted to pull their daughters out of the recreation room and away from the mesmerizing shadows, Cliff and Patricia were startled to see the hazy image of a Native American man, dressed in full tribal regalia, standing in the doorway, as if to block their escape.

"I just closed my eyes and gritted my teeth and pulled one of the girls behind me and charged right through the ghost of the Indian in the doorway," Patricia said. "Cliff and the other two girls were right behind us."

After the girls had been calmed and put to bed, Cliff and Patricia discussed the bizarre situation in which they found themselves.

"I had always been open to the idea of spirits and ghosts," Patricia explained, "but the whole haunting business was blowing Cliff's mind. He was having a very difficult time dealing with what we had just seen and heard. And it didn't help him one bit to calm his nerves when the sound of the drums seemed to come from all around the kitchen and living room."

After the Lawsons managed to get through that incredible night of visual and auditory manifestations, they decided that they would ask around about the place and check any old records available that might give them some clue as to the eerie spirit phenomena they had experienced.

"That was when we learned about the terrible deed that had been worked upon a tribal village that had once occupied the area along the river," Patricia said. "After the smallpox epidemic had done its awful work on the villagers, the bodies of the victims were dragged to a trench that had been dug by the greedy men who had engineered the disaster and unceremoniously dumped in. That trench, the mass burial site, was on our land, and the corner of the house containing the recreation room had been built over a part of it. The more we talked to some of our new neighbors, the more we began to hear stories of people who had encountered Indian spirits in the vicinity of the burial site. And a good number of folks said that they had heard the sound of drums and rattles on certain nights."

When word got around the area that the Lawsons had experienced strange phenomena at their home and were asking questions about the grim history of the mass burial site, a woman who claimed psychic abilities invited herself over to have coffee with Patricia.

"According to this lady, these manifestations have been happening around this burial site for years," Patricia said. "She suggested that there was some kind of psychic vortex that had been created because of the cruel way that the Native American tribe had been tricked out of their land and the manner in which their lives had been cut so short. She believed that the whole area around our house, the river, and the land where the village had once stood had been saturated with negative vibrations."

Patricia invited the psychic-sensitive to return that evening with some of her study group. "Around eleven o'-clock, one of the group was drawn to a particular spot on the lawn," she said. "According to the psychic, this was a power place caused by the spirits in the burial site. As we looked back toward the house, we saw incredible projections all over the place. We saw ghostly images of the Indian villagers, moving about as they must have in life—some of them dancing, some of them seeming to cook, preparing food over fires. It was an absolutely incredible experience."

Two nights later, the psychic-sensitive returned to the Lawsons' home, bringing with her a friend, a tribal Medicine priest, along with certain members of her study group. "They held a cleansing ceremony for the spirits of the dead," Patricia said. "They prayed and chanted and sought to bring peace to the troubled spirits who had been buried in that mass grave without the benefit of their death songs or prayers. After that ceremony, the thuds, noises, and other disturbances in our house stopped."

Patricia stated, however, that on nights when the moon is full—especially in August, September, and October—they could still hear the faraway sound of drums, flutes, and rattles. "None of our family finds this manifestation frightening or disturbing," she explained. "I guess, if anything, it gives us a kind of reassurance that life continues beyond the grave."

GHOSTLY ECHOES OF PEOPLE AND PLACES

Some homes and locales are so drenched in the emotions of hate, anger, lust, and bloody violence that it is difficult for the psychical researcher truly to ascertain if there are restless spirits that walk about seeking peace or if the psychic residue of such extreme human passions that led to murder, rape, and mass slaughter have given birth to ghostly images that remain attached to the area. In other instances, terrible epidemics of pestilence and disease that claimed hundreds or thousands of lives may somehow have impressed indelible images of valiant doctors and nurses and their doomed patients on the environment. There are the many battlefields where acts of courage and cowardice, patriotism and perversity, glory and greed blended together to fashion the inevitable by-products of carnage, death, and ghostly combatants who appear to fight on throughout eternity.

Dogma has no place in the mental toolbox of the psychical researcher. From time to time, the investigator will encounter areas of the unknown that may incorporate many types of phenomena in a single haunting. As I have indicated in my categorization of the various manifestations of the general phenomena we collectively term "ghosts," I believe that in many so-called haunted places, there are no spirits or multidimensional entities roaming in search of the Light but, rather, the psychic-emotional residue left by powerful human emotions. Somehow, in a manner I am convinced we will better understand, such explosively expressed feelings can supercharge an environment and endow them with a kind of memory with which certain individuals may attain a rapport that allows them to witness the long-ago scene as if they were observing it in the present.

Although they may perceive the scene of violence or intense emotion from the past as though they were seeing it occur in real time—and may even on occasion feel as if they were participating in the event—they cannot interact with the ghostly tableau, the phantom pageant, any more than they might interact with the actors they observe in dramas being enacted on their television screens. There is a mechanical kind of repetitive action that is observed when one perceives a haunting that is a result of psychic residue—that is, the ghostly figures perform the same acts, walk the same hallways, appear in the same rooms, night after night. While communication with the phantom forms may be attempted,

in such hauntings no intelligent contact can be achieved—
because there is no intelligence at work. Rather than the
spirit of a deceased man or woman haunting a locale, what
one is observing is a kind of psychic automaton, an animated
image of the deceased, caught in some imprinted memory
pattern that will continue to repeat its captured moments
until its energy eventually dissipates over time.

Ghosts Walk the Streets of Jerome

In 1876, Al Sieber, General Crook's famous guide and
chief of scouts in the campaigns against the Apache, filed the
first claim to the copper ore that existed in a mountainside
2,000 feet above Arizona's picturesque Verde Valley. Known
as a "man of iron," because of his legendary powers of en-
durance, Sieber was also as wise in the ways of metallurgy as
he was in the ways of the Apache, and he recognized the potential value of the ore in the rugged mountain terrain. As
fate would have it, Sieber never made a cent out of his discovery, but he told Angus McKinnon and M. S. Ruffner
about the area, and they began the work that would eventually lead to the excavation of $800 billion dollars' worth of
copper from the mountainside.

The city was named for a New York City financier who
never even visited the area. In 1882, Eugene Murray Jerome
invested some badly needed capital in the mining claims,
with the proviso that the camp be named after him.

For seventy-seven years, miners worked the claims, carv-
ing out an amazing 87 miles of tunnels under the town.
During those years of brutish toil there were a lot of accidents, deaths on the job, and men dying of lung problems.
Add to the above a good many men dying during the flu epidemic of 1917, and you have a powerful potential for the

kind of psychic residue that creates the ghostly echoes of the past.

At its peak in the 1920s, Jerome had a population of 15,000. When Phelps Dodge Corporation shut down the mines in 1953, the population dropped to around 120. Today, the once grand old city is occupied by folks who maintain an artists' colony, operate art galleries, run antique shops, host colorful restaurants, and staff a number of museums that preserve former glories of the mining days. The population hovers around 450 people—and a whole lot of ghosts.

As my wife Sherry and I drove up Highway 89A from the Verde Valley and first saw the houses of Jerome stacked on the hillside before us, we felt as though we were about to enter a time warp and be transported back to an earlier era. This sensation was intensified as we entered the city and saw the old gasoline signs, the antiquated posters for long-forgotten brands of soft drinks, and the turn-of-the-century architecture of the storefronts on the main street.

We soon learned that a good many stories of ghosts centered around the United Verde Hospital that sits high on Cleopatra Hill. The hospital had been used to treat miners from 1927 to 1951, and constructed of tile and cement with lots of glass windows, it obviously had been a very impressive building during its time of service. Certain of the local artists liked to paint in the old building, making good use of the light from its many windows. But in order to do so, they had to learn to ignore the ghostly manifestations that occurred around them as they worked on their canvases.

"If you want to work there," one of the artists told us, "you just have to get used to the ghostly energy that is all over the place. You make your peace with the spirits. They won't hurt you. They're just people, after all."

Although he wasn't hurt by the ordeal, another artist told us that he had been "really shook up" by the ghost that he had encountered in the hospital. He had bad dreams about the ghost for weeks after the frightening encounter.

Another told of being in the hospital one night after dark and having heard the sounds of coughing, labored breathing, as well as cries and moans of pain. "A lot of miners developed lung problems from their work," he said, "and I think I heard the ghostly sounds of their suffering."

As Sherry and I spoke with the residents of Jerome, we learned that in the opinion of many percipients of ghostly activity, the encounters were more numerous when there was a full moon and a low pressure system.

A young woman told us that she didn't know about the low pressure system being a factor, but she had had a chilling experience one night during a full moon as she walked by an older hospital farther down on Cleopatra Hill. She knew that a lot of manifestations had been reported from the predecessor to the United Verde Hospital and she didn't really know why she had decided to walk by the place, but she had suddenly felt "an incredible energy" coming from the old building.

In retrospect, she told us that she felt as if she were being drawn to the place, as if something within was telling her that she needed to have a certain kind of experience for her spiritual growth. "At first I heard the sounds of people breathing heavily," she said. "Then I could hear sighs and moans."

Even though she had a flashlight with her, she felt that she should not turn it on. There was enough moonlight filtering in through the windows for her to see quite clearly the dim shapes of several bodies lying covered with blankets in a hallway. She could see doctors and nurses rushing around the bodies, bending over them. The whole scene, she estimated, lasted only ten or twelve seconds, then it was gone.

"I knew that there had been accidents in the mines," she said, "but when I did some research on the history of Jerome, I read about the awful influenza epidemic that struck around 1917 and '18—and I had an inner knowing that I was seeing a scene from that terrible time."

Headless Charlie, the ghost of a miner who was decapitated in a gruesome mine accident, has been seen by quite a number of Jerome residents, as has the shade of a prostitute who, legend has it, was knifed in the old redlight district. Especially when the moon is full, people see the ghostly hooker walking from where the crude shacks of the prostitutes used to be to within a few feet of the Little Daisy Hotel—when she disappears.

Before we left the mining town that had once been called the "wickedest city in the West," Sherry felt as though it was important to climb Cleopatra Hill one more time and to train her camera lens on the doorway of a building near the old Episcopal church. Later, when the developed film was returned, Sherry saw what appears to be a figure standing in the doorway, thus providing us with our own ghostly memento from Jerome.

Yankee Jim's Noose Still Swings at Whaley House

There is little question in our minds that the entire area of Old San Diego is haunted, but the Whaley House, constructed in 1857, is certainly the most active. In fact, the Thomas Whaley mansion, completely furnished with antiques from the days of early California, ranks among the most haunted houses in the United States.

Immediately after its construction was completed, the mansion had become the center of business, government, and social affairs in Old San Diego. The oldest brick house in Southern California, the Whaley House served as a courthouse, a courtroom, a theater, and a boarding house—as well as the family home of Thomas and Anna Whaley and their children.

June Reading, who at the time of our visit was the director of the Whaley House, told us of footsteps being heard in the master bedroom and on the stairs. Windows, even when fastened down with three four-inch bolts on each side, would fly open of their own accord—often in the middle of the night, triggering the burglar alarm. People often reported having heard screams echoing throughout the second story of the mansion, and once a large, heavy china closet had toppled over by itself.

Numerous individuals had sensed or psychically seen the image of a scaffold and a hanging man on the south side of the mansion. According to Mrs. Reading, ten years before Thomas Whaley had constructed his home on the site, a sailor named Yankee Jim Robinson had been hanged on the spot of what would later become the arch between the music room and the living room in the mansion. Whaley had been an observer when Yankee Jim kept his appointment with the hangman.

Some visitors to the Whaley House had reported seeing a gaudily dressed woman with a painted face lean out of a second-story window. In Mrs. Reading's opinion, that could well be an actress from one of the theatrical troupes that had leased the second floor in November 1868.

The Court House Wing of the mansion is generally thought to be the most haunted spot in the Whaley House, due to the violent emotions that were expended there in the early days of San Diego. Many individuals who have visited the old house had heard the sounds of a crowded courtroom in session and the noisy meetings of men in Thomas Whaley's upstairs study. The fact that this one single mansion served so many facets of city life, in addition to being a family home, almost guarantees several layers of psychic residue permeating themselves upon the environment.

June Reading told us that other sensitive visitors to the Whaley house have also perceived the image of Anna Whaley, who, many feel, still watches over the mansion that she loved so much. And who, according to a good number of those who have encountered her presence, deeply resents the intrusion of strangers.

Mrs. Reading informed us of the night in 1964 when television talk show host Regis Philbin and a friend saw Anna Whaley as they sat on the Andrew Jackson sofa at 2:30 A.M. The ghostly image floated from the study, through the music room, and into the parlor. At that moment, Philbin, in nervous excitement, dissolved the apparition with the beam of his flashlight. Since that time, Mrs. Reading said, night visits have not been permitted in the Whaley House.

In addition to the sightings of the primary spirits of Thomas and Anna Whaley, Mrs. Reading said that the other ghosts most often seen include those of Yankee Jim, who walks across the upstairs sitting room to the top of the stairs; a young girl named Washburn, a playmate of the Whaley children; and "Dolly Varden," the family's favorite dog. And then there are the screams, the giggles, the rattling doorknobs, the cooking odors, the smell of Thomas Whaley's Havana cigars, Anna's sweet-scented perfume, the sound of footsteps throughout the house, and the music box and piano that play by themselves.

Throughout our visit to the Whaley House, Sherry kept being drawn to the area between the music room and the living room—the spot where we later learned Yankee Jim had been hanged in the days before the mansion had been constructed. On one of the photographs that she took of the room, what seems to be the glowing form of a rope appears to be dangling from the ceiling.

APPARITIONS

There is usually agreement among psychical researchers that when one refers to an apparition, he or she is generally speaking of a "ghost" that is known to the percipient.

Among the most common and universal of all psychic phenomena is that of the "crisis apparition," that ghostly image which is seen, heard, or felt when the individual represented by the image is undergoing a crisis, especially death. A classic example is that of a man who is sitting reading in his home in Dearborn, Michigan, who glances up from his newspaper to see an image of his father, dressed in his customary mechanic's coveralls, waving to him in a gesture of farewell. Our percipient is startled, for his father lives in Austin, Texas. However, within the next few minutes the telephone rings, and it is a call from his sister in Austin, informing him that their father has just passed away.

It may well be that at the moment of death the soul, the essential self within all humans, is freed from the confines of the body and is able to soar free of time and space and, in some instances, is able to make a last, fleeting contact with a loved one. These projections at the moment of death betoken that something nonphysical exists within us that is capable of making a mockery of all accepted physical laws—and even more importantly, is capable of surviving physical death.

POLTERGEISTS

As I described earlier in this chapter, a poltergeist is a psychokinetic [mind influencing matter] projection of psychic energy that finds its explosive center often in the hormonal surges of adolescence, a teenager's frustrated creative expression, and sometimes the stresses of marital adjustment. The poltergeist, therefore, quite likely emanates from the living, rather than the dead. The poltergeist [pelting or throwing ghost] is a ghost only in common parlance, which links the two because of the "spooklike" nature of the poltergeist that causes the invisible pseudo-entity to prefer darkness for its violent exercises of tossing furniture, objects, and people about the room. On occasion, though, hauntings may precipitate poltergeist activity and the energy of the poltergeist may in some cases recharge dormant memories and set a ghost in motion.

The Home on the Edge of Hell

It began one night in November 1986 in a suburb of Spokane, Washington, when Donna Fencl was awakened by the sounds of what she thought at first was someone dragging some heavy furniture across the attic floor. She nudged her husband Vernon awake and told him that someone was after the antiques they had stored in the attic.

Grumbling at first after being awakened from a sound sleep, Vernon sat upright and was soon wide awake when he, too, heard the peculiar noises issuing from above their bedroom. He grabbed a baseball bat he kept at the side of the bed and a flashlight from the drawer of a nightstand and cautiously began creeping up the attic stairs, ordering Donna to stay by the telephone, ready to dial 911.

They were both relieved when Vernon returned to report that there was no sign of burglars or any indication that any furniture had been moved. What had awakened them, he theorized, was air locks in the pipes of their old hot-water heating system. Perhaps, Vernon speculated, it really was time to install a new furnace with forced-air ducts.

Air locks in the pipes seemed a satisfactory answer, and after checking to see that their twelve-year-old daughter Amy slumbered undisturbed, the Fencls went back to sleep.

But the next evening the sounds returned, much louder than before and unmistakably in the attic directly above their heads. Once again, it sounded as though a crew of furniture movers was at work, but when Vernon went upstairs to investigate, there were no intruders to be seen and nothing had been moved.

However, on this occasion, Donna and Vernon were summoned to Amy's bedroom by her screams of terror. According to their daughter, she had felt something moving in her bed. When it had brushed up against her, it had seemed to her to feel both cold and furry. She imagined it to be some animal, such as a rat.

Although they had never been bothered by rodents in their home, both Donna and Vernon carefully searched Amy's room for any signs that they were serving as unwilling hosts to a rat or a mouse. They found no visible traces of any such creature in her room, so they assured Amy as best they could that she must have been dreaming.

They were no sooner back in their own beds when Amy's screams brought them once again rushing to her bedside. This time she said that something had lifted the end of her bed and slammed it back down several times in succession. For the second time that evening, they did their best to pacify her and assure her that she had been having a troubled dream, perhaps caused by her hearing the odd thumps and knocks caused by the air locks in the pipes of the heating system.

Two nights later, when Donna and Vernon were returning from the movies, they were barely inside the door when the eighteen-year-old girl they had hired to sit with Amy met them with the frightening accusation that their house was haunted. She would never sit for them ever again.

When the Fencls calmed her and asked what she was talking about, she told them how the television set had gone off and on when no one was near it. Footsteps had sounded upstairs and doors had opened and closed in second-floor bedrooms while she and Amy had sat cowering downstairs in the living room. Amy had refused to go to her room and was sleeping on the sofa.

Vernon paid the sitter double to compensate for her anxiety, but he couldn't accept her analysis of their home as haunted. As he drove her home, he tried to explain about the knocking sound in the pipes and how they could have sounded like footsteps walking around upstairs.

"Hey, Mr. Fencl," she told him as they pulled up in front of her house, "I know what I heard and what I saw. You've got a spook loose in your house."

Vernon could see that she could not be persuaded otherwise, and he chalked the "ghost" up to two young girls alone at night permitting themselves to become frightened by strange noises and allowing their imaginations to run wild. But when he drove into the driveway of his home, he was surprised to see the upstairs lights blinking on and off. Rushing inside, he found Donna sitting ashen-faced on the stairs, a sobbing Amy huddled next to her.

"I saw it with my own eyes," Donna said. "A gray, shadowy figure coming down the stairs toward us. I screamed with fright, and the thing vanished. But it's been turning the lights on and off upstairs ever since."

Over the next week, the shadowy figure was seen frequently, moving about in different rooms of the house. Vegetables and cooking utensils would go flying around the kitchen. Appliances would mysteriously turn themselves on and off. Doors would open and shut of their own volition.

The morning after some invisible force snatched Amy out of bed and spun her across the room, the Fencls summoned a priest to bless their home and drive away the evil entity. In the opinion of Vernon and Donna, their household had been invaded by a demonic entity and their home had somehow been moved to the edge of hell.

After the visit by the priest only seemed to provoke even more violent disturbances, Vernon called a friend of his, Karl Liekweg, a former policeman, and beseeched him to come to spend the night with them and be their bodyguard, so to speak.

"Ghostbuster had never been in my résumé," Liekweg wrote in his report of the haunting, "but I have an interest in the paranormal and I was curious to see if the kind of things that Vernon described to me were really happening, so I agreed to come."

Liekweg was dozing in the big armchair that had been moved to the foot of the stairs. At around 3:00 A.M. he was awakened by noises from above. As he moved to investigate, he noticed that the air in the house had taken on an eerie chill.

With his flashlight in hand, he moved toward the bedroom occupied by twelve-year-old Amy, the room from which the sounds were emanating.

"When I opened the door and scanned the room with my flashlight, I saw little Amy curled up in bed with her back to the headboard, horrified by the weird demonstration going on before her," Karl Liekweg said. "The furniture was dancing. The girl's bed was elevated. Dresser drawers floated across the room as if they were filled with helium. Dolls, books, and other objects were spinning around the room. As soon as I turned on the overhead lights, the spooky shenanigans stopped."

After Vernon and Donna entered the room to calm their daughter, Liekweg followed through on police procedure and checked the furniture and other objects that he had seen in motion. He found no wires, no strings, no pulleys.

"I know that I myself was not strong enough or dexterous enough to make all the furniture move about as I had seen it dancing around the room, so I could not perceive how a slight twelve-year-old girl could have done so," he said. "It seemed to me like a genuine poltergeist case with the girl, Amy, providing the energy center. As discreetly as I could, I inquired of her mother about any onset of puberty, and I learned that Amy had been quite upset and frightened with the advent of certain of her new bodily functions."

Familiar enough with the literature of the paranormal to recognize that so often the energy of the poltergeist is set free by a girl entering puberty, Karl Liekweg suggested that Mrs. Fencl explain to her daughter in greater detail and with a lot of tender loving care the hormonal and other changes that came with her womanhood. He also wisely suggested that the entire family take a few days away from the house on a holiday.

"I spent a night in the house after the Fencls were away," Liekweg wrote, concluding his report of the poltergeist haunting, "and there were no manifestations of any kind. I did a follow-up check after the family returned, and I was pleased to learn that everything was quiet once again in their home. The poltergeistic energy had been spent, and once Amy had come to terms with adolescence and realized that things that were happening were all right and normal, the haunting had ended."

The Poltergeist That Wanted to Kill

On August 8, 1989, television cameraman Barry Conrad was asked to accompany respected psychical investigator Dr. Barry Taff and a number of other researchers to a reputed haunted house in San Pedro, California. Conrad accepted the assignment in the hope that he might be able to capture some authentic paranormal phenomena on videotape. He ended up getting footage that was far more frightening than he could have foreseen in his wildest imaginings.

When the group of researchers arrived at the alleged haunted house, Jackie Hernandez, the woman who had requested the investigation, told them of lamps and other objects flying across rooms, the apparition of a decaying elderly man in the children's bedroom, and a ghostly disembodied head in the attic.

Conrad considered her accounts to be a bit in the unbelievable category, and Jeff Wheatcraft, the photographer he had brought to assist him, proclaimed himself a complete skeptic of things ghostly and otherworldly. Disbelief and skepticism would soon disappear.

Shortly after Wheatcraft ascended into the attic opening by standing atop a washing machine in the small laundry room at the rear of the house, all those assembled below heard his screams of terror. Something, he declared after he had jumped down from the attic, had pulled his Canon 35mm camera from his hands.

As frightened as the former skeptic Wheatcraft was, he joined Barry Conrad in another foray into the attic. The two photographers crawled up into the overhead space, videotape rolling, ready to record anything between heaven and earth that might be occupying the darkened recesses of the attic.

Then, as Conrad states in his report of the haunting, without warning, his camera went dead. Although he quickly replaced the batteries, the camera remained inoperative. "Usually when a battery goes out, the green pilot light will change to red with the picture gradually fading to black," he noted. "In this case, the pilot light failed altogether, a highly unusual occurrence."

Wheatcraft found the camera that had been "taken" from him in a dusty old grape box in the northwest corner of the attic. Eerily though, the lens had been removed and placed in a space just behind the trap door to the attic.

Just then a foul stench permeated the attic space, and Wheatcraft emitted another scream that something was touching him, and he stumbled toward the attic's trap door. Somehow the two photographers managed to get down from the attic to safety below without falling and injuring themselves. Shaken, Wheatcraft stated that what felt like a bony hand had applied tremendous pressure to his lower back.

Once downstairs, Conrad's camera began again to function, and he was able to record what sounded like the heavy footsteps of an angry giant thundering across the attic floor. When Wheatcraft stood on the washing machine to peer into the attic crawlspace, he shouted in awe that he was seeing three brilliant flashes of light and then an eerie black mass "the size of three adult men standing side by side."

According to Barry Conrad's report, for days afterward Jeff Wheatcraft continued to suffer pain in his lower back from the pressure that had been applied by the "bony hand," and when he visited a chiropractor, it was confirmed that his lower back had indeed suffered massive internal bruising.

Nearly a month later, on the evening of September 4, Conrad received a desperate call from Jackie Hernandez. She said that she was undergoing a vicious poltergeistic seige in her home. A soft drink can had been thrown at her while doors opened and slammed closed of their own volition. The night before, she claimed, an "invisible force" had held her down on the floor for several minutes and attempted to smother her.

Jeff Wheatcraft and another friend, Gary Boehm, happened to be visiting Conrad at his apartment when they all heard Jackie's frantic call. They decided that they must leave at once for San Pedro and do their best to help the beleagured woman and her two small children.

The men arrived in San Pedro around 1:00 A.M. At first, everything in the bungalow seemed to be calm. Then Jeff Wheatcraft wanted to show Gary Boehm the grape box in the attic where he had discovered his camera after it had mysteriously vanished from his hands.

Barry Conrad remained downstairs in the laundry room with Jackie and her neighbor, Susan. Then Conrad said, "A bright orange comet of light suddenly flashed before us and flew through a small door that led outside."

A loud moan sounded from above them in the attic. It was Jeff Wheatcraft's voice crying out that he had to get out of there. *"It's put something around my neck!"*

"My heart almost froze with fear as I noticed a weathered clothesline cord dangling from my friend's swollen neck as he stiffly emerged from the [attic] hole above," Barry Conrad writes in his report of the harrowing experience. "It was at this instant that we all felt the pangs of incredible disbelief."

According to Gary Boehm, who had come to Wheatcraft's rescue, something had wrapped a clothesline cord tightly around Jeff's neck and then hanged him on a nail protruding from one of the rafter beams. "If I had not been there," Boehm said, "Jeff would have been strangled in that attic. He didn't know what was going on, and the cord was wrapped so tightly that it was very difficult to get him down. I had to bend the nail in order to release him."

Wheatcraft was left with red friction burns encircling his neck as a result of the attack by the vicious entity. Later, when Barry Conrad examined the tapes of that evening, he was startled to observe a "bright comet of light" traveling through a doorway behind Wheatcraft shortly after the bizarre hanging episode.

"Another orb of light can be seen buzzing over the top of Jeff's head while standing in the living room discussing his ordeal," Conrad said. "And yet another light was found zooming across the kitchen above Susan moments after Wheatcraft had descended from the attic space."

"In the history of paranormal research," Dr. Barry Taff has observed, "there have only been a handful of cases in which phenomena have deliberately and maliciously attacked human beings. And [the San Pedro poltergeist case] is one of them."

PHANTOMS

As we explore the paranormal, we find that most types of phenomena appear to be universal, the individual circumstances of the accounts fitting themselves to the unique cultural interpretations of whatever area in which they manifest. Certainly, stories of phantom hitchhikers constitute one such category of ubiquitous tales, having been reported around the world.

Chicago's "Resurrection Mary" has been hitching a ride and spooking motorists since the 1930s. Said to be the spirit of a beautiful, blond Polish girl, Mary has been picked up by smitten young men at dances and asked to be taken home.

The problem is, "home" always turns out to be Resurrection Cemetery on Archer Avenue on the South Side of Chicago. On occasion, the phantom hitchhiker has been bold enough to open car doors and get in, explaining to the startled driver how she desperately needs a ride into the city. Once again, as the car approaches the cemetery on Archer, Mary bolts from the car and vanishes at the gates.

For many years now, taxi drivers in Naha, Okinawa, claim that an attractive woman in her twenties, with short-cropped hair and dressed in black slacks, often hails them for a ride on the road to the U.S. Marine Camp. When the cab drivers turn to ask for a specific destination, she disappears. The phantom has been dubbed the "Nightwalker of Nago," because she most often appears on the mountain road leading from the fishing village of Nago to the marine camp.

Since 1965, dozens of drivers have slammed on their brakes to avoid hitting a pretty young woman in a flowing white dress standing in the road on Blue Bell Hill in Maidstone, England. The phantom is said to be that of Judith Lingham, who was to have been a bridesmaid for her best friend when she died in a car crash the night before the wedding. Her spirit appears still dressed in her flowing bridesmaid's gown, still attempting to get to the wedding.

A truckdriver recently told me of the time he was crossing Oklahoma late one December night in 1997 and was approached by a young man at a truck stop who said that he needed a ride to Tulsa.

"I told him, sure, get in," Jake Kleveland said. "I had been pushing the mileage and the hours and I was getting a bit groggy—in spite of the four cups of black coffee I had just chugged down. I figured that someone to talk to would help keep me alert."

Jake's passenger appeared to be in his late teens. He was clean-shaven, but wore his hair fairly long and parted in the middle. In spite of the cold, he had only a lightweight jacket.

"I asked him if he wanted I should turn up the heater, but he said that he was comfortable," Jake recalled. "I didn't want to be nosy, but I wanted to make conversation, so I asked him why he was going to Tulsa."

Jake was astonished by the young man's answer. "I'm going to enlist in the Army. My brother's over there now, over in England. I know there's going to be a big invasion soon, and I want to get enlisted and get in on it."

Puzzled, Jake asked the teenager what invasion that might be that he wanted to "get in on."

"Then the kid looks at me real peculiar, like I am some idiot," Jake said. " 'Well, sir,' he says in this soft voice, the kind you use for little children and slow-witted folks, 'if you read the newspapers you just have to know that the Allies are going to be invading Europe—maybe in France or Italy— and getting after old Adolf and his crew pretty damn soon.' "

Jake took a really good look at his passenger for the first time. In the light from the dashboard he could see that his hair was slicked down with some greasy hair dressing. He wore old corduroy trousers and a faded flannel shirt. And there was a rolled-up newspaper in his jacket pocket.

"That a new paper?" Jake found himself asking against his better judgment.

"Sure is, mister," the teenager answered. "Pa gave it to me just before I walked down the lane and started hitching for Tulsa."

Jake shifted uncomfortably behind the wheel. Suddenly the cab space in his eighteen-wheeler seemed to shrink and, in spite of the heater, to become very cold. "What's the date?" Jake asked. "I kind of lose track when I'm on the road."

The kid unfurled the newspaper, and Jake caught a glimpse of a news photo of Winston Churchill and Franklin D. Roosevelt and a bit of a headline about some meeting in Cairo. "It's December 4, 1943," the teenager said.

Jake found himself blurting out that that was exactly *fifty-four years ago to the day.*

"Then the kid just looked at me with these very sorrowful eyes," Jake said. "I mean, he was looking like he was about to cry, but at the same time, his eyes just seemed to be piercing, as if he was looking right through me and at some other place way off in time."

Within the next few moments, Jake saw that his strange passenger was becoming less material in form, almost translucent. His voice was barely a whisper when he said, "I guess . . . I'm not going to make it to Tulsa this time . . . either."

And then he vanished.

"I had hoped that the kid would give me someone to talk with and to help keep me awake," Jake said. "Man, believe it when I say that I was now as wide awake as I had ever been in my life. I saw that kid's eyes every night before I went to sleep for months."

Jake concluded his account by stating that he did ask around truckstops in the area about such a phantom of a young teenager trying to get to Tulsa to enlist in World War II, but he had no luck in tracking down any other truckers who claimed to have had such an experience.

"Maybe we just happened to connect that night and come together from our respective moments in time and space," Jake said. "I know that I will never forget the experience as long as I live."

*   *   *

In the next chapter, we shall see that those men and women who have encountered strange half-human, half-animal creatures have found the experience as unforgettable as the percipients of ghost and hauntings have found their meetings with those eerie entities from out of the dark.

Two

MANIMALS

On the night of October 4, 1998, seven hunters were roasting marshmallows around a fire at their camp near Mud Springs, a desolate area of Trinity County about 200 miles north of San Francisco, when they heard a rustling in the bushes.

When one of the men got his flashlight and went to investigate the noise, he saw an enormous manbeast that he estimated to be about nine feet tall standing about 50 yards away on the other side of a creek.

Later, two of the hunters told California Department of Fish and Game officials and a reporter from the *Redding Record Spotlight* that the creature stayed a distance from their campsite most of the night, but it remained near enough so that they could hear its eerie screams. The men also stated that they were convinced that the thing was not a bear, for they were able to see its arms, which hung past its knees. The next morning, the hunters were able to find humanlike tracks in the area that measured six inches wide and twenty inches long.

* * *

Reports of such incredible, monstrous "manimals," half-human, half-apelike creatures appearing to witnesses from out of the darkness have been with us since the demon-haunted Middle Ages. In those days, the giant, hairy beings who lived in the forest caves of Europe were believed to be Satan's spawn. The monasteries rang with angry cries about the giant demons with their ugly shapes and bestial faces that had kidnapped villagers and pious monks. Abbots and Bishops penned angry diatribes against these entities and condoned their death when captured.

In 840 C.E., Agobard, the Archbishop of Lyons, told of three such demons, "giant people of the forest and mountains," who were stoned to death after being displayed in chains for several days. In his *Chronicles*, Abbot Ralph of Coggeshall Abbey, Essex, England, wrote of a "strange monster" whose charrred body had been found after a lightning storm on the night of St. John the Baptist in June 1205. He stated that a terrible stench came from the beast with "monstrous limbs."

Villagers of the Caucasus Mountains have legends of an apelike "wildman" going back for centuries. The same may be said of the Tibetans living on the slopes of Mt. Everest and the Native American tribes inhabiting the northwestern United States.

The Gilyak, a remote tribe of Siberian native people, claim that there are animals inhabiting the frozen forests of Siberia that have human feelings and souls. The Gilyaks say that these half-human beasts travel in family units and that their greatest desire is to learn the secret of fire.

The humanlike creature—whether sighted in the more remote, wooded, or mountainous regions of North America, South America, Russia, China, Australia, or Africa—is most often believed to be a two-footed mammal that constitutes a kind of missing link between *Homo sapiens* and the great apes, for its appearance is more primitive than that of Neanderthal.

The descriptions given these manimals by witnesses around the world are amazingly similar. Height: six to nine feet. Weight: 400 to 1,000 pounds. Eyes: black. Dark fur or body hair from one to four inches in length is said to cover the creature's entire body with the exception of the palms of its hands, the soles of its feet, and its upper facial area, nose, and eyelids.

Based on the eyewitness descriptions of hundreds of reliable individuals who have encountered these creatures over the last fifty years especially, it would seem that the manimals are more humanlike than apelike or bearlike. For one thing, these entities are repeatedly said by witnesses to have breasts and buttocks. Neither apes nor bears have buttocks—nor do they leave flatfooted humanlike footprints.

COULD THESE CREATURES BE AN UNRECOGNIZED SPECIES?

Is it possible for such large humanlike beings to exist without being fully credited and catalogued by orthodox zoologists and biologists? In recent decades we have witnessed the official "discovery" of a large number of animals previously unrecognized by the experts, although well known to the aboriginal inhabitants of the creatures' natural habitats.

Although hunters in Kamchatka, Manchuria, and Sakhalin had long been telling excited stories of the giant carnivorous brown bear they had encountered, European scientists did not accept the existence of the great bear until 1898. The largest land animal next to the African elephant is the white rhinocerous, which remained officially unacknowledged until 1900. The largest of the apes, the mountain gorilla, was considered a silly native superstition until 1901. The dragons of Komodo Island, Indonesia, were considered the creations of a strange myth conjured up by the islanders until 1912. And the British zoologist who described the bizarre "royal hepard"—a half-leopard and half-hyena beast long claimed by the natives of Rhodesia to be an actual beast of prey— wondered how such a large animal, and one so distinct from other species, could have remained "unknown" for so long.

In June 1994, the first living specimen of the Vu Quang ox was caught in a rugged area on the Vietnamese-Laotian border, and its verified existence was hailed as the zoological find of the half-century. This horned mammal, weighing over 200 pounds with cinnamon, black, and white coloration, is a hemi-bovid, a species ancestral to both oxen and antelope that was thought to have become extinct four million years ago. Zoologists estimated their present population to be in the hundreds.

In July 1999, zoologists saw the first photographic evidence that the Javan rhinoceros, thought completely wiped out on the Asian mainland in the 1960s, still thrived some 130 kilometers north of Ho Chi Minh City in the Lam Dong province of Vietnam. These huge animals, which can weigh over 3,000 pounds, have somehow been misplaced or missed for nearly forty years.

In December 2000, Thai scientists set out to search the northern jungles of Thailand for conclusive proof of the sightings of large, hairy elephants that witnesses claim strongly resemble the long-extinct woolly mammoth. What these scientists and forestry officials may discover is either a new species of elephant or long-lost descendents of the great-tusked mammoth of the Ice Age.

Since at this point no one is really quite certain whether

Bigfoot, Sasquatch, and the other manimals are animal or human, it should be recalled that no Westerner had set eyes on the Pi Tong Luang people of northern Thailand until the late 1930s. At the time of their "discovery," the Pi Tong Luang were assessed as a primitive people, possessing no weapons, speaking only in monosyllabic spurts, and living in small, nomadic family groups. It seemed not to matter at all to them that their official existence was denied and that they had been relegated to the misty corridors of folk myth.

But could small bands of humans truly avoid official discovery in the United States?

In California, in 1872, the last of the Yahi tribe gave up their fight against the steadily growing numbers of the white settlers and, rather than surrendering, simply disappeared into a small valley on the slopes of Mt. Lassen. There the little community lived in peace until 1884 when the continuous loss of hunting land forced the Yahis to raid the ranchers' cabins in search of food. Remarkable as it may seem, during the next decade of nocturnal raids on the ranchers, the Yahi were seen only once.

In 1894, the last surviving members of the tribe made their home on two pieces of land half a mile wide and three miles long. Although they had established a permanent camp in an area that was becoming increasingly heavily populated, their presence remained undiscovered until some surveyors happened on them in 1909.

In 1911, when Ishi, the last surviving Yahi walked into a small California town to surrender, it was determined that he had lived on the fringe of civilization for thirty-nine years. In the four decades since the Yahi ceased their war with the United States, tribal members had been seen only twice. Yet Ishi and his people had kept permanent camps, had made daily use of fires, had foraged among the white community, and had even conducted elaborate cremation rituals for their dead.

By contrast with the Yahi, the manimals around the world seem to require no permanent home or camp, do not seem to have mastered fire, and have a virtually unlimited area of remote wooded and mountainous areas in which to roam—yet these giant, hairy beings have been frequently sighted and reported.

A persistent question arises out of all this: If the manimals really exist, why is there so little physical evidence in addition to casts of huge humanlike footprints? Why haven't some hunters found skulls or skeletons?

Any accomplished hunter or woodsperson will answer this question by pointing out that Mother Nature keeps a clean house. The carcasses of the largest forest creatures are soon eaten by scavengers and the bones, hooves, and antlers scattered.

The late zoologist Ivan T. Sanderson suggested that if these manimals are members of a subhuman race, they may gather up their dead for burial in special caves. Dr. Jeanne-Marie-Therese Koffman agreed that the creatures may bury their dead in secret places. It may be, she theorizes, that they may throw the corpses of the deceased into the rushing waters of mountain rivers or into the abysses of rocky caverns.

Then, too, it is not unusual for certain of the higher animals to hide the bodies of their dead. Accounts of the legendary "elephants' graveyard" are well known; and in Ceylon, the phrase "to find a dead monkey" is used to indicate an impossible task.

Proving the existence of such manimals also seems to many scientists to be an impossible task. And there is always the question of whether or not these creatures are truly physical beings or if they are nonmaterial creatures who enter our dimension only sporadically from some dark and mysterious spirit world out of space and time.

BIGFOOT

In 1920, the term "abominable snowman" was coined through a mistranslation of yeti "wildman of the snow," the Tibetan word for the mysterious apelike monster. For the next two decades, reports of the creature were common in the Himalayan mountain range, but it was not until the close of World War II that world attention became focused on the unexplained humanlike bare footprints that were being found at great heights and freezing temperatures. The Himalayan activity reached a kind of climax in 1960 when Sir Edmund Hillary, conqueror of Mt. Everest, led an expedition in search of the elusive yeti and returned with nothing to show for his efforts but a fur hat that had been fashioned in imitation of the snowbeast's crest.

Reports of a large apelike creature in the United States and the Canadian provinces are to be found in the oral traditions of native tribes, the journals of early settlers, and accounts in regional frontier newspapers, but wide public attention was not really called to the creature until the late 1950s when road-building crews in the unmapped wilderness of the Bluff Creek area north of Eureka, California, began to report a large number of sightings of North America's own "abominable snowman." Once stories of giant humanlike monsters tossing around construction crews' small machinery and oil drums began hitting the wire services, hunters, hikers, and campers came forward with a seemingly endless number of stories about the shrill-squealing, seven-foot forest giant that they had for years been calling by such names as Bigfoot, Sasquatch, Wauk-Wauk, Oh-Mah, or Saskehavis.

In North America, the greatest number of sightings of Bigfoot have come from the Fraser River Valley, the Strait of Georgia and Vancouver Island, British Columbia; the "Ape Canyon" region near Mt. St. Helens in southwestern Washington; the Three Sisters Wilderness west of Bend, Oregon; and the area around the Hoopa Valley Indian Reservation, especially the Bluff Creek watershed, northeast of Eureka, California. In recent years, extremely convincing sightings of Bigfoot-type creatures have also been made in areas of New York, New Jersey, Minnesota, South Carolina, Tennessee, and Florida.

Strange Encounters with Beasts That Shouldn't Be

Reports of Bigfoot-type creatures in California go back to at least the 1840s when miners reported encountering giant two-legged beastlike monsters during the goldrush days. Sightings of the Oh-Mah, as the native tribes called them, continued sporadically until August 1958, when a construction crew was building a road through the rugged wilderness near Bluff Creek, Humboldt County, and discovered giant humanlike footprints in the ground around their equipment.

For several mornings running, the men discovered that something had been messing with their small equipment during the night. In one instance, an 800-pound tire and wheel from an earth-moving machine had been picked up and carried several yards across the compound. In another, a 300-pound drum of oil had been stolen from the camp, carried up a rocky mountain slope, and tossed into a deep canyon. In each instance, only massive sixteen-inch footprints with a fifty-to-sixty-inch stride offered any clue to the vandal's identity.

When media accounts of the huge footprints were released, people from the area began to step forward with their own plaster casts of massive, mysterious footprints and to relate their own frightening encounters with hairy giants. Two physicians swore that they had almost run over such a monster when the creature stepped out in front of their automobile as they traveled on Route 299. A woman and her two daughters reported sighting a large, hairy, two-legged giant on a slope above the Hoopa Valley.

A Frightening Body-to-Body Collision with Bigfoot

In February 1962, at the residence of Mr. and Mrs. Bud Jenkins, who lived about four miles from Fort Bragg, California, Robert Hatfield, a logger from Crescent City, was staying the night when he heard the Jenkins' dog yelping in fear.

Hatfield stepped outside and came face-to-face with a hairy monster with a humanlike face. He said later that the creature had to be more than six feet tall because it was peering over a fence of that height. Believing at first that a large bear had wandered into the yard, Hatfield dashed back into the house and awakened Bud Jenkins.

The two men rushed back outside. Seeing no sign of the big animal, they raced around the house, each one in a different direction. Hatfield turned a corner and collided with the creature.

Knocked sprawling to the ground, Hatfield looked up into the strange features of the Bigfoot and yelled at Jenkins to get back inside the house. The thing was no bear, but something half-man, half-beast.

Hatfield managed to scramble to his feet and run for the door. The massive creature was just a few steps behind him as he dashed into the house. Both men pressed against the door with every ounce of their weight and strength, but they could not close it with the howling monster pushing against it from the outside.

Suddenly, the pressure against the door eased, and Jenkins ran to get his rifle. When they returned, the men found that the frightening visitor had disappeared—but they found a number of huge footprints to corroborate their story, as well as a muddy handprint on the side of the house. Measurements of Bigfoot's handprint revealed it to be eleven inches across.

Later, when Hatfield spoke to reporters about the nightmarish ordeal, he said that he would never forget the face that had looked down on him after he had collided with the beast. He described the Bigfoot's facial flesh as being almost black in color with dark hair around its mouth and cheeks. He also remembered two large black eyes and features that were almost human.

The Strange Crouching Thing at the Side of the Road

Some years ago when I was teaching in college, one of my former students told me a most remarkable account of his meeting with a Bigfoot. Bob, at that time a senior, had been in my freshman English class, and I knew him to be a quiet, intelligent fellow, who gave every evidence that his interests lay in science, rather than in creative compositions and imaginative literature. I was not surprised that he had gone on to major in biology—which made his story of his bizarre encounter all the more convincing.

Bob had been driving on Highway 52, traveling some distance from Rochester, Minnesota, about ten o'clock in the evening when his headlights picked up the form of what he had first thought was a person crouching at the side of the road. He pulled his car onto the shoulder of the highway and stepped out to offer his assistance if it should be needed.

It was then that Bob saw that the "person" he had seen

crouching at the roadside was hardly a member of the brotherhood of man. The features were apelike, the shoulders heavy, and the creature loped up the steep embankment to the shelter of the woods as easily as if a stairway had been carved in the rock.

Bob saw that the creature had been kneeling over a dead rabbit. As he knelt to examine the body, the thing raised itself to its full height and gave a harsh bark of protest as if to frighten Bob away from its meal. The strange cry startled Bob and he ran back to his car.

Bob told me emphatically that he was convinced that the creature was neither wolf nor bear: "It had been crouching in a humanlike manner at the side of the road. At my approach, it had turned to look at me over its shoulder. Its head had definitely turned on a neck. Neither a wolf nor a bear can look over its shoulder without turning its body.

"The physiognomy of the creature was apelike, humanoid. When it was crouching and when it was running, I noticed that it had well-developed buttocks. It was this distinctly human characteristic that made me discard any alternate theories. What I saw was something that could only be described as a naked, hairy wild man."

Meeting the "Grand-Daddy" of All Bigfoot Monsters

Two truckdrivers from Oklahoma told me that they had seen the "grand-daddy" of all Bigfoot-type monsters when they were driving east of Winona, Mississippi, in November 1966.

Bill and Jim, two brothers, said that their pickup was going slowly up a very steep incline when they caught sight of some movement in the pines ahead of them. "Then this creature came rushing up to the edge of the highway. It stood at least eight feet tall and it weighed between six hundred to eight hundred pounds. Its face was a cross between a man's and a gorilla's. Its chest was an easy three-feet thick. Its legs and arms were huge. It was fast, running beside us. Then it wheeled and ran down the far ditch on my left—then here it came again! This time getting really close to the cab and looking us over real good!"

In their written report to me, the men expressed their fear that the monster would smash in the windows of the cab and mangle them. Although they considered themselves pretty rugged fellows, they said they doubted if six or eight men could handle the creature in hand-to-hand fighting.

They also wished to make the point that the Bigfoot ran and walked like an erect human. "The thing was shaped like a man," they wrote, "but there was definitely some animal mixed in there. Also [in their opinion] the creature could see in the dark and had sensitive ears. It seemed to hate the noise of our radio—so we turned it up full blast. And although it seemed hard to believe, the Bigfoot seemed more afraid of us than we were of him. But we imagine that it would be extremely dangerous if it were ever cornered or surprised."

The Missouri Monster

The monster that interrupted eight-year-old Terry Harrison's afternoon play in Louisiana, Missouri, on July 11, 1972, was described in the press as being ". . . at least seven feet tall with a pumpkin-shaped head . . . covered with shaggy black hair," and was said to have startled the boy with a "low, throaty growl."

At the time that "Momo," the Missouri Monster, was making headlines, I had formed a research group called Other Dimensions, and I sent our director of field investigations, Glenn McWane, to the site of the Bigfoot sightings to talk firsthand to the witnesses. Edgar Harrison, the boy's father, told McWane that Terry had run into the house and called out his alarm to his sister, Doris. "She got on the phone to my wife at our café, and Betty called me," he said. "Then Doris looked out the bathroom window. The thing was standing up the hill from the house."

Harrison was home within 30 minutes after receiving the telephone call from his wife, standing at the exact spot where the monster had stood. He found a stamped-down circle, but no other evidence of the giant forest creature.

On the evening of July 11, the Harrisons hosted a church meeting at their home. "About fifty people heard the thing roar that Friday night," Harrison said. "You could hear this growling getting closer and closer. Pretty soon you could hear the trees and the brush crackling up on Marzolf Hill. Then there was a loud *EEEeeerrrrr!* About five minutes later, it did the same thing over again. Three times in a row. Then that was it for the night."

By July 18, monster reports had proliferated.

One area resident said that he had seen Momo walk across Highway 79 with either a sheep or a dog in its mouth.

Numerous people claimed to have seen giants with red eyes staring at them from out of the darkness. Again and again came the reports of a strange, foul odor associated with the monster.

Huge three-toed tracks were discovered to confuse the question of the number of digits on the Bigfoot's feet.

A man swore that Momo had picked up the back end of his small foreign car.

On July 19, a "posse" of about twenty-five men scoured Marzolf Hill—the snake-infested, cave-packed terrain where the Harrison children had first sighted Momo—and didn't even find a rabbit. Police Chief Shelby Ward told the media that he was satisfied that there was no longer a monster on Marzolf Hill. He also announced that he would keep the hill barricaded from general public usage in order to keep curiosity seekers from going up there after dark and injuring themselves.

But sober, ostensibly reliable witnesses kept seeing Momo—or his kin—and they continued to spot him in an ever-widening range from Louisiana to Missouri. Serious researchers of the Bigfoot enigma argued that there was well-established data on such creatures and that sightings in that particular area went back at least as long ago as twenty years.

When Glenn McWane returned to our offices, he reported that while some of the accounts of Momo had been exaggerated, he didn't believe that all the witnesses had been suffering from overworked imaginations. "I believe that they did smell an odor foreign to them, that they did find unfamiliar footprints, that they did see an animal alien to their environment," he said. "The majority of these men and women are extremely well acquainted with the wildlife native to their section of Missouri. If the creature had been an animal that belonged, someone surely would have identified it."

"Whatever It Is, It Doesn't Belong Around Here"

In the summer of 1976, some law enforcement officers in Whitehall, New York, were among those who were surprised by the appearance of a Bigfoot-type entity. According to Paul B. Bartholomew, co-author of *Monsters of the North Woods*, the incident began on August 24, 1976 along Abair Road in rural Whitehall when two teenagers were startled by an unidentified creature walking along the roadside. They later described the thing as standing seven to eight feet tall, walking upright like a man, and swinging its long arms at its side. The monster's eyes gave off a reddish glow and it made a sound like a pig squealing.

Spooked by the giant creature, the two teenagers picked up a friend, who expressed his complete skepticism of their claims. After parking their vehicle and turning their lights off, the trio didn't have long to wait for a second appearance of the monster. Frightened, the teenagers drove into Whitehall and alerted the authorities.

"The following evening," Bartholomew writes in the *IRAAP Messenger*, the newsletter of the Independent Researchers' Association for Anomalous Phenomena, "an off-duty patrolman and a New York State trooper staked out the area. Parked with their lights off, the pair waited until they heard some noises. Quickly they snapped on their lights and saw that the creature had approached to within twenty-five feet of their car. The lights caused the creature to run off screaming."

Whitehall Police Chief Wilfred Gosselin stated that there was "something" out there, and "it's no animal that belongs in the northern part of this state."

Eight Feet Tall and Smelling "Pretty Bad"

In July 15, 1997, two teenaged brothers from Neeses, South Carolina, heard the family's dogs howling and went to investigate. That was when they spotted "a large, brown-yellow Bigfoot, eight feet tall . . . that smelled pretty bad." Fourteen-year-old Jackie Hutto told the Neeses *Times and Democrat* that he saw the monster lift the chain-link dog kennel out of the ground in which it was embedded, then turn and run into the woods.

About thirty-six miles south of Columbia, the state capital, the area around Neeses is covered with small creeks, rivers, and swamp land, bordering large farms, perhaps an ideal hiding place for a Bigfoot.

Tracks Made by a Giant of the Woods

When Janet Gamble spotted the huge footprints as she was jogging near her home in northern Saskatchewan on

July 26, 1998, she told the *Regina Leader Post* that she panicked, for she realized that she had come across the track of a Bigfoot. Alerting her husband Dennis to her chance discovery, he and his brother videotaped the tracks to establish a permanent record.

Although neither the Royal Canadian Mounted Police nor the anthropology department of the University of Saskatchewan seemed particularly interested in the giant fourteen-inch by seven-inch footprints with a six-foot stride, Archie Baptiste, a tribal elder of the Red Pheasant Reserve, told the Gambles that the tracks had been made by a *mistysen*, a legendary giant of the woods that avoids humans. While there was no official interest in the Gambles' evidence of a Bigfoot, some area residents made a correlation between the massive prints and a number of missing livestock and dogs.

"Early in the spring," according to Eugene Gardypie, a friend of the Gambles, "a nearby farm had a bull go missing. It was later found dead with several bites taken out of it." Gardypie added that another bull had disappeared the week of July 26.

The Controversial Patterson-Gimlin Film of Bigfoot

On October 20, 1967, near Bluff Creek, north of Eureka, California, Bigfoot hunters Roger Patterson and Bob Gimlin were packing into one of the greatest wilderness areas in the country. The two men were on horses, following a creek into the remote mountains.

At around 3:30 that afternoon, they were 20 miles beyond the end of a dirt road that had been slashed through the forest for logging trucks. The two men were moving through the dense underbrush when their horses suddenly reared and tossed both of them to the ground. Patterson got to his feet and scrambled for his 16mm movie camera, for directly ahead of them was a gigantic, hairy animal walking upright like a man.

Patterson dashed through the brush toward the Bigfoot, hand-holding his camera, trying to keep focus on the creature that was walking away from him. He managed to shoot several feet of movie film of what appears to be a female Bigfoot. Glossy black hair shining in the bright sun, it walks away from the camera with a stride that is very human. It has pendulous breasts, and it looks back at the cameraman as it walks steadily toward a growth of trees. It does not appear to be frightened, it is not running away in panic, but it is obvious that it wishes to avoid contact. Experts say that the creature in the filmclip is over seven feet tall and estimate its weight at around 400 pounds. It left footprints seventeen inches long, and it had a stride of forty-one inches.

After his examination of the Patterson-Gimlin film, Dr. John R. Napier, director of the Primate Biology Program of the Smithsonian Institution, commented that while he saw nothing that pointed conclusively to a hoax, he did express some reservations about the exaggerated, fluid motion of the creature. He also said that he thought the Bigfoot was a male, in spite of the pendulous breasts, because of the crest on its head, a signature of male primates.

Dr. Osman Hill, director of Yerkes Region Primate Research Center at Emory University, stated his opinion that the Bigfoot in the filmclip was hominid (humanlike) rather than pongoid (apelike). If the being in the film was a hoax, Dr. Hill commented, it had been incredibly well done.

Technicians at the Documentary Film Department at Universal Pictures, Hollywood, said that it would take them a couple of million dollars to duplicate the monster in the filmclip. First, they stated, they would have to create a set of artificial muscles, train an actor to walk like the thing on the film, then place him in a gorilla skin.

Most scientists remained skeptical. Don Abbott, an anthropologist with the Provincial Museum in Victoria, British Columbia, said that it was as difficult to admit that the film was real as it was to admit that such a creature as Bigfoot existed. He, like so many other biologists and anthropologists who viewed the film, was not ready to place his reputation on the line until something "concrete" showed up—like bones or a skull.

And so the controversy raged for thirty years. Then on October 19, 1997, the day before the thirtieth anniversary of the Patterson-Gimlin filming of Bigfoot and just prior to a release by the North American Science Institute that would announce their analyses that the creature depicted on the film was genuine, stories appeared in the media claiming that John Chambers, the makeup genius behind such classic motion pictures as *The Planet of the Apes*, had been responsible for creating the gorilla suit that had fooled the monster hunters. According to Howard Berger of Hollywood's KNB Effects Group, it was common knowledge within the film industry that Chambers had designed the costume for friends of Patterson who wanted to play a joke on him. Mike McCracken Jr., an associate of Chambers, stated his opinion that he (Chambers) was responsible for the gorilla suit.

Roger Patterson died in 1972, never doubting that he had caught a real Bigfoot on film. None of the "friends" who allegedly asked John Chambers to design a gorilla costume in order to hoax Patterson have ever stepped forward and identified themselves. Chambers himself, who was living in seclusion in a Los Angeles nursing home when the story of the gorilla suit hoax broke, refused to confirm or deny the reports.

Chris Murphy, a Bigfoot researcher, told the *Sunday Telegraph* (October 19, 1997) that "very high computer enhancements of the film show conclusively that, whatever it was, it was not wearing a suit. The skin on the creature ripples as it walks."

Other Bigfoot experts have weighed into the fray and declared the Patterson-Gimlin film to be an authentic documentary of a genuine female hominoid. Two Russian scientists, Dmitri Bayanov and Igor Bourtsev, minutely analyzed every movement of the female Bigfoot on the controversial film and concluded that it had passed all their tests and scrutinies and their criteria of "distinctiveness, consistency, and naturalness." Who, they ask rhetorically in their article in *The Sasquatch and Other Unknown Hominoids*, "other than God or natural selection is sufficiently conversant with anatomy and bio-mechanics to 'design' a body which is perfectly harmonious in terms of structure and function?"

So it is that the Patterson-Gimlin Bigfoot film remains controversial. But it has not been disproved. The jury must still be considered out on the final decision as to its authenticity.

Researchers Obtain Bigfoot Body Cast

On September 22, 2000, a team of fourteen researchers that had tracked the elusive Bigfoot for a week deep in the mountains of the Gifford Pinchot National Forest in Washington state found an extraordinary piece of evidence that may end all arguments about whether or not the mysterious creature exists. There, in a muddy wallow near Mt. Adams, was an imprint of Bigfoot's hair-covered lower body as it lay on its side, apparently reaching over to get some fruit. Thermal imaging equipment confirmed that the impression made by the massive body was only a few hours old.

The team of Bigfoot hunters who discovered the imprint—Dr. LeRoy Fish, a retired wildlife ecologist with a doctorate in zoology; Derek Randles, a landscape architect; and Richard Noll, a tooling metrologist—next made a plaster cast of the body print, what appeared to be impressions of the creature's left forearm, hip, thigh, and heel. More than 200 pounds of plaster were needed to acquire a complete three-and-one half-by-five-foot cast of the imprint. Dr. Jeff Meldrum of Idaho State University stated that the imprint had definitely not been made by someone getting into the mud wallow and squirming around.

On October 23, Idaho State University issued a press release stating that a team of investigators, including Dr. Meldrum; Dr. Grover Krantz, retired physical anthropologist from Washington State University; Dr. John Bindernagel, Canadian wildlife biologist; John Green, retired Canadian author and long-time Bigfoot hunter; and Dr. Ron Brown, exotic animal handler and health care administrator, had examined the plaster cast obtained from the mud wallow and agreed that it could not be "attributed to any commonly known Northwest animal and may present an unknown primate."

According to the university press release, after the cast had been cleaned, "extensive impressions of hair on the buttock and thigh surfaces and a fringe of longer hair along the forearm were evident." In addition, Dr. Meldrum, associate professor of anatomy and anthropology, identified what appeared to be "skin ridge patterns on the heel, comparable to fingerprints, that are characteristic of primates."

While the cast may not prove without question the existence of a species of North American ape, Dr. Meldrum said that it "constitutes significant and compelling new evidence that will hopefully stimulate further serious research and investigation into the presence of these primates in the Northwest mountains and elsewhere."

SASQUATCH

Stories about Canada's Sasquatch, a tribal name for Bigfoot, have been cropping up in the accounts of trappers, lumberjacks, and settlers in the Northwest Territories since the 1850s. Long before the frontier folk discovered the giant of the woods, the Sasquatch had become an integral element in many of the myths and legends of the native people. Even today, certain tribal members can recite the genealogy of the "giant, hairy men," and emphasize that at one time these creatures were very numerous in Canada.

Perhaps the most remarkable and most thoroughly documented account of a Sasquatch from those early days occurred in 1884 and was recorded in the *Daily British Colonist*. In the immediate vicinity of Number 4 tunnel, twenty miles from Yale, British Columbia, a group of railroad men captured a creature that could truly be called half-man and half-beast.

The men called him "Jacko," and described him as looking very much like a gorilla, standing about four feet, seven inches and weighing 127 pounds. The only sound that issued from him was a kind of half-bark and half-growl.

According to the *Daily British Colonist*, July 4, 1884:

"[Jacko] has long, black, strong hair and resembles a human being [with the exception that] . . . his entire body, excepting his hands . . . and feet are covered with glossy hair about one inch long. His forearm is much longer than a man's forearm, and he possesses extraordinary strength. . . ."

No one really knows what happened to Jacko, a remarkable creature that may have put the controversy over Sasquatch/ Bigfoot to rest in favor of either a subspecies of human or an unknown species of North American ape over 120 years ago. It is known that the man who became Jacko's "keeper," George Telbury of Yale, British Columbia, announced his intention to take the man-beast to London, England, to exhibit him. Whatever fate had in mind for either Telbury or his unusual property, all traces of Jacko vanished after the rash of news stories recounting the details of his capture.

Shortly after all the media excitement over the Bigfoot tracks and giant hairy man sightings in California and the Northwestern states in the late 1950s, Canadians began coming forward with their own startling encounters with Sasquatch. *The Nelson News* for October 4, 1960, told of the frightening run-in that John Bringsli, for more than thirty-five years an experienced woodsman, hunter, and fisherman in the Kootenay district, had with an unknown monster while he was picking huckleberries near Lemon Creek. According to Bringsli, the sight of the unusual animal paralyzed him with fear:

"It was seven to nine feet tall, with long legs and powerful arms covered with hair," Bringsli said. "It had very wide shoulders, and a flat face with ears flat against the side of its head. At first I thought it was a strange-looking bear, but then I saw that it looked more like a big, hairy ape."

The huge creature just stood there, staring at Bringsli. "It was about eight in the morning, and I could see very clearly," Bringsli said. "Astoundingly, I saw that it had hands, not claws. Its long hair was a peculiar bluish-tinge. Its apelike head appeared to be fashioned directly to its huge shoulders."

After a long two minutes of staring at one another, the Sasquatch began slowly to walk toward the paralyzed huckleberry hunter. It was then that John Bringsli decided it was time to sprint to his car and to find another location for his berry picking.

When he returned to the scene the next day with a group

of friends armed with high-powered rifles and cameras, the strange beast did not reappear. Bringsli and his party did find one footprint, sixteen to seventeen inches long, with a "sharp toe print."

Sometimes the Monster May Hunt Its Hunters

Perhaps the most eerie tales in all of Sasquatchery are grouped around Canada's mysterious Nahanni Valley, located in the southern end of the Mackenzie Mountains. Hot sulfur springs keep the valley's 250 square miles verdant during the entire year, even though the Nahanni is situated above 60 degrees latitude.

The Native American tribes in the area have avoided the Nahanni since the times of their forefathers. Even today, tribal hunters are reluctant to follow their quarry into the valley's warm mists. To both the tribal villagers and the whites who live near the Nahanni, the mysterious place is known as "The Valley of Headless Men."

According to shadowy accounts amassed over the years, there have been too many prospectors and fur trappers lured into the valley in search of fabled gold deposits and rich catches of furs, who have been found with the flesh stripped from their bones and their heads missing. Often, say the old stories, search parties have found the deep indentations of giant, humanlike footprints around the decapitated skeletons.

A few bold trappers who have managed to escape the dangers of the valley and returned with valuable bundles of furs have said that they would never enter the Nahanni again under any circumstances. They complain of the mist that seemed to swirl around them night and day and eventually caused them to see things that they hoped could not be there.

They also state that they could not shake the feeling that someone or something was spying on them, watching them, all the time.

"Hell, you can't find anyone from any of the tribes who'll go with you into the Nahanni," one trapper said. "They say the valley is filled with evil spirits. You know, I think they just might be right."

Could it be that a band of the usually docile and shy Sasquatch have developed hostile attitudes toward humans, especially those who would violate their Nahanni Valley? Is it possible that the Sasquatch of the Nahanni have begun to collect the skulls of humans for use in primitive religious ceremonies, just as Neanderthals severed the skulls of the cave bear to use as totems? Whatever may be the reason and whatever or whoever may be responsible, some accounts state that more than a dozen prospectors and fur trappers are known to have been decapitated in the eerie mists of the Nahanni Valley. And although the giant footprints near the skeletal remains constitute only circumstantial evidence, it remains evidence of a most uncomfortable sort.

THE SKUNK APE—FLORIDA'S OWN BIGFOOT

The two teenagers were supposed to be attending a dance in New Port Richey, Florida, on that star-dusted, moon-marvelous night, but because of their youth and because of the beauty of the night, they had decided not to come back after intermission but to take advantage of a lovers' lane near Elfers.

They had not been parked long when the girl complained of a disagreeable odor. "There's a terrible smell around here," she said, crinkling her nose in a sign of disapproval. "Can't you smell it?"

Her date had to admit that he did. It smelled kind of like a skunk, but it had the stench of the swamp to it, as well. Whatever it was, it was a powerful, stifling, nauseating odor.

Just as he was about to start the car and drive to a spot with a more agreeable aroma, the young couple were startled by a large, apelike creature that rose from the bushes beside them and emitted a high-pitched squealing growl. The panicked boy somehow managed to start the motor and lean on the horn at the same time. Seemingly repelled by the loud blaring of the horn and the roar of the engine, the creature turned and ran back into the woods.

As with Bigfoot in the Northwestern United States and Sasquatch in Canada, legends of an apelike monster that haunts the more remote areas of Florida have been in circulation since the early days of that state's history. As with the legends of the hairy giants of the North, members of Native American tribes insisted the centuries-old tales were true.

Legend appeared to dramatically come to life in February 2001 when the Sarasota County Sheriff's office released two remarkable photographs of a mysterious creature that had been taken by an elderly woman who sighted an apelike entity in her backyard. For two nights, the large hairy monster had made strange noises, emitted a strong odor, and snitched apples from her back porch. On the third night she managed to take two photographs of the creature that her husband thought looked something like an orangutan. While Steve Otto of the Tampa *Tribune* admitted on February 13 that the pictures provided "absolute kinda irrefutable proof of Skunk Ape," he, along with other reporters and Skunk Ape hunters, recalled earlier encounters with the elusive Bigfoot of the South. My own files contained such accounts as follows:

* * *

Around 9:30 in the evening on November 30, 1966, a woman who wished to remain anonymous was changing a tire on a lonely stretch of Route 491 near Brooksville, Florida. The nearby wooded area made the scene an uncomfortable, eerie place to have to change a tire.

Then she became aware of an awful stench. There was a heavy crashing of brush, and she turned to see a large, hairy creature walking toward her. To her great relief, the huge apelike beast simply stood by the side of the road and seemed content merely to stare at her as she leaned weakly against the side of her automobile.

Within another few moments, the sound of an approaching vehicle caused the thing to turn and walk back into the woods.

On December 5, 1966, *Orlando Sentinel* staff writer Elvis Lane commented that the many sightings of the creature that had been dubbed the "Florida Sandman," in contrast to the "Abominable Snowman," had created a "Loch Ness–like atmosphere" in Osceola County. Lane wrote of two hunters who claimed to have wounded the monster. Although it left a trail of blood, the creature seemed relatively unscathed by their volley, and the two men fled in the opposite direction.

In another report, Lane described how the son of a ranch hand had gone to investigate the sounds of someone opening their garage and had surprised the hairy giant raising the door. When the young man shouted his alarm, the monster threw a heavy tire at him.

Area residents also complained about the Sandman or Skunk Ape peeping in their windows at night. Others said that they had had garbage cans upset by a huge creature that retreated into the night when they clicked on yardlights. The more observant eyewitnesses described the nocturnal marauder as standing between six and seven feet tall and weighing somewhere between 300 and 400 pounds. Nearly every witness mentioned the terrible stench that accompanied the giant intruder.

According to some who have attempted to pursue the Skunk Ape into the wilds of the Everglades, the creature lives in muddy and abandoned alligator caves deep in the steamy swamp. The gators leave the rotting remains of their kills behind to putrefy in the heat of their hideaways, and the Skunk Apes absorb the stench into their hair, thus accounting for their awful smell.

Although the Skunk Ape is said to be primarily a vegetarian and often steals produce from area gardens, Everglades hunters claim to have seen the giant kill a deer and split open its belly to get at the liver and entrails.

In 1980, large footprints, complete with the impression of toes, were found in the Ocala National Forest. The Sheriff's Department estimated that the unknown creature that had made the prints was around ten feet tall and weighed around 1,000 pounds.

On Monday evening, July 21, 1997, Vince Doerr, chief of the Ochopee Fire Central District, told the *Miami Herald* that he had seen "a brown-looking tall thing" run across the road ahead of him. He was certain that the thing was not a bear.

Ochopee borders the Everglades, and a few days after Doerr's sighting, a group of six British tourists and their guide, Dan Rowland, saw a Skunk Ape on Turner River Road, just north of the town. According to Rowland's statement in the *Miami Herald* [July 28, 1997], the unknown apelike creature was between six and seven feet tall, "flat-faced, broad-shouldered, covered with long brown hair or fur and reeking of skunk." The seven witnesses observed the Skunk

Ape "in a slough covered with bald cypress trees." Rowland added that ". . . it loped along like a big monkey or gorilla, then it disappeared into the woods."

The guide said that the Naples Trolley Tour out of Marco Island also sighted the Skunk Ape and that the driver "was really shook up."

No doubt, the Skunk Ape will continue to "shake up" Floridians and tourists to that state for many years to come.

Winged Manimals

In the early 1970s, I received a fascinating report from writer Don Worley, who told me that his informant, PFC E.M. was a young man of twenty-one whom he had known all his life. Worley went on to preface the young Marine's account by stating that E.M. had no knowledge of the paranormal nor did he have any interest in the strange or unknown. "E.M. is a reliable observer," Worley said, "and he swears this event is true."

In August 1969, E.M. was with a group of Marines who were on a defensive perimeter near Danang, Vietnam. "There were three of us sitting on top of the bunker, looking west at our part of the perimeter," the young Marine stated in his report. "It was about one-thirty A.M. There was a half-moon in the sky. Visibility was good, and there were no limiting factors except darkness."

All of a sudden for some inexplicable reason, the three Marines looked up in the sky and saw an astonishing figure coming toward them:

"It had a kind of glow, and at first we couldn't make out for sure what it was," E.M. said. "It looked like a gigantic bat. After it got close enough, so we could see what it was, it looked like a woman, a naked black woman with big wings and a kind of greenish cast to her. She glowed and threw off a radiance."

According to E.M., the winged woman's arms appeared not to have any bones in them "because they were so limber," and when she flapped her wings, "there was no noise."

As she hovered over their heads, E.M. estimated that the winged lady was only six or seven feet above them: "We just froze. We couldn't believe it, because we had never seen anything like this before in our lives. When she was maybe ten feet away from us, we started hearing her wings flap. The total time we watched her until we lost sight of her must have been between three and four minutes."

In his transcript of his interview with the young Marine, Don Worley asked if they had reported the incident to anyone.

"We told everybody," E.M. responded emphatically. "We told our lieutenant and junior execs—and they kind of looked at us like we had been on dope or something."

Could they see if the winged visitor had been truly a solid, material woman?

"Definitely!" E.M. answered. "She was a well-developed woman! She was completely naked, but there was a kind of down or fur covering her body. She glowed a greenish color, and even though her skin color appeared to be ebony, her hair was straight like a Caucasian's, rather than curly like a black person's."

While it may be easy to imagine three Marines on guard duty fantasizing about a well-developed woman visiting their lonely post at night, it is difficult to perceive why they would visualize her coming equipped with wings to keep herself out of their reach. While it may also be easy for the skeptics to write off other accounts of winged entities visiting humans on lonely and shadowy country roads as difficult-to-fathom fantasies, the flying manimals have scared the bejabbers out of those who claimed to have seen them.

Winged Birdman in His Melon Patch

In July 1980, Joe Pierce, who farms in a rural area outside of St. Louis, Missouri, told of his encounter with a tall humanlike creature with wings that was feasting on his crop of prize watermelons. "I had worked hard nurturing the melons in that special patch behind the barn, carefully weeding between the rows, seeing that they had plenty of water, and so forth," Pierce said in his report of the incident. "I wasn't like the old-timers who loaded their shotguns with rock salt to sting the behinds of any kids who came by night to steal a couple of melons, but I did keep a watchful eye on those melons."

Around eleven o'clock one night, he heard his old Border collie Angus barking and whining at something in the melon patch behind the barn. "I was puzzled by Angus's whining," Pierce said, "because he was still a feisty old guy. I thought that maybe one or two of the melon rustlers might be known to Angus—and they were confusing him at his guard duties by calling his name and talking gentle to him."

Pierce set out with a flashlight to investigate the disturbance in the melon patch, and as he turned the corner of the barn, he nearly stumbled over Angus, who was cowering and shivering next to the building. "I knew then that he had been frightened by someone in that patch," Pierce said, "and I was afraid Angus might have been hurt by a watermelon thief."

Pierce knelt briefly beside his dog, checked quickly for any injury, then, relieved at finding no wounds of any kind, he stood up and directed the beam of the flashlight toward the sounds of movement in the melon patch. He will never forget what he saw.

"At first it looked like a man with a blanket wrapped around him, bending over and chomping into a melon," Pierce said. "I thought it was too dad-blamed hot for anyone to be covering himself with a blanket, but then I figured he had done it to disguise himself. I yelled at him to get the hell out of my watermelon patch—and when he stood up I could see that he was a tall manlike creature with dark wings that had been folded around his torso. As he stretched himself to his full height of well over six feet, each wing unfolded to a width of what appeared to be seven to eight feet—at least fourteen feet from one wing tip to the other."

Pierce recalled that he was struck dumb by the sight of the winged creature. "My mouth was open, but I couldn't seem to yell or make any sound at all. I dropped the flashlight, and I can remember leaning back against a wall of the barn. I really felt like I was going to pass out. My knees just buckled, and I slid down to the ground."

Fearing that the thing would attack him, Pierce was relieved when it emitted a terrible screeching sound, then lifted off into the night sky. "Its wings made a sharp leathery slapping sound as it flew away," Pierce said. "I was close to an eagle once as it flapped its wings before flying off, but this creature's wings would easily have drowned out the sound that eagle made."

The few family members and neighbors to whom Pierce confided advised him that he had probably startled a large barn owl into flight and had exaggerated its dimensions in the darkness. "I know that some barn owls can develop some mighty large wing spans," Pierce said, "but they don't stand over six feet tall. And I can't remember owls ever going after watermelons. This thing was some kind of freak of nature— half-human and half-bird."

THE "THINGS" FROM ATLANTIS

When some people hear such reports of creatures that appear to be half-human and half-animal, they recall the old Greek mythological figures such as the centaur, with the head and upper torso of a man and the lower body of a horse; the satyr, with a horned human head and body supported by the hairy legs of a goat; and the Harpy, with the head of a once lovely human female that screeches destruction from atop a large, winged body. The student of metaphysics, however, recalls the teachings of the great American prophet Edgar Cayce concerning a time in the fabled Atlantis when grotesque mixtures of animals and humans were created. These entities were called "Things" and exactly how such beings should be treated remained a central issue throughout the history of Atlantis, dividing the nation into two groups— the Children of the Law of One and the Sons of Belial.

According to Cayce, the Sons of Belial enslaved these manimals—many of whom carried physical deformities such as feathered appendages, webbed feet, and other animal-like features—and treated them little better than robots. The Children of the Law of One, however, taught that these beings were not objects, but imprisoned souls containing the divine spark of the Creator. As such, they were to be helped out of their miserable existence, not kept there for purposes of exploitation. This difference in attitude and treatment of the Things persisted all the way up to the time of the First Destruction of Atlantis, in approximately 50,000 B.C.E.

During the Second Destruction in 28,000 B.C.E., the continent of Atlantis broke up into five major islands, the largest and most advanced of which was Poseidia. It was at this time, Cayce said, that the Sons of Belial discovered cybernetic control of the human brain. Soon thereafter, they cracked the DNA code, enabling them to shape heredity. Such control, resting in their unethical hands, resulted in the creation of more Things. There are those who have studied the Cayce material who insist that the pig was an Atlantean creation, with human DNA serving as the base material. Proponents of this theory will point out that pork is the meat most similar in substance to human flesh—and the most difficult for humans to digest. They will also call attention to the ancient Jewish taboo applied to the ingestion of pork. And then there is the Greek myth of Circe, the enchantress who turned men into swine.

Then, as Cayce perceived in his visions, the Sons of Belial had become such an effrontery to nature that the Creative Forces brought about the complete destruction of Atlantis. The volcanic eruptions and the breaking up of the land masses occurred over several months around 10,000 B.C.E. As each tremor became increasingly more damaging, the Children of the Law of One heeded the signs and began to migrate to the Pyrenees Mountain range, Egypt, the Yucatan, and what is now Peru.

After the once mighty nation had disappeared beneath the waters of the Atlantic, it was discovered that the majority of the survivors had made their way to Egypt. Here, the priest-craft of the Children of the Law of One purified the Things that had followed them there in the Temple of Sacrifice and the Temple Beautiful. In the first, physical corrections were made, feathered appendages and other animal features were removed. In the second temple, the entities' souls were purified and they were taught to develop their creativity.

WILL OUR OWN SUPERSCIENCE CREATE HYBRID MONSTERS?

But what of the Things that did not go down beneath the ocean with the great cities of Atlantis? What of those hybrid monsters who managed to make it to other lands far away from the ministrations of the Children of the Law of One and their two healing temples? Are they the creatures that we today call Bigfoot or Sasquatch? Are they the mysterious winged entities that haunt our nights? Are all these manimals that taunt our conventional biologists and zoologists the surviving creation of a once-powerful ancient superscience that defied nature and mocked the Creative Forces?

Before we can state that such ideas are farfetched, we know that many surgeons have experimented with livers and hearts from pigs as living organs for transplanted surgeries into humans. And before we can laugh off the Atlantean legend of the Things, we must absorb the fact that in January 1999, Amrad, an Australian biotech company, took out a Europe-wide patent on a process that would allow human-hybrid animals to be developed with body parts that originated from humans.

On November 26, 2000, the London *Observer* reported that the European Patent Office had stated in the previous month that it would never grant a patent on mixed-species embryos, considering such biological blendings "against public order and morality." But a researcher in Greenpeace's German office had discovered Amrad's patent and its subsequent sale to the U.S. company Chemicon International.

Church groups reacted with outrage when word of the patent became known to the public. A spokesman for the Roman Catholic Church called the process "morally indefensible." Dr. Donald Bruce, a spokesman for European churches on bioethics, said that such a patent should never have been granted. To speak about using human cells in animals, Dr. Bruce stated, "is completely unacceptable."

Thomas Schweiger, representing Greenpeace, issued a call to the European Patent Office to withdraw the patent. "The chimeras [creatures made of the parts of various animals and humans] may be nonhuman, but they may contain human organs, body parts, nerve cells, and even human genetic codes. The company does not give concrete medical uses and obviously intended to [receive] . . . broad monopoly rights on the process and chimeric creatures."

Although an expressed intention of the process may well be to grow human organs in animals for surgical transplantation, experts warn that there is no doubt that the potential is there to create hybrid human-animal creatures.

If one day in the not-too-distant future our science should introduce such manimals to a brave new world, then our society may well prove itself to be Atlantis reborn—and our nation will have come full circle from the shadows of an ancient wrong to the darkness of a blighted tomorrow.

Three

LAKE AND SEA MONSTERS

In March 1998, Scottish pet food salesman Richard White won a prize award of $825 for the best photograph of the Loch Ness Monster of the year. White had been on his way to the village of Foyers above the loch when he noticed an unusual disturbance in the water halfway across the loch toward Urquhart Castle on the opposite bank. He stopped to take a look, grabbed his camera, and began snapping photos of the monster in the water.

Gary Campbell, president of the Official Loch Ness Monster Fan Club, declared White's photos of "Nessie" to be among the best that he had ever seen. The fact that scientists using computer enhancement techniques had been unable to assess exactly what the pictures showed, Campbell said, only added to the mystery of Loch Ness.

Sightings of Nessie, most often described as a long-necked monster resembling a prehistoric brontosaurus, have been sighted in and near Loch Ness since the fifteenth century, and nearly two million tourists each year come to Scotland to test their luck at obtaining a glimpse and a photograph of the elusive water beast.

Because international hunts for Nessie seem to increase with each passing year, on January 5, 2001, Scottish Natural Heritage announced that it would establish a panel of environmental experts to form a Loch Ness Monster Board. Among the primary duties of such a panel will be the examination of the many applications for Nessie hunts and to draw up an official list of guidelines for such endeavors. Members of the Monster Board, such as the representatives from the Scottish Environment Protection Agency, have expressed their growing concern that the wildlife that shares the loch with Nessie—the otters, seals, and fish—might be adversely affected by some of the traps and other devices employed by the monster hunters.

OBSESSED WITH NESSIE FOR THIRTY YEARS

While science may remain highly skeptical of Nessie's actual existence, Dan Taylor of Hardeeville, South Carolina, says that there is nothing like having your miniature submarine moved around by a giant water beast to make you a true believer in sea serpents and lake monsters. That was what happened to him in Scotland's Loch Ness in 1969, and he told J. R. Moehringer of the *Los Angeles Times* (August 16, 1998) that he had been obsessed with the legendary Loch Ness monster ever since. Taylor even sold his house to finance the construction of a special submarine that he hopes will be able to establish proof of Nessie's existence once and for all.

Taylor had accompanied University of Chicago biologist Roy Mackal on the 1969 quest for Nessie that was sponsored by Field Enterprises, publishers of the *World Book Encyclopedia*. He had been selected to become a part of the expedition because of his expertise with submarines, and he brought with him a small fiberglass sub that he had built to explore the murky depths of Loch Ness. Regardless of his considerable skills as a submariner, however, there was little that he could do to see more than a few feet out of the portholes because the water was thick and dark with mud and peat.

It was on one of his last futile runs around the loch that Taylor encountered Nessie. The submarine was hovering around a depth of 250 feet when he said that he felt the craft beginning to turn, unnaturally, "like the secondhand of a clock being pushed backward by a finger." Taylor knew that *something* had pushed up against the submarine and turned it around, but he said that it didn't dawn on him that it had been Nessie until he surfaced.

It was that brief "haunting, tantalizing" encounter that has driven Dan Taylor ever since to create a submarine designed to bring back proof of the existence of the huge water beast with which he "bumped and twirled" on the bottom of Loch Ness over thirty years ago. According to Taylor, he has "unfinished business" with Nessie.

SEEKING SOLID PROOF OF THE LOCH NESS MONSTER

Solid proof of the fabled Loch Ness monster has been sought by those who have seen the creature with their own eyes since St. Columba made the first recorded sighting in 565. For the past several decades, volunteer Nessie spotters work in relays from mid-May to mid-October. Each volunteer is equipped with log pads, field glasses, and video cameras with telephoto lenses.

Some years ago, Clem Lister Skelton, resident technician of the Loch Ness Phenomena Investigation Bureau, Ltd., claimed to have seen Nessie many times. "We have one of the largest creatures in the world in this loch's confines, and we don't know what it is," he observed. "[The quest for the monster] is challenging, exciting—and infuriating."

Could "one of the largest creatures in the world" actually be living in a lake in Scotland? Loch Ness is certainly large enough and deep enough. It is twenty-four miles long by about a mile across. It has a mean depth of 433 feet, twice that of the North Sea into which it flows through the River Ness at its eastern end. Loch Ness is fed by five rivers and fifty mountain streams. The loch never freezes, and snow rarely lies near its shores. Its temperature remains fairly constant at about a chilling 42 degrees Fahrenheit, summer or winter.

What about the fact that no monster carcasses have ever been washed ashore? Well, as local inhabitants and Nessie researchers point out, the sides of the loch are steep, the bottom is deep with mud, and there are no tides in the loch that would push dead hulks the size of the monster ashore.

One of the more verifiable of the sightings of a large creature in Loch Ness was made in the mid-1960s by Tim Dinsdale, a member of the Defense Ministry's Joint Air Reconnaissance Center (JARIC), who said that the twelve-to-sixteen-foot-long thing that he photographed traveling at a speed of ten knots was "almost certainly animate."

On January 24, 1966, the Royal Air Force issued its analysis of the Dinsdale film, stating that the movement in the water of the "hump" of the creature indicated that the object was moving at a speed of about ten miles per hour. After much technical discussion about the relative size and perspective of the "solid black, approximately triangular shape" (the hump) and a comparison of the unidentified creature with a motorboat moving in the same area (filmed immediately after the creature had swum past), the RAF conceded that the object was "not a surface vessel." And: "One can presumably rule out the idea that it is any sort of submarine vessel for various reasons, which leaves the conclusion that it probably is an animate object."

In the spring of 1968, David James, a former member of the British Parliament and head of the Loch Ness Phenomena Investigation Bureau, stated that in the studied opinion of the bureau, it should be made clear that there was no single monster that had lived in Loch Ness for a few thousand years. What the bureau was investigating was the possibility of an unidentified creature, "breeding, evolving like any other species . . . cut off from the sea, for 5,000 to 7,000 years." The Loch Ness Phenomena Investigation Bureau also wished to make one assertion very clear: "There is something there. Too many reliable persons have seen too much, with too little possibility for coincidence, connivance, or conjuration to pass the entire matter off as only a figment of someone's imagination."

In 1968, Dr. Roy P. Mackal, University of Chicago biologist and head of the U.S. branch of the bureau, received the three-year grant from Field Enterprises Educational Corporation of Chicago that incorporated the services and the submarine of Dan Taylor. Although the expedition had sophisticated photographic equipment, biopsy darts, and other advanced research materials, as we have already stated, the murky brown waters of Loch Ness rendered all the underwater devices relatively useless. Dr. Mackal has theorized that the type of creature that most neatly fits the mass of descriptive evidence and photos compiled by researchers and witnesses has to be some kind of large aquatic mammal that would be capable of thriving above 50 degrees north latitude.

However, David Tucker, head of the electronic engineering department at Birmingham University, and a team of sonar experts did have better luck finding evidence of Nessie in the peat-stained loch waters with the special equipment that he had developed. After two weeks of probing Loch Ness with sonar, Tucker's study appears to provide evidence that a family of monsters does indeed inhabit the loch. In one thirteen-minute period, Tucker stated, sonar echoes defined large objects moving underwater. A massive object was recorded swimming at a speed as high as 17 miles per hour and diving at a rate of 450 feet a minute. "From the evidence we have," he concluded, "there is some animal life in the loch whose behavior is difficult to reconcile with that of fish."

On June 6, 1996, sixteen guests and staff members at the Craigcarroch House Hotel on the shore of Loch Ness reported having seen the powerful wake of some large marine creature moving across the lake for five to ten minutes. Although none of the witnesses to the event said that they actually saw Nessie, Kate Munro, one of the hotel's owners, said that it had to have been a very large creature to create such a frothy disturbance and to move in a zigzagging motion on an otherwise placid lake surface.

LAKE MONSTERS AROUND THE WORLD

Although Nessie is far and away the most famous of all monsters inhabiting inland bodies of water, there are reports of equally large, equally strange aquatic creatures in lakes all over the world.

Russia's Lake Brosno

Residents of Benyok, a village on the shores of Lake Brosno, about 250 miles northwest of Moscow, have reported a "dragon monster" lurking in the lake. Both local inhabitants and tourists visiting the picturesque lake have said that the creature's body is snakelike, approximately sixteen feet long. Its head looks like that of a huge fish, with two large bulbous eyes.

Siberia's Lakes Vororta and Labynikir

Reports from Lake Vororta speak of a monster that terrorizes the local inhabitants. The huge water beast is said to emit a horrible roar and is described as spherical in shape. According to news stories from the area in the 1950s, the creature had eaten a swimming dog, a reindeer, and an undetermined number of humans.

Geologist Viktor Tverdokhlebov was quoted in a United Press International story in 1953 as saying that the creature that he had seen in Lake Labynikir was an "ominous-looking dark gray sphere that showed slightly above the water [and] inspired nearly uncontrollable fear as it approached.... There were two bulging protrusions that must have been eyes approximately seven feet apart on the head. The creature reached the bank, stopped, then went into a series of convulsions which raised waves and fountains of water as it disappeared below. There was no question about the monster's intentions. It was heading straight for us—and only when the ripple of water it had stirred reached our feet was its terrible hypnotic spell broken. We were able to flee the water and escape—not a moment too soon!"

"Issie" in Lake Ikeda, Japan

Although reports of a lake monster nearly a hundred feet long and about three feet around had been made by startled witnesses for hundreds of years, the first sighting of Issie by a large group of people occurred on September 4, 1978, when over twenty people saw the massive, snakelike creature splashing in Lake Ikeda. An Issie Information Office in Kago-shima Prefecture states that some of those who have reported the serpent over the years have described it as mostly black, while others say that it is brown with yellow stripes.

Lake Pohenegamook, Quebec

In this lake country 200 miles east of Quebec City, many people have described the same creature—an animal be-tween 12 and 18 feet long, brown or black in color, with a round back two or three feet wide, and a sawtooth fin down the center. Anytime anyone approaches the thing, it slithers away and sinks down below the lake's surface.

Lakes Manitoba and Winnipegosis, Manitoba

These lakes have a long, continuing history of something big and strange frightening fishermen. In 1960, Professor James A. McLeod, head of the Department of Zoology of the University of Manitoba, decided to investigate the tales, pro-claiming before his departure that the "monster" was proba-bly just a large snapping turtle.

But then McLeod discovered a fisherman who had made a replica of a peculiar-looking bone that he had found near the shore. The original had been destroyed in a fire, but either the fisherman was an astute paleontologist or he had actually made a model of a bone from a creature that had been extinct for millions of years. The professor was no longer interested in searching for giant snapping turtles. He even went so far as to speculate that giant prehistoric reptiles that had once lived in the area might somehow have survived. "Of course," he emphasized, "we are skeptical, but it is a possibility."

"Ogopogo," Okanogan Lake, British Columbia

Native Americans called it N'haaik, and the tribespeople

in that area have been aware of this long-necked creature's existence for centuries. In fact, they regarded it as a kind of demon to which sacrifices must be made if any canoes were to make it across the lake in safety.

In July 1989, after three centuries of reported sightings, a salesman captured the beast on videotape, and the footage so convinced the Canadian government of the lake monster's existence that Ogopogo was placed on the nation's protected wildlife list.

"Selma," Seljord Lake, Norway; The Great Lake, Sweden

Sightings on Norway's Seljord Lake date back to 1750 when a man was attacked by a "sea horse" while rowing on the lake. In 1880, two people washing clothes on the beach killed a "strange-looking lizard" that had crawled out of the water. Over the passing of time, hundreds of witnesses have seen the sea serpent that the locals have nicknamed "Selma." Descriptions vary from those who say that it has several humps, a crested neck, and an eel-like head to those who swear that it has the features of an alligator with two horns protruding from its head.

In July 1998, Swedish journalist and lake monster hunter Jan Sundberg gathered an eleven-man team to spend seventeen days trawling the lake in southern Norway with a minisubmarine fitted with cameras and a host of the state-of-the-art technology. Sundberg told Reuters (July 19, 1998) that the echoing equipment that he had used on his expedition to the lake in 1977 had detected large objects moving under the water in unison and separating in different directions.

According to Sundberg, the Seljord serpent lifts its head above the surface of the lake and "travels very fast, up to 25 knots." The creature doesn't fit any species presently known to science and "has several qualities not seen before, such as travelling on the surface at a high speed and moving vertically up and down."

During the 1998 expedition, Sundberg and his crew managed to record "some mysterious whale-like noises," but admitted that evidence was not enough to prove the lake serpent's existence to a hardcore scientist, "who wants the evidence of a dead or live" monster.

While Sundberg plummed the depths of Norway's Seljord Lake seeking Selma, a fleet of fifteen vessels with researchers and divers set out to plum the depths of Sweden's Great Lake in an effort to identify the lake monster that had been seen by 450 people since 1653. Some witnesses described a large gray-brown eel about ten feet long by three feet wide while other claimed to have sighted a serpent up to about fifty feet long with humps and a small doglike head.

In August 2000, Sundberg returned to Seljord bringing with him a special eighteen-foot-long tube-shaped trap for Selma, the legendary horned serpent of the lake. Sundberg adapted the trap from a fish trap for eels. "If anything up to about six meters long swims in one end, the opening closes— and it won't be able to get out," he said (Reuters, August 2, 2000). Two biologists from the University of Oslo were on standby to fly down by helicopter and take DNA tests of the serpent, Sundberg explained. "Then we'll release it back into the lake. We will be very careful not to hurt it."

In January 2001, Sundberg and his team announced their plans to leave the lakes of Sweden to pursue the Loch Ness monster in Scotland. According to Sundberg, his Global Underwater Search Team would begin "Operation Clean Sweep" on March 20, 2001. The Swedes plan to place a large funnel-shaped net in the loch and use it to trap any "Nessies" swimming in the shallows.

"Champ," Lake Champlain, New York

Interestingly enough, the first white man to see Champ, the monster of Lake Champlain, was Samuel de Champlain, for whom this lake, which separates Vermont and New York, is named. In his journal entry for July 1609, he describes his sighting of a serpentine creature about twenty feet long, as thick as a barrel, with a horselike head. The tribespeople who accompanied Champlain's expedition were quite familiar with the serpent and called it *chousarou*.

In the nearly 400 years since the French explorer had his encounter with Champ, there have been over 600 sightings of the unknown beast. Some area residents argue that the monster is in reality a giant sturgeon or a group of otters swimming in single file. Others name the misidentification of such floating objects as buoys, tree stumps, or barrels.

School teacher Joseph W. Zarzynski has been among the most vocal and persistent defenders of Champ and his kin as "something strange and wonderful" dwelling in Lake Champlain. His efforts were no doubt quite influential in the October 6, 1980, decision of the Port Henry Village Board of Trustees to pass a resolution granting protection of the serpentine creatures along the shores of the 109-mile lake. Their resolution said, in part, that "all the waters of Lake Champlain which adjoin the village of Port Henry are hereby declared to be off limits to anyone who would in any way harm, harass, or destroy the Lake Champlain monsters."

Apparently Champ appreciates his protected status and continues to flourish in the lake. Seasonal resident Elizabeth

Wilkins reported sighting a "large humped, crocodile-like creature . . . about thirty or forty feet long" in the lake as she ate breakfast on the morning of November 26, 2000.

Champ Quest, a Panton, Vermont-based nonprofit group that keeps records on the monster, reported sixteen sightings in 2000. Director Dennis Hall told Lohr McKinstry, staff writer for the Plattsburgh, New York, *Press-Republican* (December 12, 2000) that he had personally spotted Champ on July 23 "over a four-minute period" as the creature "stuck its neck straight out of the water and remained on the surface."

"Memphre," Lake Memphremagog, Vermont

Early colonists soon learned that tribal villagers would not bathe in Lake Memphremagog because of their fear of a monstrous creature with a horselike head, a long neck, and a large humped body. Biologist Gary Mangiacopra from Southern Connecticut State University has theorized that Memphre is a member of a species of giant invertebrate amphibians that has survived in the lake since the last ice age. Such water beasts can grow to weigh as much as 4,000 pounds, range in length from 20 to 40 feet, and live for about seventy-five years. Since the bodies of such invertebrates as Memphre and its fellow lake monsters fall apart within hours of their death and are quickly eaten by other marine creatures, Mangiacopra states, no fleshy gobs of the beasts wash ashore to "prove" their existence. Neither are there any skeletal remains available to examine, because, as invertebrates, they have no skeletons.

After hundreds of sightings of Memphre had been reported since colonial times, the Vermont Legislature unanimously passed a law in 1987 to protect Memphre and her family of water creatures "from any willful act resulting in death, injury, or harassment."

"Ogua," Monongahela River, West Virginia

According to local tradition and written accounts, sightings of this long-necked serpent were extremely common in the colonial period. In the late 1700s, a group of settlers killed an Ogua with clubs and found it to be about 20 feet in length and to weigh nearly 500 pounds. Although sightings are not as frequent as they were in earlier times, reports of Ogua continue in the Monongahela and other waterways of the state.

"Meshekenabek," Lake Manitou, Indiana

The Potawtomi tribe would neither hunt nor fish in Lake Manitou, and they told the early settlers to beware of the evil spirit that made its home in the lake. In 1827, during construction of a corn mill on the lake, several workmen claimed to have sighted a dark-colored serpentine creature over 30 feet in length with a long neck and a horselike head. In 1838, George Winter, a noted painter of Native American life, sketched his conception of the huge, snakelike monster. In recent years, reports of Meshekenabek have lessened, but it lives on in folklore of the area.

Black Mystery Monster in Lake Erie

Although there seems to be no long-standing history of reports of a lake monster in Lake Erie, residents of a number of Ohio communities have claimed since at least 1990 to have sighted a large blackish beast about fifty feet long with bulging eyes swimming through the water like a monstrous snake. Witnesses describe the creature as possessing a reptilian head atop a long, tapered neck.

The Dragon, Lake Elizabeth, Angeles National Forest, California.

Since the days of the early Spanish explorers, there have been reports of a dragonlike creature in the waters of Lake

Elizabeth. Local legends describe the monster as being about 30 feet long with greenish skin and exuding a sulfurous odor.

Flathead Monster, Flathead Lake, Montana

Sightings of a large, dark, eel-shaped creature, 20 to 40 feet long, have been reported in Flathead Lake since 1889, but in 1993, an astonishing claim issued forth from the lake that the Flathead Monster had saved the life of a three-year-old boy.

According to Cindy Johnson, she and her sister were getting ready to take a boat ride on the lake when they both stepped back inside the house to get some items, leaving little Andrew, her son, on the dock. When she glanced out the window and saw Andrew nowhere in sight, a terrified Cindy ran down to the dock, fearing that he had fallen into the lake.

Relieved, but baffled, she saw a soaking wet Andrew making his way up the ladder. Since her son didn't know how to swim and the water was well over his head at the end of the dock—and he was not even wearing a life jacket—she could not imagine how he had managed to get out of the lake. Andrew's response was direct and startling in its implications: He had lost his balance, fallen into the lake, threshed about helplessly in the water—and then the Flathead Monster had lifted him to the safety of the ladder with its tail. Andrew added that old Flathead had a baby of her own with her.

In February 1996, Mrs. Johnson told researcher Dr. Franklin Ruehl that Andrew was now a healthy, normal six-year-old first grader, but "the story of the monster saving his life has been burned into his memory forever."

While it is pleasant to think of the various Nessies, Champs, and Ogopogos as benevolent and cheerful creatures from some Disney animated feature, alert beasts who are always there to save the lives of folks who accidentally fall

overboard into the water, judging from the generally frightening, nightmarish descriptions of the massive, long-necked
serpentine leviathans, there would be very few witnesses who
would care to test the "benevolent monster" hypothesis in
actual practice.

And what about the even more massive, more hideously
described monsters of the sea? While it has become fashionable in some circles to go to swim with the dolphins—and
even the sharks in some advertised underwater excursions—I
would not suggest an organized program to swim with the
sea serpents.

SEA SERPENTS

In the May 1965 issue of *Fate* magazine, Edward Brian
McCleary told of his harrowing escape from a sea monster.
According to McCleary, he and four friends left on the pleasant Saturday morning of March 24, 1962, to go skindiving at
the ruins of the sunken *Massachusetts* in Pensacola Bay, Florida. A sudden storm sent the young men into the ocean, and
they clung desperately to their rubber raft. After the squall
had subsided, a heavy, oppressive fog settled over the sea.

Suddenly the misty air became filled with the odor of dead
fish—and about forty feet away they heard a tremendous
splash. Whatever the thing was, it had created waves that had
reached the raft and splashed over the sides.

They knew that no boat had made the sound. They heard
the splash again, and through the fog they could make out
what appeared to be a ten-foot pole with a bulbous head on
top. It remained erect for a moment, then bent in the middle
and dove under the surface. A sickening odor permeated
the air.

From out of the fog came a strange, high-pitched whine. The five young men knew that they had never before heard anything like that sound. They panicked, slipped on their fins, and dove into the water. They decided to keep together and try for the portion of the wrecked *Massachusetts* that remained above water. In back of them, as they swam, they could heard *whatever it was* making a strange, hissing sound.

Then they heard a terrible scream. McCleary remembered that it lasted about half a minute. "I heard Warren call, 'Hey! Help me! It's got Brad! I've got to get outta here . . .' His voice was cut off sharply by a short cry."

The three remaining swimmers clustered together, not knowing how many feet of water separated them from whatever was down there waiting for them. Then McCleary gasped: "Eric! What happened to Larry? He was here a minute ago!"

The two dove for their friend, but found no trace of him. Eric got a cramp in his leg, and McCleary wrapped his arm around his neck to help support him as they continued swimming toward the wreck.

A wave broke and separated them. When McCleary surfaced, he saw Eric swimming ahead of him.

The horror that happened next will be forever etched in Brian McCleary's brain. Breaking water next to Eric was the sea monster. "I could see the long neck and two small eyes," McCleary said, recalling the time of terror in the water. "The mouth opened and it bent over. It dove on top of Eric, dragging him under. I screamed and began to swim past the ship. My insides were shaking uncontrollably."

Somehow McCleary managed to swim the remaining two miles to shore. He remembers a jumbled montage of images, sprawling on the beach, stumbling to a tower of some sort, spending the night in a fitful slumber, then falling on his face before a group of boys. When he opened his eyes, he was in the Pensacola Naval Base Hospital.

McCleary wrote that none of the journalists told all the facts of the five divers' encounter with the hideous and terrible sea beast. Each of the local newspapers carried the story of the tragedy, but they attributed the young men's deaths to accidental drowning.

Later, McCleary asked E. E. McGovern, the director of the search and rescue units, if he believed his story about the monster. According to McCleary, the veteran of many sea encounters replied: "The sea has a lot of secrets. There are a lot of things we don't know about. People don't believe these things because they are afraid to. Yes, I believe you, but there's not much else I can do."

Ancient Survivors of the Deep

During the first week of April 2000, while on a morning drive along Cape Bonavista, Newfoundland, Canada, Bob Crewe sighted a creature in the water that he estimated as measuring about 30 feet across. Intrigued by the strange beast, Crewe stopped his truck on a cliff overlooking the ocean and honked his horn to gauge the thing's response. According to Crewe, it raised its head at the sound of the blaring horn, and he was able to see that the creature had a neck about four or five feet long. He went on to describe the sea serpent as very much resembling a huge snake with some kind of snout protruding from its head.

"Any fool can disbelieve in sea serpents," wryly observed Victoria, British Columbia, newspaper editor Archie Willis in 1933. Willis's pronouncement came as a sharp rejoinder to the skeptics who laughed at the hundreds of witnesses who swore that they had seen a large snakelike creature swimming in the waters off the coast of the Pacific Northwest. Willis christened the sea monster "Cadborosaurus," and the moniker stuck.

The creature with its long serpentine body, its horselike head, humps on its back, and its remarkable surface swimming speed of up to 40 knots, has been a part of coastal lore from Alaska to Oregon for hundreds of years. While the waters of the Pacific Northwest border one of the deepest underwater trenches on the planet—where almost any massive sea beast could reside—the greatest number of sightings of Cadborosaurus have occurred in the inland waters around Vancouver Island and the northern Olympic Peninsula.

In *Cadborosaurus: Survivor of the Deep*, Vancouver biologist Dr. Edward L. Bousfield and Dr. Paul H. Leblond, professor of oceanography at the University of British Columbia, describe the creature as a classic sea monster with a flexible, serpentine body; an elongated neck topped by a head resembling that of a horse or giraffe; the presence of anterior flippers; and a dorsally toothed or spiky tail.

The Monster of Gloucester

On the opposite shore on the Atlantic seacoast of North America, there is a sea serpent that has been paying periodic visits to the Cape Ann area and Gloucester, Massachusetts for more than 340 years. An Englishman named John Josselyn, who was returning to London, made the first sighting of the creature as it lay "coiled like a cable" on a rock at Cape Ann. Seamen would have killed the serpent, but two Native American crew members protested such an act, stating that all on board would be in danger of terrible retribution if the sea creature was harmed.

On August 6, 1817, Amos Lawrence, founder of the mills which bore his name, sighted the sea monster and issued a proclamation to that effect. Col. Thomas H. Perkins, one of Boston's wealthiest citizens, also testified to the reality of the great serpent, stating that it was about 40 feet in length with a single horn nine to twelve inches long on its head.

On that same August day, a group of fishermen spotted the marine giant near Eastern Point and shouted that it was making its way between Ten Pound Island and the shore. They said later that they could clearly see the thing's backbone moving vertically up and down as it appeared to be chasing schools of herring around the harbor. Shipmaster Solomon Allen judged the serpent to be between 80 and 90 feet in length.

Generations of Gloucester residents and tourists have sighted the Cape Ann sea serpent, very often as they sailed the harbor and nearly always stating that they were frightened by the appearance of a huge snakelike creature at least 70 feet in length. In April 1975, some fishermen saw the monster up close and were able to provide one of the more complete descriptions of the monster.

According to Captain John Favazza, they had sighted a large, dark object on their starboard side, about 80 feet away, that they had at first thought was a whale. Then a serpentlike creature lifted its head from the surface, saw the fishing boat, and began to swim directly toward them. Favazza later told reporters that the sea serpent was black, smooth rather than scaly, with a pointed head, small eyes, and a white line around its mouth. It swam sideways in the water, like a snake. It was longer than his 66-foot boat, and he estimated its girth as about 15 feet around.

Lost: One Pickled Sea Serpent's Head

If a strange twist of fate on the unforgiving seas had not intervened, the skeptic's tiresome challenge of why, if such monsters exist, doesn't some bold seaman bring one back dead or alive would have been answered 150 years ago.

On January 13, 1852, two New Bedford whaling vessels, the *Monongahela* and the *Rebecca Sims*, were drifting slowly in the Pacific doldrums, their sails limp from lack of wind. When the lookout's shout of "something big in the water" caused Captain Seabury of the *Monongahela* to bring his telescope to bear on the object, he could distinguish only a huge living creature, thrashing about in the water as if in great agony. The captain's immediate deduction was that they had come upon a great whale that had escaped another whaler's longboats but was now succumbing to the fatal wounds of a harpoon.

Captain Seabury ordered three longboats over the side to end the beast's pain, and he was in the first boat as it pulled alongside the massive thing that he still believed was a wounded whale. He drove the harpoon deep into the leviathan's flesh as the crewmen pulled hard on the oars to get the longboat safely away from the waters that would soon be churning with the pain-maddened movements of the sea giant.

The instant the harpoon struck home, a nightmarish head ten feet long rose out of the water and lunged at the boats. Two of the longboats were capsized in seconds. The terrified whalers realized at once that they were dealing with a sea creature the likes of which they had never seen, but they were much too busy escaping from the violent strikes of its ghastly teeth-studded jaws to theorize about what it was that was trying to devour them.

Then the monster sounded. The heavy line smoked over the bow as the sea beast dove for the bottom. Captain Seabury was able to tie on the spare coil with only seconds to spare. More than 1,000 feet of line were out before the massive thing ceased its descent.

Unfurling her sails to catch what little wind there was, the *Monongahela* had managed to come alongside the capsized longboats and began to pick up the frightened seamen who were bobbing in the water, fearing that the hideous beast might at any moment resurface and make a meal of them. Captain Seabury made the line fast on the vessel, though he couldn't be certain that his monstrous prey was still impaled by the harpoon. The *Rebecca Sims*, under the command of Captain Gavitt, pulled alongside her sister ship, and the crews of the two ships began discussing the strange monster that they had encountered.

The next morning, Captain Seabury ordered the line taken up. The crewmen had pulled in only about half of the line when the massive carcass suddenly popped to the surface. It was much greater in length than the *Monongahela*, which measured 100 feet from stem to stern, and it had a thick body that was about 50 feet in diameter. Its color was a brownish gray with a light stripe about three feet wide running its full length. Its neck was ten feet around, and it supported a grotesque head that was ten feet long and shaped like that of a gigantic alligator. The astounded crewmen counted ninety-four teeth in its ghastly jaws—and each of the three-inch, saberlike teeth was hooked backward, like those of a snake.

Ever the practical Yankee, Captain Seabury ordered his crew to render the creature as if it were a whale—but the monster was possessed only of tough skin, stringy flesh, and no blubber.

Captain Seabury was fully aware of the ridicule accorded to sailing masters and their crews who claimed to have encountered "sea serpents," so he gave orders that the hideous head be chopped off and placed in a huge pickling vat in order to preserve it until they returned to New Bedford. In addition, he wrote a detailed report of their harpooning the sea monster and he provided a complete description of the thing that they had brought aboard the *Monogahela*. Since Captain Gavitt and the crew of the *Rebecca Sims* were homeward bound, Captain Seabury gave him the report in order to prepare New Bedford for the astonishing exhibit that he and his men would bring with them upon their own return.

If only Captain Seabury would have transferred the grisly head to Captain Gavitt's vessel along with his report of the monster, the doubting world would have had its first mounted sea serpent's head 150 years ago. But the sea was not yet willing to yield the answer to one of its most stubborn and perplexing riddles.

Captain Seabury's account of the incredible sea serpent arrived safely in New Bedford and was entered into the records along with the personal oath of Captain Gavitt. But the *Monogahela* never returned to port with its incredible cargo. Years later her nameboard was found on the shore of Umnak Island in the Aleutians.

The Sea Serpent and the Two Zoologists

When the crew of the yacht *Valhalla* sighted a sea monster off Parahiba, Brazil, on December 7, 1905, they were fortunate to have among their passengers E. G. B. Meade-Waldo and Michael J. Nicoll, two expert naturalists, Fellows of the Zoological Society of Britain, who were taking part in a scientific expedition to the South Atlantic and Indian Ocean.

Meade-Waldo prepared a paper on the sighting, which he presented to the Society at its meeting on June 19, 1906. In his report, he told how his attention was first drawn to a "large brown fin . . . sticking out of the water, dark seaweed-brown in color, somewhat crinkled at the edge." The creature's fin was an astonishing six feet in length "and projected from eighteen inches to two feet from the water." Under the water and to the rear of the fin, the zoologist said that he could perceive "the shape of a considerable body. A great head and neck did not touch the [fin] in the water, but came out of the water in front of it, at a distance of certainly not less than eighteen inches, probably more. The neck appeared to be the thickness of a slight man's body, and from seven to eight feet was out of the water."

The head, according to Meade-Waldo's expert observation, had a "very turtlelike appearance, as had also the eye. . . . It moved its neck from side to side in a peculiar manner; the color of the head and neck was dark brown above and whitish below." Meade-Waldo also stated that since he saw the creature, he has reflected on its actual size and concluded that it "was probably considerably larger that it appeared at first."

Nicoll discussed the incident of the *Valhalla* sea monster sighting two years later in his book *Three Voyages of a Naturalist:* "I feel certain that [the creature] was not a reptile . . . but a mammal. The general appearance of the creature, especially the soft, almost rubberlike fin, gives one this impression."

COULD DINOSAURS SURVIVE IN OUR LAKES AND SEAS?

A popular theory to explain the existence of sea monsters is that they may be survivors of one of the giant reptiles of the Mesozoic Age. Philip Gosse, the famous nineteenth-century naturalist, was an avid exponent of the possibility that plesiosaurs could still be thriving in our oceans. While the Mesozoic Age ended tens of millions of years ago, he argued, there was no *a priori* reason why some of the descendents of the great sea reptiles could not have survived. Gosse's theory has been given added credence in our own century by the discovery off the coast of southeast Africa of *coelacanth* (crossopterygian fish), which have survived almost unchanged for 70 million years—from a time even before the Age of Reptiles.

Other marine zoologists favor the unverified existence of an aquatic mammal related to the whales as their candidate for the mantle of sea monster. They maintain that the horselike mane often reported on the so-called sea "serpents" would be an unlikely appendage for a reptile—and quite convincingly, they argue that only a warm-blooded mammal would be able to survive in the cold water of the North Atlantic, where so many sea monster stories originate.

Still other marine researchers have expanded the theory of the monstrous sea mammal and combined it with another candidate for survival from prehistory. They hypothesize the survival of an ancient species of whale known as *Zeuglodon* or *Basilosaurus*, whose fossil remains are well known. Well-equipped for the role of a sea monster, *Basilosaurus* was a huge beast with a slim, elongated body measuring over 70 feet in length. Its skull was long and low, and the creature propelled itself by means of single pair of fins at its forward end. This massive marine monster is known to have survived into the Micene Epoch, just over 30 million years ago. If the *coelacanth* has survived for 70 million years, it seems possible that the relatively young *Basilosaurus* could still be inhabiting our seas—and scaring the wits out of unsuspecting mariners.

After years of researching Nessie and Champ and similar long-necked lake creatures all around the northern hemisphere, Dr. Roy Mackal has come to believe that rather than beholding "monsters" in the waters, people are witnessing small, remnant bands of *Zeuglodons*, the primitive ancestor of the whale, long thought to be extinct. In Dr. Mackal's theory, the creatures migrate from oceans to lakes, following prey such as spawning salmon. Lake Champlain is linked to the Atlantic Ocean by the Richelieu and St. Lawrence Rivers of Quebec. Loch Ness is connected to the sea, and so is Lake Okanagan in British Columbia, where Ogopogo is frequently sighted.

Smaller than the *Basilosaurus*, a later development on the evolutionary ladder, *Zeuglodons* bear little resemblance to modern whales. Dr. Mackal said that the fossil remnants of the creature at the Smithsonian Institution "looks like a big anaconda [a large semiaquatic boa constrictor] with a ridge down its back."

THE "ONE WHO STOPS THE FLOW OF RIVERS"

For at least 200 years now, stories have emerged from the swamps, rivers, and lakes of African jungles that there is a brownish-gray, elephant-sized creature with a reptilian tail and a long, flexible neck. The native people call it *mokele-mbembe* ("the one who stops the flow of rivers") or *emela-ntuka* ("the one who eats the tops of trees"). In 1980, Dr. Roy Mackal led an expedition into African swamps that are "Mokey's" hangouts and stated later that the descriptions of the beast would fit that of a *sauropod*, the giant plant-eating reptile that supposedly became extinct about 60 million years ago.

J. Richard Greenwell, an expedition member from Tucson, told of having discovered huge tracks that led into the Likouala River. In his opinion, no animal smaller than an elephant could have left such a path through the thickets near the river, and, Greenwell noted, elephants always leave an exit trail when they leave a river. Whatever left these massive prints made no such sign of an exit, which may indicate that Mokey is a marine, as well as land, creature.

Tracking even dinosaur-sized creatures is not that simple in the Likouala swampland, which is twice the size of Scotland, and thick with venomous snakes and disease-bearing insects. On November 28, 1981, Herman Regusters, an aerospace engineer from South Pasadena, and his wife Kia claimed to have seen and to have photographed a dinosaur-like animal in a remote African lake. Mrs. Regusters said that the gigantic reptile was a dark red with a long, thick neck, and longer than two hippopotamuses. Unfortunately, the photograph taken by the Regusters was rather fuzzy, and their tape recording of the "roaring trumpeting noise" heard frequently around Lake Tele was impossible to identify.

In 1996, zoologist Professor Michelle Gupton told the British press that she was attacked by a huge water monster as she investigated the shoreline of Lake Tele. According to Ms. Gupton, the brownish-gray creature about the size of an elephant suddenly rose out of the waters of the lake right in front of her. Awestruck, she reached out to touch its smooth skin.

That was a nearly fatal mistake on the part of the zoologist. The monster snapped at her with its huge teeth, slashing out a foot-long slice of skin on the side of her stomach. Ms. Gupton said that she passed out from the pain and was later rescued by members of her party who had been searching the surrounding jungle for signs of *mokele-mbembe*. She was rushed to a hospital, where her wound was treated. In her considered opinion, her experience proves that dinosaurs are far from extinct.

Dr. Bill Gibbons, a zoologist who specializes in attempting to track down new species, told the *London Sunday Times* (June 3, 1999) that he is certain that *mokele-mbembe* exists. "The main problem, aside from the inhospitable terrain, is that it mostly lives underwater in areas with very few people and in countries which are politically very unstable."

Only recently, Dr. Gibbons said, cryptozoologists had heard reports that hunters from the Kabonga tribe had killed a *mokele-mbembe* and had tried to eat it. Its flesh proved inedible and the carcass was left to rot and be gnawed and pecked at by scavengers. But now, he hopes, a most unusual skeleton awaits them. If it is still there when their expedition manages to arrive in the largely inaccessible swamps of central Africa, then we may all discover that there truly are more monsters awaiting us in the darkness—monsters that should have been extinct 60 million years ago.

Four

BLOODSUCKERS

I had my first "interview with a vampire" in 1969. I was in a large Midwestern city doing television and radio interviews for a new book release, when a local police officer of my prior acquaintance, knowing of my research into the paranormal, called my hotel room and asked if I would like to talk to a "real vampire" that they had just arrested for vagrancy.

"We can't hold her for long," he said, "so if you want to talk with her, come down to the precinct house right away."

My police officer friend explained that the only thing that had allowed them to arrest the "vampire" was the fact that she was loitering outside the gates of a cemetery late at night and presenting an unsettling disturbance to passersby. He told me in confidence that they could also have busted her on prostitution charges, because she was offering to exchange her physical favors for the blood of the men who stopped to speak with her. As a compassionate police officer, however, he chose to view the young woman as a "crazy, mixed-up kid" and only placed her in lockup for the night.

The vampire, we'll call her Vonda, was in the final process

of gaining her release when I arrived at the precinct. There was no question that she certainly dressed the part of a vampire in her long black evening dress and the skillfully shaded makeup that shadowed facial hollows and accentuated her high cheekbones. Her fingernails were painted black, and I assumed that it was colored contact lenses that made her eyes appear dark and feral and that expensive visits to a dentist had capped and lengthened her canine teeth.

My officer friend introduced us, and I offered to buy her some breakfast if she would allow me to ask her some questions about her vampirism. Since it was nearly noon and the rays of sunlight had not caused her to burst into flame, it was apparent that she was not really a member of the undead and that I would be safe enough to be in her presence without crucifix, holy water, or a wooden stake.

Vonda told me between sips of hot coffee and nibbles of toast and eggs that she was really a vampire. She slept in a coffin and hungered for warm, human blood—though she would settle for animal blood that she sometimes acquired from a neighborhood butcher shop. Although she appeared to be in her midtwenties, she swore that she was really 59 years old. It was the drinking of blood, she declared, that kept her young.

When I asked her if she believed herself to be immortal, Vonda smiled, nicely displaying the pointed "fangs" that modern dentistry had so eerily enhanced. "That remains to be seen," she answered, "but I believe that by ingesting human blood, I can delay—even reverse—the aging process. I plan to be seducing young men into giving me their blood when I am chronologically in my nineties and beyond."

Vonda said that she most often withdrew blood—around a pint—from those who agreed to trade their vital fluid for sex. She made the men comfortable in her apartment and made certain to observe the highest of sanitary methods in extracting the blood from their arms. She had once been a student nurse, and she was confident that she was employing regular medical procedure in the process of withdrawing the blood from her compliant and cooperative partners. Vonda added that she would grant special sexual favors for those more adventurous males who allowed her to slash their arm with a razor and suck the blood from the open wound.

Vonda told me that there were many women and men in the city who were vampires and who supplemented their regular diet with as much human blood as they could acquire. Under no circumstances, she swore, had she or any of her fellow brother and sister blood-drinkers ever forced any of their "donors" to give blood against their will. None of the vampires of whom she was aware had ever killed any victims and drained their blood. They were bloodsuckers who sometimes became desperate for human blood, Vonda conceded, but they were not murderers.

Regretfully, as we will see in this chapter, not all vampires follow such a benign code—neither the classic bloodsucking creatures of the night that have terrorized humankind for centuries nor the contemporary cult of blood-drinkers that strive to emulate vampiric immortality in their bizarre alternate lifestyle.

THE LEGEND OF THE VAMPIRE

Few of the monsters of legend and lore that stalk us from out of the dark fill us with as much dread and apprehension as those creatures that seek to suck our blood and drain away our life force. When we realize there are real-life vampires and a host of other strange, unidentified blood-drinkers out there—hideous night-stalkers that exist outside the parameters of fright-night motion pictures—then even the most stalwart among us want to tack garlands of garlic and dozens of crucifixes to the doors and windows.

The vampire legend is universal, and every culture has its own name for the monster. The word itself rises from the slavonic Magyar—*vam*, meaning blood; *pir*, monster. To cite only a few other appellations for the vampire from different languages, there is the older English variation, *vampyr*; the Latin, *sanguisuga*; Serbian, *vampir*; Russian, *upyr*; Polish, *Upirs*; and the Greek, *Brucolacas*. From the villages of Uganda to Haiti, to the Upper Amazon, all indigenous people know the vampire in its many guises. Traditional Native American Medicine priests, Arctic Eskimo shamans, Polynesian Kahuna, all know the vampire and take precautions against those who were once human who are now undead and seek blood by night to sustain their dark energies.

While contemporary science may look askance at tales of vampires rising from their coffins by night to dine on the blood of the living, in the eighteenth century the respected French philosopher Jean Jacques Rousseau wrote that ". . . if there was ever in the world a warranted and proven history, it is that of vampires." Rousseau stated that nothing was lacking to prove that such monstrous creatures exist. There were hundreds of ". . . official reports, testimonials of persons of standing, of surgeons, of clergymen, of judges; the judicial evidence is all-embracing."

From prehistoric times when primitive hunter-gatherers came to equate a fatal attack from a cave bear's claws and jaws and the flowing of a victim's vital fluid with the release of the life force itself, blood has been considered sacred. Throughout history, a large number of magical and religious rituals have centered around the shedding of blood, and thousands of members of ancient priesthoods have raised chalices filled with the dark, holy elixir of life over thousands of altars stained with both animal and human blood.

As respect for the spiritual quality of human life evolved, the sacrifice of men, women, and children was considered forbidden. While in less civilized times the drinking of an animal's vital fluid had been deemed an appropriate way in which to absorb the strength or virility of the lion, the bear, or the boar, religious law now admonished against both the drinking of animal blood and the eating of meat from which the blood had not been thoroughly drained.

The Old Testament book of *Leviticus* [17:14] acknowledges that blood is "the life of all flesh, the blood of it is the life thereof," but the children of Israel are instructed that they "shall not eat of the blood of no manner of flesh; for the life of all flesh is the blood thereof: whosoever eateth it shall be cut off." Again, in *Deuteronomy* 12:20–24, the Lord warns, ". . . thou mayest eat flesh, whatsoever thy soul lusteth after. . . . Only be sure that thou eat not the blood: for the blood *is* the life; and thou mayest not eat the life with the flesh. Thou shalt not eat [blood]; thou shalt pourest it upon the earth as water."

Similar warnings against the ingesting of blood for religious or health reasons became a part of the teachings of all major faiths and cultures. Therefore, after hundreds of years of such prohibitions concerning animal blood, what could be more ghastly and repulsive to the human psyche than those monsters that wait unseen in the dark to bite the throats and drink the blood of men, women, and children?

With each succeeding generation, the dark powers of the vampire grew. His hypnotic powers were irresistible. Once his eyes fixed on his victims, they were under his control. There would be no use for anyone caught by his grasp to try to fight free, for his strength was that of a dozen normal, living men. He could transform himself into the form of a bat, a rat, an owl, a fox, and a wolf. He was able to see in the dark and to travel on moonbeams and mist. Sometimes, especially when cornered, he had the power to vanish in a puff of smoke.

What could the populace do if they suspected that a vampire was rising from his grave or coffin at night to seek warm human blood?

There were such precautions as liberally applying wolfsbane and sprigs of wild garlic at every door and window. Wearing a crucifix about one's neck and placing others prominently on several walls were highly recommended. If one were truly serious about putting a stop to the nocturnal predator, one would hunt down his grave or coffin and place thereon a branch of the wild rose to keep him locked within. If that didn't work, then the only courses of action remaining were to pry open his coffin during the daylight hours while the vampire lay slumbering and pound a wooden stake through his heart—or perhaps a bit safer, destroy the coffin while he was flapping about during the darkness and allow the rays of the early morning sun to scorch him into ashes.

Contrary to the glamorous image popularized by motion pictures depicting handsome vampires and their voluptuous "brides," the traditional appearance of a vampire is grotesque, a nightmarish creature of the undead with twisted fangs and grasping talons. Rather than the seductive, attractive, formally dressed aristocrats of Hollywood and popular fiction, the vampire of legend is a demonic presence, wrapped in a rotting burial shroud, intent only on sating its bloodlust. The vampire is also a shapeshifter, assuming most often the form of a bat or a wolf.

The cinematic depiction of the vampire in F. W. Murnau's *Nosferatu* (1922) is a much more accurate characterization of the traditional vampire. In this motion picture, actor Max Schreck appears not as the suave, handsome, continental Count Dracula in formal evening dress, smiling seductively at the ladies in the parlor, then, later, materializing in their bedrooms. Schreck's loathsome vampire skitters about in the shadows with dark-ringed, hollowed eyes, pointed devil ears, and hideous fangs. With his long, bloodstained talons, his egg-shaped head, and pasty white complexion, Schreck's Nosferatu looks exactly like the creature of the undead as seen in the collective nightmares of humankind throughout the centuries. Is it just a convenient coincidence that Schreck in German means "terror" or "horror"?

After Bram Stoker's novel *Dracula* (1897) became an extremely popular stage play, and in 1931, a classic motion picture with Bela Lugosi portraying the Count as a sophisticated aristocrat, the image of the vampire as a monstrous demon of the night had been transformed in the collective mass consciousness into that of an attractive, sensual, immaculately dressed stranger who possesses a bite that, while fatal, also promises eternal life. Eternal, that is, if one can avoid those persistent vampire hunters with their wooden stakes.

The occasional stake through the heart has never seemed to keep the cinematic Dracula in his casket for very long. In the final scene of dozens of motion pictures, we have seen the indefatigable Dr. Von Helsing, the academic and scholarly vampire slayer, put an end to the monster once and for all time—until the next film in the series is ready to be released. Cinematically, at least, it seems that nothing can kill a vampire or keep it in its grave for very long. At least as long as its seductive fangs continue to bite off large chunks of box office booty.

As the name "Casanova" has become synonymous in the common vernacular with a great lover, and the name "Quisling" to represent a traitor to a cause, the name "Dracula" has come to symbolize a person who comes from out of the dark and murders through seduction, deceit, and torture, regardless of whether any bloodsucking occurrs. In March 1999, in Ciudad Juarez, Mexico, a twenty-six-year-old bus driver was given the title of "El Dracula" when he was arrested and accused of killing as many as 190 young women whom he kidnapped and subjected to rape and sexual torture before he strangled them and dumped their bodies in the desert.

Some years before, in Monteros, Argentina, another "Dracula," swathed in a black cape, crept into the bedrooms of at least fifteen women, bit deeply into their throats, and sucked the blood which he drew. When police finally tracked the vampire to his lair in a cave on the outskirts of the city, they found a twenty-five-year-old stonemason sleeping in a coffin, his eyes closed in a deep sleep. On his lips was the blood of his most recent victim.

In 1979, motion picture director Werner Herzog remade Murnau's *Nosferatu* with Klaus Kinski applying the classic makeup made famous by Max Schreck, and thus appearing, as *Entertainment Weekly* would later state, "as an oversize vermin." In that same year, director Tobe Hooper utilized the same kind of traditional undead "Schreck look" for the vampire in his adaptation of Stephen King's *Salem's Lot* for television.

E. Elias Merhige's *Shadow of the Vampire*, released on December 29, 2000, tantalizes audiences with the unsettling suggestion that the monstrous Nosferatu (Willem Dafoe), who assumed the title role in the classic film by F. W. Murnau (John Malkovich), was, in reality, actually portrayed by a real vampire, rather than an actor.

And yes, as we have seen, there are real vampires. Not all of them sleep in coffins, and they don't require a wooden stake in their hearts to dispatch them—but they do believe that they must have blood in order to survive and to thrive.

On July 26, 2000, just outside of Santa Cruz, California, a motorist picked up a transient who was thumbing a ride. Things were calm during the 90-minute ride to San Francisco, but when it was time to drop off the hitchhiker, things became very strange.

Stating that he wanted to give the driver a "thank-you hug," the hitchhiker pinned the man's arms to his sides, lunged for his throat, and began biting and sucking at his jugular. After a two-minute struggle, the driver managed to break free of the bloodsucking hitchhiker and the would-be vampire fled the scene on foot.

The driver flagged down a police car and told them of the vampiric attack by the strange individual to whom he had given a ride. The hitchhiker was apprehended a short time later at an entrance to the Golden Gate Park. "I need blood," he told officers by way of explanation for his attack on the motorist.

On February 7, 1998, the *Milwaukee Journal Sentinel* carried a story of a man accused of sucking the blood out of a teenaged girl's arms after he had enticed her to slash her flesh with a razor blade. According to police reports, this same "vampire" hosted parties for teenagers, during which he encouraged them to cut themselves and lick or suck their blood.

THE VAMPIRE ARCHIVES

Verzini: "I Take Delight in Drinking the Blood of Women"

The lust for human blood overcame Vincent Verzini during the years 1867 to 1871. The twenty-two-year-old Italian vampire grasped each of his female victims by the throat, first choking her, then tearing at her flesh with his teeth. He then proceeded to suck the blood through the wound.

Verzini had murdered two women, strangling and horribly

mutilating them, when he began to stalk Maria Previtali, his pretty nineteen-year-old cousin. Although he seized her, threw her to the ground, and began to strangle her, Maria was able to bring up her knee and kick him in the stomach.

The thwarted vampire muttered obscenities and threats and staggered off across a field. Maria hated to believe that her cousin could be responsible for the terrible attacks on women that so terrified the countryside, but she ran home and told her mother of Vincent's attempt to strangle her. Mrs. Previtali immediately took her daughter to the village prefect and Vincent was arrested.

After being questioned at length, Vincent Verzini made a full and detailed confession in which he admitted that he enjoyed "an unspeakable delight" in strangling women and that he received "real sexual pleasure" from the act. He "took great delight" in drinking their blood, he said. "It satisfied me to seize the women by the neck and suck their blood." Verzini was tried, convicted, and sentenced to life imprisonment.

Harrmann: Chewing at Their Throats, Biting Them to Death

Although he was officially charged with only twenty-four murders, Fritz Harrmann, the famous Vampire of Hanover, was unofficially credited with more than fifty deaths. The newspapers of the day noted, however, that during the year 1924, when Harrmann's morbid murders came to light, over six hundred young boys had disappeared in Hanover, Germany, then a city of about 450,000.

During his six-year reign of savagery from 1918 to 1924, Harrmann performed acts of sadism on his victims, chewing at their throats and often biting them to death, sometimes nearly gnawing the head away from their bodies before he cannibalistically ate their flesh. In this perverse regard, he is as much a werewolf as a vampire.

How could Harrmann have disposed with what may have been as many as fifty to several hundred bodies?

Fritz Harrmann also ran a small combination butcher shop and restaurant, and it was known throughout Hanover that Fritz's butcher shop always had the choicest cuts of meat available. One can only imagine the queasy stomachs of Haarmann's clientele when they learned that after he had enjoyed a few choice meals from his victims' bodies, he transformed the remaining chunks of the cadavers into steak and sausages for sale in his shop and restaurant.

Haigh: Religious Fanaticism and a Thirst for Human Blood

By the time the British vampire John George Haigh had been delivered to the hangman in 1949 for having killed nine people, he had been analyzed by enough doctors and psychologists to allow some authorities to express their opinion that his thirst for human blood was somehow linked to his religious fanaticism. Haigh had become obsessed with the Old Testament admonition to "drink water out of thine own cistern and running waters out of thine own well," and through some twisted process of thought, he interpreted these passages to mean that he should begin drinking his own urine and blood.

Haigh was a vampire whose first taste of human blood was his own. He had become involved in an automobile crash in which he suffered a scalp wound which bled profusely. The blood flowed down his face and into his mouth, initiating a bizarre hunger that would lead him to the gallows. As if to offer additional proof of his need to drink of his own "cisterns" and "wells," as well as those fountains of others, shortly after the accident he had a dream which he understood to mean that his religious fervor had sapped his strength. The only process by which he might rejuvenate his bodily resources, he believed the dream to say, was to partake in a regular consumption of fresh human blood.

In keeping with the religious casting of his delusions of vampirism, Haigh evolved a ritual to be observed in the sacrifice of each of his victims. First, he would sever the jugular vein, then he would carefully draw off the blood of the victim a glassful at a time. The actual act of drinking the vital fluid was observed by Haigh with great ceremony. He later became convinced that his religious faith, as well as his physical energies, could be sustained by the sacrifice of others and by the drinking of their blood.

Riva: Roaming the Countryside by Night to Find Blood

On October 30, 1981, in Brockton, Massachusetts, Superior Court Judge Peter F. Brady sentenced twenty-four-year-old James P. Riva II to a mandatory life sentence at Walpole State Prison on the second-degree charge of murdering his grandmother by shooting her with gold-tipped bullets, then attempting to drink her blood from the wounds. Long before his trial began, James did not hesitate to declare himself a vampire.

His mother, Janet Jones of Middlebury, Vermont, testified that James had claimed to have been a vampire for four years. He told her that voices had solemnly informed him that he had no choice in the matter. He must be a vampire and he must drink blood for a long time. The source of such commands, James said, had come to him directly from a devil.

Defense psychiatrist Dr. Bruce Harry testified before the court that James Riva had been insane at the time that he murdered his grandmother. He had been obeying the demonic voices that said that he could not become a good person until he had killed someone and drunk their blood.

Riva's attorney, James T. Spinale, explained to the court that James believed that he was to subsist only on animal and human blood. He envisioned himself as a vampire who could not eat normal meals, but who must roam the countryside at night, eating whatever he could find that still contained animal blood.

Ferrell: A 500-Year-Old Vampire Named "Vesago"

On November 9, 2000, the Florida State Supreme Court reduced the death sentence of self-professed vampire Rod Ferrell, 20, to life in prison because he was only 16 when he clubbed Richard and Ruth Wendorf to death with a crow bar on November 25, 1996, and drove off in their Ford Explorer with Heather, their 15-year-old daughter, and his vampire cult. The high court had established a precedent in a 1999 ruling that defendants must be at least 17 at the time they committed the crime in order to be executed.

During his trial in February 1998, Ferrell, the leader of a coven of teenaged vampires, had provided graphic testimony of the Wendorf murders, as well as the ritualistic lifestyle of his coven members, which included the Wendorfs' own daughter, whom he had initiated into the cult with a blood-drinking ritual in a graveyard. When the trial judge sentenced Ferrell to death for the murders, he ventured his opinion that the young man, then 17, proved that "there is genuine evil in the world."

Ferrell was a second-generation vampire. His mother, Sondra Gibson, had pleaded guilty in 1997 to charges of attempting to seduce a 14-year-old boy into a vampire cult. Ferrell claimed that as a young child he was introduced to occult rituals by his father and his first stepfather—and he swore that he had even witnessed human sacrifices.

After his mother's second divorce, Ferrell became serious about practicing occult rites, especially focusing on vampiric practices. He took to wandering in cemeteries late at night, posing as one of the undead, pretending to be a 500-year-old vampire named "Vesago." Within a brief period of apprenticeship to an older vampire, Ferrell was cutting himself, offering his blood to others, and asking them to reciprocate in the ritual of exchange.

THE NEW BREEDS OF VAMPIRES AMONG US

In 1982, the late parapsychologist Stephen Kaplan, director of the Vampire Research Center in Elmhurst, New York, estimated that there were approximately twenty-one "real" vampires living secretly in the United States and Canada. Kaplan had spoken to many of these self-professed creatures of the night, some of whom claimed to be as old as 300 years, and established the demographics as Massachusetts in the lead with three vampires, followed by Arizona, California, and New Jersey, with two each, the remaining fifteen scattered throughout the other states and provinces.

A feature article by Angela Aeliss (Ft. Worth *Star-Telegram* January 5, 2001) interviewed Nicholas Strathloch, who claimed to be one of 300,000 worldwide members of an ancient vampire religion. Strathloch, a Vampire Master Adept, "the highest grade of recognition within the Temple of the Vampire," told the journalist that among those of his particular vampiric creed, killing is strictly forbidden. While he freely admits to feeding off the emotional energies of other people, he denies ever biting anyone in the neck and feasting on human blood. Nor would he ever take energy from anyone who was ill, because they themselves would require all their bodily resources. In fact, Strathloch told Ms. Aeliss, vampires may also be healers, projecting energy to those who need it.

In the United States, according to vampire researchers and self-professed vampires, Los Angeles has the greatest population of those attracted to the vampiric lifestyle. There are also heavy concentrations of vampires in Rome, Vienna, and London. Japan ranks high in numbers of practitioners of the vampire religion, and India has always had a large number of vampires among those who worship Kali, the Hindu goddess of creation and destruction. In addition to the international gatherings of the Temple of the Vampire, there also exist such orders as Order of the Dragon, the Vampire Church, the House of Kheperu, and the Vampire Grove.

Among those vampire religionists who reject the drinking of human blood and who feed only on the energy of willing or unwilling volunteers, many claim potent psychic abilities, especially the power to project their spiritual essence from their own physical vehicles to possess the body of another.

The Attractive, Alluring Undead

Today, in 2001, vampire research has taken on entirely new and extremely diverse sets of definitions and demographics. With the ever-growing popularity of the Gothic movements, the various vampire role-playing games, the continuing bestseller status of the Anne Rice vampire novels, the high ratings of television series based on vampires and the occult, it would be an impossible task to estimate the population of those who define themselves as some facet of the term "vampire," or to establish any but the most approximate demographics. Millions of readers and viewers have agreed with Ms. Rice that the vampire is a romantic, enthralling figure. The author's major vampire character, Lestat de Lioncourt, and her series of books in the "Vampire Chronicles" series, portray the undead as far from grotesque. Ms. Rice has stated that she perceives the vampire as an individual who never dies, who exerts a charm over people, then accepts their blood as a sacrifice that he might live. In her opinion, the image of the vampire is alluring, attractive, and seductive, and the idea of being sacrificed to keep such an entity alive becomes rather romantic. We long to be one of them, to be one of the undead, forever youthful, attractive, and seductive.

Apparently, Anne Rice's vision of identification with the vampire is an accurate one for thousands of contemporary men and women, for it has been a highly contributive element in establishing an entire subculture of those who wish to become bona fide children of the night.

In the November 24, 2000, issue of the *New York Times*, Margaret Mittelbach and Michael Crewdson report on the city's vampire scene "that has been going strong since the mid-90s" and the many nightclubs that cater to the "daylight-challenged" in their article, "Vampires: Painting the Town Red." The journalists describe the activities in such "dens" as CBGB's, Downtime, the Korova Milk Bar, the Pyramid, the Limelight, and True, "a club in the Flatiron District, where as many as 300 undead heads dance, drink and make merry late into the night." The dress code in such establishments is "gothic," "dark-fetish," "faerie," "Wiccan," or "Celtic" and the overwhelmingly predominant color is black: "And that's not your average New Yorker black. We're talking head-to-toe coal black. Black nail polish. Black bustiers. Black watchbands . . ."

And on the "rare occasion" when a patron of these vampire havens smiles, Mittelbach and Crewdson note, one can make out "the glint of white fangs."

Perhaps few of those New York "vampyrs" prefer blood to

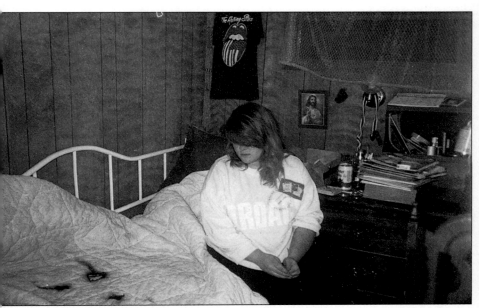

Charred spots remain where the poltergeist haunting Jackie Hernandez's San
Pedro, CA, bungalow set fire to a blanket.
(*Photo courtesy Barry Conrad,* Unknown Encounter, *Barcon Video*)

Ghost stretched a clothesline noose around Jeff Wheatcraft's neck and attempted
to hang him from an attic rafter in the bungalow.
(*Photo courtesy Barry Conrad,* Unknown Encounter, *Barcon Video*)

Hernandez's vinyl lawn chair glows with an eerie light. (*Photo courtesy Barry Conrad,* Unknown Encounter, *Barcon Video*)

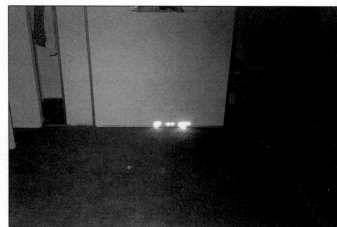

A trio of silent, glowing objects floated around in the Hernandez children's bedroom. (*Photo courtesy Barry Conrad,* Unknown Encounter, *Barcon Video*)

Professional television cameraman Barry Conrad, witnessed phenomena while producing a documentary of the San Pedro haunting and had one of the entities follow him home. (*Photo courtesy Barry Conrad,* Unknown Encounter, *Barcon Video*)

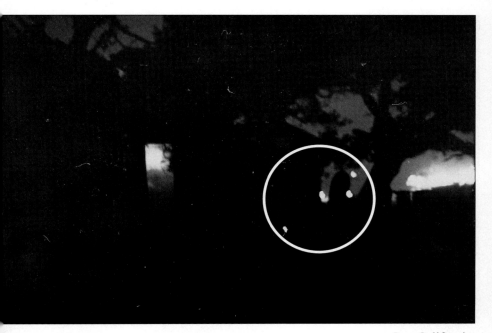

In a California cemetery, psychical researchers photographed a mysterious glowing light in the doorway of a crypt and illuminated orbs moving around the headstones.
(*Photo courtesy Nocerino and Pelton*)

Frank "Nick" Nocerino, the Dean of West Coast psychical researchers, has spent a lifetime investigating haunting phenomena throughout the world.
(*Photo courtesy Nocerino and Pelton*)

During a séance, a phenomenon becomes visible over a chair in the room. (*Photo courtesy Nocerino and Pelton*)

Soon after, the ethereal outline of a male entity can be seen sitting in that chair. (*Photo courtesy Nocerino and Pelton*)

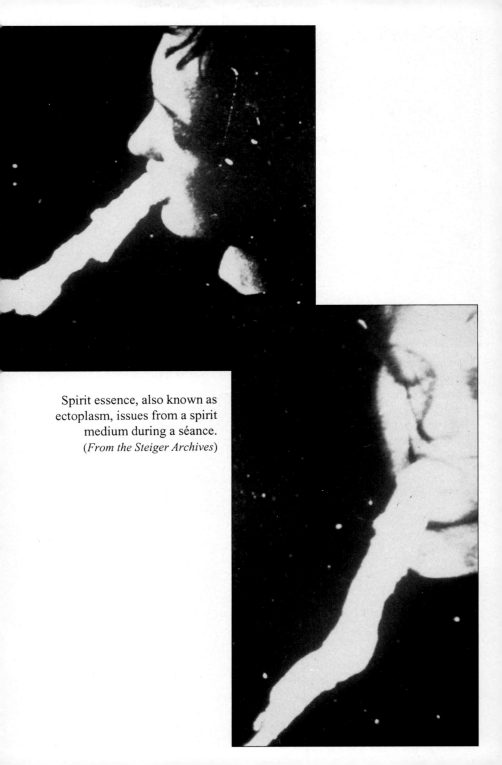

Spirit essence, also known as
ectoplasm, issues from a spirit
medium during a séance.
(*From the Steiger Archives*)

Medium Clarisa Bernhardt
achieved early fame for the
accuracy of her earthquake
predictions and her impressive
demonstrations of spirit contact
during seances. (*Photo courtesy
Clarisa Bernhardt*)

Bernhardt used an autofocus
camera to photograph this spirit
essence in Kansas during
Halloween week in 1998.
(*Photo courtesy Clarisa Bernhardt*)

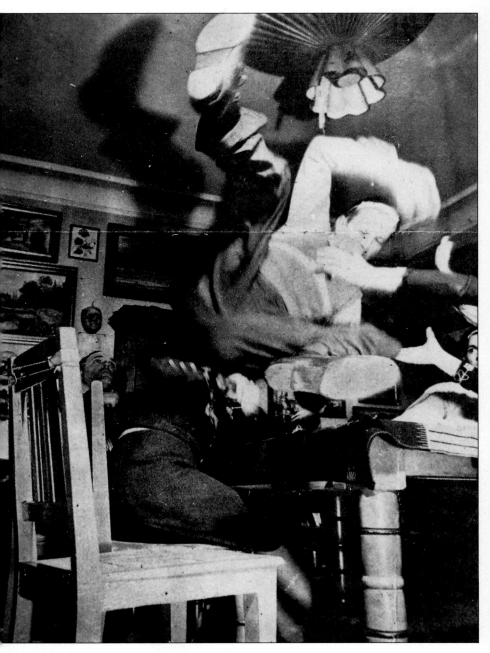

The late psychic sensitive Olof Jonsson participated in this impressive demonstration of levitation during a spirit séance. (*From the Steiger Archives*)

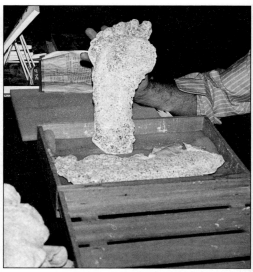

On March 9, 1985, Bigfoot tracks measuring over 20 inches in length and 9 inches across were found in the snow in Whitehall, NY. (*Photo courtest Robert Bartholomew*)

Casting made by Bruce Hallenbeck in Kinderhook, NY, in 1981. (*Photo courtesy of Paul Bartholomew*)

Casting of one of the 14-inch long West Rutland footprints taken on September 20, 1985. (*Photo courtesy Paul Bartholomew*)

Paul Bartholomew, co-author of *Monsters of the North Woods*, holds a 20-inch casting of the "Ye-Ren," China's Bigfoot creature. (*Photo courtesy Paul Bartholomew*)

Photo of a Bigfoot-type creature was taken at a bridge site in rural Chittendon, VT.
(*Photo courtesy Ted and Jeff Pratt*)

Close-up of the creature. (*Photo courtesy Ted and Jeff Pratt*)

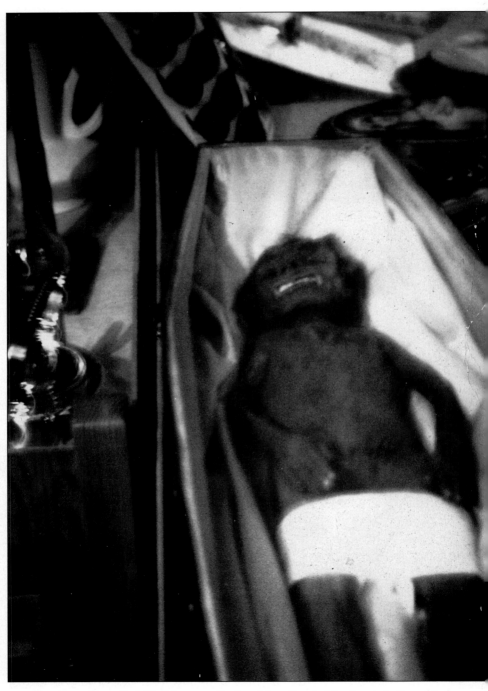

Creature, allegedly killed in an undisclosed location in Mexico, is believed to be the elusive bloodsucking Chupacabra.
(*Photo courtesy Commander X, Inner Light Publications*)

Fairy photographed near psychic-sensitive Diane Tessman boosted its energy to make a clear photographic portrait impossible.
(*Photo courtesy Global Communications*)

Humanlike footprints are scattered worldwide in geological strata more than 250 million years old, predating all known humans. (*From the Steiger Archives*)

Ghostly image of the "woman in black" photographed in a ladies rest room in a political embassy in Washington, D.C. (*From the Steiger Archives*)

Police officers investigate a UFO landing site near Glassboro, NJ, on September 4, 1964. (*Project Bluebook Files*)

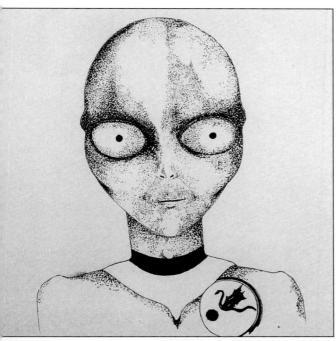

A flying-serpent insignia is often mentioned by witnesses in UFO contact and abduction cases involving reptilian-like creatures. (*From the Steiger Archives*)

Dale Russell and Ron Seguin of Canada's National Museum of Natural Sciences at Ottawa fashioned a creature that might have evolved from Stenonychosaurus, a small dinosaur that lived near the close of the Age of Reptiles 65 million years ago. The four-and-a-half foot biped greatly resembles the descriptions of UFO crewmembers. (*From the Steiger Archives*)

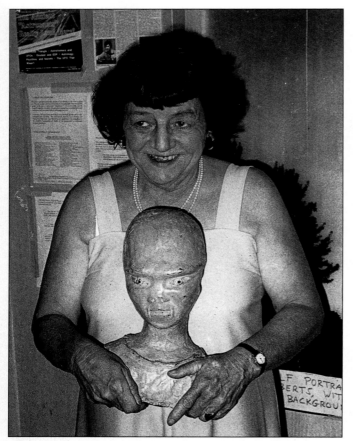

Betty Hill holds bust modeled after the entities who abducted her and her husband, Barney, as they drove from Canada to New Hampshire on September 19, 1961. (*Photo courtesy Global Communications*)

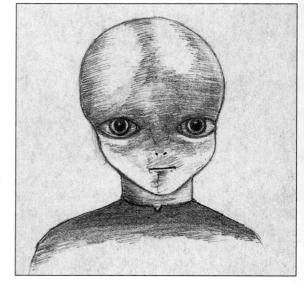

Sketch of alien entity who abducted Travis Walton near Heber, AZ, on November 5, 1975 eerily resembles the entities who abducted the Hills fourteen years earlier. (*From the Steiger Archives*)

Phantom-like entity photographed near a UFO landing site in Canada. (*Photo courtesy Global Communications*)

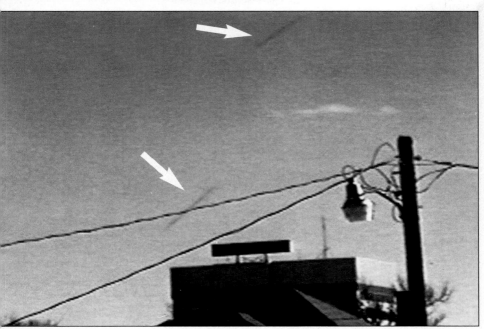

Intelligent sky creatures nicknamed "rods" or "orbs" may account for many UFO or spirit sightings. Here, two rods streak overhead. (*Photo courtesy Jose Escamilla*)

A "rod" photographed traveling through deep rocky abyss.
(*Photo courtesy Jose Escamilla*)

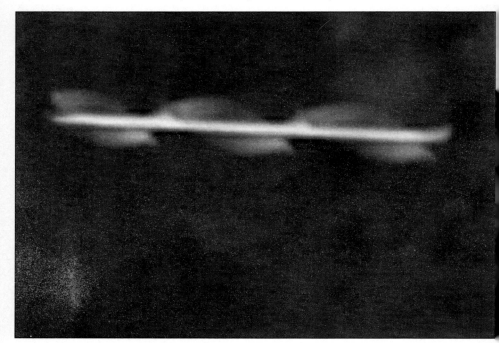

Close-up of "rod" showing what could be fins, wings, or an unknown spiral
mechanism for rapid propulsion. (*Photo courtesy Jose Escamilla*)

beer or wine, but the blood drinkers are there among them. The "Human Living Vampires" believe that they require blood in order to function at their highest level of proficiency. They realize that they are not immortal beings, but they may feel that they have extrasensory abilities that border on the supernatural that are accentuated with the ingestion of human blood. Most often the vital fluid is obtained from willing donors who permit the vampires to make small cuts or punctures in their flesh and lick or suck the blood.

The vast majority of those enthralled by the vampire lifestyle are those young people who find dressing the part of an attractive and seductive member of the undead to appeal to their romantic sensibilities. For these individuals, attending a vampire den one night a week may be akin to being able to dress up for Halloween fifty-two nights of the year. An occasional bit of blood-letting and licking may be a kind of aphrodisiac and intensify their lovemaking.

Men who enjoy emulating the vampire legend as epitomized in the twentieth century by the various motion picture Draculas—Bela Lugosi, Frank Langella, Christopher Lee, and Gary Oldman—dress in elegant capes and evening clothes as they role-play the character of the mysterious and handsome stranger who can promise eternal life and lust to their ladies who also role-play by donning the classic cinematic ethereal gowns with the plunging necklines of the innocent Lucy Westerna—Frances Dale, Kate Nelligan, Barbara Shelley, and Winona Ryder—eager to be seduced by the kiss to the neck that will bestow passion beyond their wildest dreams. It is interesting to note that in these games of "let's pretend we're vampires," no one visits these clubs and parties dressed as the hollow-eyed, pasty-faced, grotesque Nosferatu.

While the above role-playing as vampires and victims may be considered quite harmless as long as the participants know when to draw the line between fantasy and reality, those men and women who cross the boundaries of mental aberration into blood fetishism and obsessive blood-drinking may gradually develop a psychosis that can force them to mutilate or even kill others.

According to psychologists, the desire to assume the guise of a vampire, the restless soul of a member of the undead who must drink the blood of the living to sustain its life, is highly suggestive of pathologically immature, dependent personalities, who cannot fend for themselves in the normal business of living, but who must attach themselves to a more productive personality, just as the vampire attaches itself to those hosts on whose blood it feeds. Such individuals almost always subconsciously desire to return to the state of complete dependence characteristic of the prenatal state. Psychoanalysts often discover that in those pathological cases in which subjects believe themselves to be vampires, the grave or coffin comes to symbolize the womb. The vampire's dependence upon the grave or coffin as a place of safety seems again to betray a deep longing for the prenatal security of the womb.

To such students of the mind, the vampire's fangs are clearly phallic, both in form and function. The vampiric predilection for young people and children, often their own relatives, reveals a form of infantile sexuality and possibly incestuous cravings. The act of sucking a victim's blood is in itself significant, for many psychologists state that such an act would be a sign of a mother fixation. And the fear that one's life will end with someone driving a stake through one's heart, these researchers suggest, may well be a hatred of the father figure.

It would appear that the true lair of the vampire must be sought in the hidden and forgotten recesses of the human mind, rather than in secluded burial vaults and the cobweb-laced ruins of deserted mansions; and that the terrible hunger of real-life vampires must be understood in the light of the frustrations and misdirection of the most basic of human needs: the need to love and to reproduce one's own kind.

PSYCHIC VAMPIRES

Perhaps the archetypal vampires are truly those nocturnal demons that have been visiting the resting places of humans for thousands of years, draining the vital fluids and life energies of their victims who lie helplessly under their seductive ethereal forms. These creatures of darkness are known as "incubi," who often appear to their female prey as handsome men, and "succubi," who manifest as rapturous feminine vessels of delight to receive the seminal fluid of males. We shall explore the nefarious pursuits of such demonic entities in Chapter 7, but for the present, let us examine another kind of vampire, perhaps equally as deadly as the ones who drain their victims' blood, for these, the "psychic vampires," steal the spiritual life force from their unsuspecting prey.

There is one kind of psychic vampire in nearly every office environment or any setting where a number of humans gather to work or to exchange social amenities. You've all seen such an insidious siphon of energy at work. Everyone comes into the office, trying his or her best to be cheery and upbeat first thing in the morning, but Old Grumpo sits there, frowning, matching every greeting with a dour response. But by lunchtime—and you've all witnessed this incredible transformation—Old Grumpo is now perky and cheery, but those seated near this vampire are now feeling very low-energy, even depressed and down. Once again this psychic vampire has "sucked" up all the positive energy that it needed from its office mates and it has been nurtured and fed and is ready to work at full force. The only way to protect yourself from the psychic vampire is to move your desk to the far side of the office or to practice the mental exercise of shielding yourself by visualizing a barrier of Light between yourself and Old Grumpo.

There is a much more dangerous kind of psychic vampire that can select a likely victim and steadily drain the person's life force until the prey has fallen fatally ill. Callously leaving the once vigorous individual depleted and lying in a co-matose state, the psychic vampire moves on to feed on a new victim's vital energy.

In the files of the *Steiger Questionnaire of Mystical, Paranormal, and UFO Experiences*, I have a fascinating account that was given to me some years ago by a very spiritually adept metaphysician who found himself defending a young woman who had fallen prey to a practitioner of black magic who was psychically draining her energy as she slept.

"Everyone at the office loved Yolanda," Neil said, beginning his report of the incident. "She was a beautiful Hispanic girl in her early twenties, and when she had begun working with us, she just sparkled with energy. After the first few weeks, she had become very subdued and quiet. Where she had been outgoing and friendly, she was now withdrawn and nearly indifferent to the responses of others. Where she had been moving briskly about the office, she now seemed to be carrying a great weight on her shoulders."

When Neil mentioned his concern for Yolanda to a coworker, the woman just shrugged and commented how the "honeymoon" was over and the girl was just settling down to being a drone in a dull office routine. Neil believed Yolanda's apathy and lethargy to be caused by something much more sinister.

"I have always kept very quiet about my interest in meta-physics," he said. "Only my closest friends are aware that I have been studying the occult and the paranormal for over twenty years. I had become extremely adept at astral projection [conscious and controlled out-of-body experience] and I considered myself a rather skilled practitioner of white magic. Unbeknownst to my office coworkers, I had placed many a healing spell on them and accelerated the improvement of their various ills and allergies."

Neil said that he had had certain suspicions about Jeremy, one of the department heads, for quite some time. "Jeremy was a rather stout, middle-aged man in his early fifties, who had been with us for less than a year—and there was something about him that just didn't feel right. I had noticed that certain people felt very uncomfortable in his presence—for reasons they could never quite explain. Those same people also seemed often to suffer from sudden headaches or upset stomachs—even occasional fainting spells. I strongly suspected that he was drawing energy from them when he needed an extra boost to complete a heavy workload of his own—and on some level of consciousness, I also felt that he was somehow responsible for Yolanda's malaise."

Neil suspected that Jeremy might be a conscious or unconscious psychic vampire, but he had no idea of the extent of the man's true powers until one night when he was out of his body during a deep, meditative state.

"I had been lying before the altar that I had constructed in a corner of my apartment when I suddenly felt my astral body being pulled in a certain direction, as if I were being sucked into a vortex," Neil said. "At first I became alarmed, but then I heard a voice telling me that I was being taken somewhere to help someone."

Neil found himself in a bedroom. A young girl lay on the bed, and Neil caught the shadowy figure of a man approaching her bedside. For a moment, Neil thought that he was witnessing a thief breaking into a woman's apartment, but then he realized that the situation was much more insidious than that. He saw that the other man in the room was also out of his body, and he was given to understand why he had been summoned there by some higher power. The young woman tossing fitfully on her bed was Yolanda. The shadowy figure was Jeremy.

"A small whimper escaped Yolanda's lips as Jeremy's form hovered over her," Neil said. "I knew at once that he was a very powerful magician of the darkside and that he had visited her before. I could perceive that he was invading her unconscious mind as she lay sleeping and that he was projecting an image of himself as a handsome young man of great seductive powers."

The sleeping victim tossed off her covers, as if she had suddenly grown too warm. The black magician hovered above her like a dark cloud, and Neil became very aware of the mental images with which Jeremy was bombarding his prey. Yolanda moaned, as if trying to resist the impressions flooding her unconscious, but Jeremy was clever, a master magician at manipulating someone who lay in the dream state. She sighed and lifted her nightgown, opening her naked thighs to receive her unseen exploiter.

"That was when I moved to Jeremy's side," Neil said. "The unscrupulous magician had been draining Yolanda's psychic energy by forcing her to have astral sex with him in the dreamstate. He truly was like a vampire on many levels, and I knew that I must stop him."

Jeremy became aware of Neil at once and swung about, perturbed and defensive, like a hungry wolf prepared to fight for its conquered prey.

"I didn't know if I was up to doing psychic combat with a darkside magician of Jeremy's obvious prowess," Neil said, "but I felt confident that those other forces that had drawn me there were also standing by to assist me. When I saw the fear come into Jeremy's eyes, I knew that I was correct. Glancing behind me, I saw the images of three etheric masters, each of whom held flaming spirit swords. Jeremy beat a hasty retreat, leaving Yolanda to awaken wide-eyed and trembling, as if she had just emerged from a terrible nightmare."

At the same instant, Neil felt a tugging at his astral body, and he knew that he was being pulled back to his physical body lying before the altar in his own apartment. "I awakened pleased that I was able to serve and to assist the White Brotherhood in combating such a powerful magician as Jeremy who had succumbed to the power of the darkside," Neil concluded his story. "I was not at all surprised when I arrived at the office the next morning to learn that Jeremy had resigned and had already cleaned out his desk and vacated the premises. And I am happy to report that Yolanda's health and vibrant spirit were soon restored to their previous high levels."

CHUPACABRA

Although certain purists of monsterdom will insist that Chupacabra is but an elder creature of darkness that has been resurrected in our modern era, it seems to other students of the arcane that the world had been waiting for a new blood-sucking beast to manifest upon the scene. When Chupacabra first burst upon the scene in Puerto Rico in the summer of 1995, it achieved instant popularity and a creepy kind of celebrity status. Named for a seeming initial penchant for attacking goats and drinking their blood, the Chupacabra ("goat sucker") both terrified and fascinated the public at large. Soon there was a song dedicated to Chupacabra to be sung to the tune of "Macarena," and comedians were coming up with their own translations of the creature's name, such as humor columnist Dave Barry, who stated that the word was Spanish for "attorney."

However, for those farmers and ranchers who entered their corrals and pens to find their livestock slaughtered, mutilated, and drained of blood, Chupacabra was hardly a laughing matter or a folk legend to celebrate in song. From August 1995 to January 2001, the monster was credited with at least 3,000 deaths of animals ranging from goats, rabbits, and birds to horses, cattle, and deer.

The beast is nightmarish in appearance, and it was observed by numerous eyewitnesses as it attacked their livestock. Many of the firsthand descriptions make the creatures sound very much like some kind of miniature, bipedal dinosaur, minus a tail. Standing erect on its powerful goatlike legs with their three-clawed feet, seizing a helpless sheep in three-clawed hands at the end of its thin arms, Chupacabra could almost be a much smaller version of Tyrannosaurus Rex.

The monster is generally described as slightly over five feet in height, though some reports list it as over six and a half feet. Its head is oval in shape and it has an elongated jaw with a small, slit mouth and fangs that protrude both upward and downward, which, in certain accounts, sound similar to the grotesque monster in the *Alien* motion picture series. A few witnesses claimed to have seen small, pointed ears on its reptilianlike head, but nearly all who have seen the Chupacabra state that they will never forget its red eyes glowing menacingly in the dark.

A most unusual attribute of the Chupacabra is its chameleonlike ability to change colors even though it appears to have strong, coarse black hair that covers its torso. Somehow, the creature is able to alter its coloration from green to grayish and from light brown to black, depending upon the vegetation that surrounds it. Another peculiarity of the beast is the row of quill-like appendages that runs down its spine and the fleshly membrane that extends between these projections, which can flare or contract and also change color from blue to green or from red to purple.

Some witnesses who have managed to drive the monster away from their livestock have claimed that the Chupacabra can fly, but others state that it is the beast's powerful hindlegs that merely catapult it over walls, small trees, and one-story barns or outbuildings. It is those same strong legs that enable the creature to run at extremely fast speeds to escape its pursuers.

It wasn't long after the night terrors in Puerto Rico before reports of Chupacabra began appearing in Florida, Texas, and Mexico, and among the ranchers in Brazil's southern states of São Paulo and Parana. In Brazil, the ranchers called the monster "O Bicho," The Beast, but there was no mistaking the brutal signature of the Chupacabra as the mutilated corpses of sheep and other livestock began to mount. The description provided by frightened eyewitnesses was also the same—a reptilian creature with thin arms, long claws, powerful hind legs, and dark gray in color.

On May 11, 1997, the newspaper *Folha de Londrina* in Parana state, Brazil, published the account of a "massacre" that had occurred at a ranch near Campina Grande do Sul when in a single corral twelve sheep were found dead and another eleven were horribly mutilated.

While some authorities scoffed at such accounts and attributed the attacks to wild dogs or cougars, other officials who had themselves been eyewitnesses to the appearance of The Beast argued that the creature that they had seen walking on its hind legs and seizing livestock by the throat had most certainly not been any kind of known canine or cat. For one thing, neither dogs nor the big cats have fangs that are equipped to suck blood from their prey.

A number of authorities began to speculate that the Chupacabra-type creatures had been manufactured by some secret government agency, a bizarre hybrid of various animals, created for God knew what purpose. Certain clergymen issued pronouncements indicating that God knew very well what the creatures were—a "wake-up call," heralding the end of the world. UFO buffs theorized that the monsters had been brought here by extraterrestrial aliens who were using their grotesque "pets" to test our atmosphere and environment preparatory to a mass invasion of Earth. Anthropologists asserted that tales of a mysterious, vampire-like creature that sucked the blood out of livestock had been common in Central America for centuries.

Whatever the bloodthirsty creature is, Chupacabra or a closely related species might range into Argentina, Chile, Nicaragua, and other South American nations, but it also continues to attack the farms of Puerto Rico. On August 11, 1998, Sra. Providencia Rivera Mercado, who lives in the Barrio Playa section of Anasco, found each of her seventeen rabbits, four guinea hens, and other assorted fowl dead and bloodless from perforations on their necks.

Luis Diaz, who resides in the Colinas Verdes section in Cayey, a small city approximately 30 miles south of San Juan, said that he had never believed in tales of the Chupacabra until Christmas Eve, 1998, when he looked outside to see a creature with dark-colored fur, long hind legs, short front legs, and a broad body hovering over a number of his chickens. Diaz speculated that either the bloodsucker could fly or was capable of extremely high jumps, for it vanished almost at once, leaving behind fifteen hens, two ducks, and a variety of other poultry, all dead and drained of their blood.

Rumors concerning Chupacabra's origin continue to circulate at a furious pace. From April to September 2000, over 800 animals were slaughtered by the bloodsucker in Chile, and both the people and the authorities were becoming concerned about what kind of monster was running amuck in their country. Some witnesses to the bloody rampages of the creature described it as a large rodent, others as a mutant kangaroo, while still others perceived it as winged, apelike vampire.

A widely popular story spread throughout Chile that Chilean soldiers had captured a Chupacabra male, female, and cub that had been living in a mine north of Calama. According to the account, a team of NASA scientists arrived in a black helicopter and reclaimed the Chupacabra family. The creatures, so the story claimed, had escaped from a secret NASA facility in the Atacama Desert of northern Chile where the U.S. Space Agency was attempting to create some kind of hybrid beings that could survive on Mars.

On August 30, 2000, Jorge Luis Talavera, a farmer in the jurisdiction of Malpaisillo, Nicaragua, had had enough of the nocturnal depredations of Chupacabra and lay in wait with rifle in hand for its return. The beast had sucked the life from twenty-five of his sheep and thirty-five from his neighbor's flock. That was an average of four sheep a night for fifteen days. That was enough!

It seemed that Talavera accomplished what no other irate farmer or rancher had been able to do. He shot and killed a Chupacabra.

Scott Corrales, Institute of Hispanic Ufology, reports that a specialist of veterinary medicine examined the carcass and acknowledged that it was a very uncommon creature with great eye cavities, smooth batlike skin, big claws, large teeth, and a crest sticking out from the main vertebra. The specimen could have been, the specialist said, a hybrid animal made up of several species, created through genetic engineering.

However, on September 5, 2000, the official analysis of the corpse by the university medical college was that Talavera had shot a dog. A furious Luis Talavera declared that the officials had switched carcasses. "This isn't my goatsucker," he groused as the college returned the skeleton of a dog for his disposal.

On October 8, someone's goatsucker or other vampiric creature from out of the dark was sighted on a rooftop in Iquique, Chile. Jesus Barrientos, 42, told the newspaper *La Cuarta* that he had gone up to the roof around 10:30 in the evening to arrange some boxes stored there. At first he thought the thing was an extremely large bat but in the moonlight he could see that it was some strange kind of animal with an elongated face, bulging eyes, and sharp teeth. Just as the poor man froze in terror and believed that the monster was about to jump on him, it spread its huge wings and flew off into the night.

Later, as he told others of his frightening experience Barrientos learned that other residents of the city had claimed to have seen the creature standing on top of the dome of the city's cathedral.

What better vantage point could any vampire or bloodsucker have to spot its next victims?

Five

WERECREATURES

Late one winter's night in 1993, Lorianne Endrizzi was driving down Bray Road in Elkhorn, Wisconsin, when she saw what she at first thought was a man crouching at the side of the road. Curious as to what he might be doing on the shoulder of the road, she slowed down to take a closer look.

Within the next few moments, she was astonished to see that the being spotlighted in the beams of her headlights was covered with fur, had a long, wolflike snout, fangs, pointed ears, and eyes that had a yellowish glow. The thing's arms were jointed like a human's, and it had hands with humanlike fingers that were tipped with pointed claws.

Lorianne Endrizzi sped off, thinking that the creature was so humanlike that it had to be some kind of freak of nature. Later, when she visited the library, she found a book with an illustration of a werewolf. She said that she was startled to see how much the classic monster of legend resembled the beast that she had seen that night on Bray Road right there in Elkhorn, Wisconsin.

Doristine Gipson, another Elkhorn resident who sighted the creature on Bray Road, described it as having a large chest, like that of a weightlifter's. She was certain that she had not seen a large dog, but a humanlike creature that had a wide chest and was covered with long, brown hair.

A twelve-year-old girl said that she had been with a group of friends walking near a snow-covered cornfield when they sighted what they believed to be a large dog. When they began to call it, it stared at them, then stood upright.

As the children screamed their alarm, the beast dropped back down on all fours and began running toward them. Fortunately for them, the monster suddenly headed off in another direction and disappeared.

While some area residents believed that the Wisconsin Werewolf was a real wolf and others reminded the concerned that bears have the ability to stand on their hind feet and to use their front paws as if they were hands, wildlife expert Don Groebner stated that neither animal was found in that area.

Myth and Mystery of the Werewolf

Psychologists recognize a werewolf psychosis (lycanthropy or lupinomanis) in which persons so afflicted may believe that they change into a wolf at the full moon. Those so disturbed may actually "feel" their fur growing, their fingernails becoming claws, their jaw lengthening, their canine teeth elongating. Perhaps the werewolf that haunted Bray Road in 1993 was such a demented individual, temporarily possessed of a psychosis that eventually passed, allowing mental equilibrium to once again become balanced.

If, however, the Wisconsin Werewolf who stalked the winter wilds between the towns of Elkhorn and Delavan was truly a member of the lycanthropic lineage of legend, then he or she could easily shapeshift back into the form of a familiar and trusted citizen of either community. The really unsettling thing about werewolves and other werecreatures of ancient tradition is their ability to appear so normal and unnoticed in their human form and their capacity to become so vicious and savage in their animal form.

What if in that savagery, such a werecreature as a werewolf should bite you one night during the full moon as you were out walking in the woods? Would you then become a werewolf, just as in such popular movies as *The Wolf Man*, *The Howling*, and *American Werewolf in London?*

Forget about it! The werewolf doesn't leave enough of its victims' body parts scattered about to allow them to become fledgling creatures of the night. The werewolf bites, slashes, tears, devours its victims. There is none of the polite and mannerly vampiric sucking of the victim's neck and leaving two small puncture marks on the throat as a kind of initiation rite into the ranks of the undead. There are no seductive promises of a life eternal or everlasting youth and sexual prowess as long as the neophyte vampire is able to subsist on the warm blood of the living. The werewolf is strictly, wham, bam, you are dead—really dead, not undead.

Unlike the traditional vampire, werewolves are not members of the undead who promise everlasting life and undimming seductive powers in exchange for a little warm blood. When they are in their human form, they can walk about tranquil forest paths or bustling city streets appearing as ordinary as anyone on his or her way to work or shopping. They needn't fear the scorching rays of the rising sun. They have no use for a moldy coffin in which to sleep during the daylight hours. They have no dread of mirrors that may not show their reflection.

Those who became werewolves in the ancient traditions were generally of two types: (1) innocent men or women who ran afoul of a sorcerer who had vengefully placed a curse of

lupine transformation upon them, or (2) power-hungry individuals who deliberately sought the ability to shape-shift into
the form of a wolf through an application of darkside magic.
Those innocents who had become werewolves against their
will may have been filled with disgust at their acts of slashing,
ripping, and often ingesting the flesh of their human victims,
but they were powerless to resist such gruesome and murderous desires while they remained under the spell that had been
placed upon them. Those who became werewolves because
of their quest for the power of transmutation from human to
animal through incantations, potions, or spells, took evil delight in their savage strength and their ability to strike fear
into the hearts of all those whom they encountered.

So how would you stop a werewolf who was stalking you
as its prey? Carry a bouquet of wolfbane? Stuff sprigs of garlic in your pockets? Ah, the pistol with the silver bullet! Only
a silver bullet can stop a werewolf cold in its tracks and kill it,
right?

Once again, forget about it! All of the above werewolf de-
terrents were imagined by Curt Siodmak for the 1941 classic,
The Wolf Man, starring Lon Chaney Jr., Evelyn Ankers, and
Claude Rains, and since that dramatic presentation, they
have been repeated as dogma in every werewolf story from
Frankenstein Meets the Werewolf to *An American Werewolf in
Paris*. Even the ancient "gypsy folklore" repeated by Ms.
Ankers, the heroine in *The Wolf Man*, was created by Siod-
mak:

> Even a man who's pure in heart and says his prayers at
> night, may become a wolf when the wolfbane blooms and
> the autumn moon is bright.

On September 2, 2000, Curt Siodmak died at his ranch in
Three Rivers, California, at the age of ninety-eight. In refer-

ring to his classic screenplay, he once observed that he had delineated the character of the werewolf, an entity that had haunted people's fantasies for over 2,000 years.

However, it is not only on the misty moors of Wales, where Siodmak set *The Wolf Man,* that the tread of the werewolf provokes troubled fantasies and nightmares. There is no known culture on this planet that has not at one time or another cowered in fear because of the savage attacks of a nocturnal predator known as a werewolf. The prefix *wer-* in Old English means "man," so coupled with wolf, it designates a creature that can alter its appearance from human to beast and become a "man wolf." In French, the werewolf is known as *loup garou;* in Spanish, *hombre lobo;* Italian, *lupo manaro;* Portuguese *lobizon* or *lobo home;* Polish, *wilkolak;* Russian, *olkolka* or *volkulaku;* in Greek, *brukolakas.*

The belief in werecreatures goes back to the dawn of humankind. Wherever early human settlements appeared, these half-human monsters also came forth from out of the darkness to steal livestock, abduct women, and devour babies.

Native American tribes tell of bear-people, wolf-people, fox-people, and so forth, and state that in the beginning of things, humans were as animals and animals as humans. Stories of women who gave birth to werecreatures are common among the North American tribal myths.

Early cultures throughout the Americas, Europe, Asia, and Africa formed totem clans and often worshipped minor deities that were half-human, half-animal. Norse legends tell about hairy, humanlike beings that live in the underworld caves and come out at night to feast on the flesh of unfortunate surface dwellers.

One of the great mysteries in revealing the true identities of the werecreatures lies in determining just where the line of demarcation exists that separates legendary accounts of hairy monsters devouring human victims from the early historical records of savage human warriors draped in animal pelts slaughtering their human foes—for there is no known nation on this planet that at some time in its evolutionary upward spiral did not adorn its warriors with the skins of wild animals as an integral element in their preparation for battle, hoping that the ferocity and strength of the beast would magically rub off on them. Most often, especially in the evolving Northern European tribes, the fierce animal of choice was the wolf or the bear.

In ancient Scandinavia, the Norse words *ulfhedhnar* ("wolf-clothed") and *ber-werker* refer to the wolf or bear skins wore by the fierce Viking warriors when they went "berserk," war-mad, and became as vicious animals among their opponents. In the Slavonic languages, the werewolf is called *vlukodlak*, which translates to "wolf-haired" or "wolf-skinned," once again suggesting the magical transference desired from wearing the skin of a brave animal into battle.

In the Middle Ages, large bands of beggars and brigands roamed the European countrysides at night, often dressed in wolfskins and howling like a pack of wolves on the hunt. In the rural areas of France, Germany, Lower Hungary, Estonia, and other countries, these nocturnal thieves were called, "werewolves." The old Norwegian counterpart to werewolf is *vargulf*, literally translated as "rogue wolf," referring to an outlaw who separates himself from society.

In our own age, we are reminded of Hitler's brutal regiment of "werewolves," men who were trained to remove all signs of human compassion from their psyches. Nor should we overlook how greatly the behavior of such serial killers as Jeffrey Dahmer, Richard Ramirez, Richard Speck, and all the other "Jack the Ripper" type of slashers and cannibals resemble the classic attack patterns of the traditional werewolf.

A Transylvanian's Strange Power over Wolves

On October 30, 2000, international news services carried a story datelined Transylvania that told how the villagers of Potingani, near Hunedoara, Romania, were living in fear of a man who they believed had a strange power over the wolves in the area. It certainly didn't help his cause when the accused "wolfman," fifty-year-old Gheorghe David, was seen running around the village at night, howling at the moon and grimacing at people with teeth that appeared to be fanglike and pointed.

According to the news reports, villagers had banded together, broken into David's house, and made a bonfire of his collection of books about magic and the occult. But ever since that ill-advised adventure, those men and women who had participated in the book burning had received nocturnal visits from wolves that prowled and howled outside their windows.

Local police stated that there was nothing that they could do to intervene unless someone could provide them with direct evidence of how David controlled the wolves. Or perhaps, until some villager provided proof that Gheorghe David was really a werewolf.

A Werewolf in Texas

Thirty-five-year-old Donald Childs had all the proof he needed that he had seen a real wolfman on the evening of February 27, 1971—and he was as serious about his claims as a heart attack. In fact, he actually suffered a heart attack when he looked out the window of his home in Lawton, Texas, and saw a werewolf on its hands and knees attempting to drink out of an empty fish pond in the front yard.

When he was released from the hospital two days later,

Childs told investigating police officer Clancy Williams that the creature had been tall, covered with a lot of hair, including its face, and it wore trousers. According to other witnesses who had also viewed the monsters, the trousers were far too small for the beast.

Childs had not been the first witness to spot the wolfman. Officer Harry Ezell later reported that the first calls had come from the west section of the city and described some kind of animal or "something" running down the street, dodging cars, ducking behind bushes, then getting up and running again. Twenty minutes after the initial calls had been logged, Officer Ezell stated that the police had received a call from a man who had come face-to-face with the creature sitting on a railing outside of his apartment.

According to Ezell, the man had thought someone was playing a practical joke on him, dressed in some bizarre ape costume, perching on the railing. But then the thing turned its head to look at him, and the witness was startled to be looking directly into the eyes of a monster with a horribly distorted face, as if it had been scarred in a fire. The creature's facial region was bordered by thick hair, and its upper body and the lower parts of its legs were extremely hairy.

To further dispel any notions that someone in a grotesque costume was playing a joke on him, the wolfman jumped from its perch on the railing onto the ground seventeen feet below. The stunned witness told Officer Ezell that the beast, wearing only trousers which covered his legs to his knees, ran from the area on all fours.

Fifteen minutes later, a group of soldiers from Ft. Still met the wolfman. They freely admitted that the monster had frightened them.

The werewolf was sighted on Friday and Saturday nights in Lawton. Sunday night was quiet, but on Monday, Major Clarence Hill, commander of the police patrol division, exercised caution and sent out an alert for all officers to be on careful watch for the wolfman.

But the nightmarish creature, whatever it was, had either once again assumed a more subtle and human appearance— or it had found its way back through the portals of another dimension of space and time, perhaps back to an age of superstition and terrible fears of the unknown.

LOBIZONS IN URUGUAY AND BRAZIL

Scott Corrales, editor of *Inexplicata: The Journal of Hispanic Ufology*, relates three interesting contemporary werewolf encounters in the October 2000 issue of *Fate* magazine.

In the first account, Corrales quotes the reports that appeared in *Paradigmas* magazine concerning an outbreak of lycanthropy in the town of Rivera, north of the Uruguayan capital of Montevideo in July 1993. Two young women had been attacked at night by the wolf man. The first victim had her dress torn and received deep claw marks on her chest. The second was "shamed" by what had apparently been a sexual assault by the *lobizon*.

On March 14, 1995, near the community of Tres Lagos (Matto Grosso do Sul), a werewolf attacked a well-known soccer player as he left a family reunion. According to Dourado de Paula and two individuals who witnessed the attack, the creature stood six and a half feet tall, was entirely black in color, and had red eyes and a pointed tail. De Paula managed to drive the monster off with a stone after it had nearly succeeded in seizing him.

Corrales writes that further reports of the *lobizon* surfaced in the rural area outside of Sao Paulo on October 7, 1996. Two witnesses had sighted a creature that resembled a large dog walking on its hind legs. The beast had large black eyes, long fangs, and a body covered by dense yellow fur. A local farmer found strange claw-shaped footprints, 13 inches long, "deeply etched into dry, hardened soil." Subsequent analysis of the footprints indicated that the beast "weighed some 440 pounds."

Is There a Werewolf in Your Family Tree?

Grant, 52, was completely serious when he told me that he was a werewolf. "It runs in my family," he said. "My grandfather was one, but the curse skipped my father, got my uncle, who was killed in a car-truck collision when he was twenty, then surfaced again in me. It seems primarily to affect the male members of our bloodline, but we have found old diaries indicating that my great-great-aunt also was afflicted with lycanthropy. We have now traced the lycanthropes in our lineage back to France in about 1450."

Grant has felt since he was a young boy that the full moon exerts a powerful influence over his personality. "During the two nights before the full moon, the two nights during, and the two nights following, I totally see myself as a wolf. It is difficult for me to stand erect, and I prefer moving about on all fours. My sense of smell becomes extremely acute, and I will subsist on meat that is exceedingly rare—preferably dripping blood. And my eyes? I seem to become colorblind during that period, and the whites of my eyes acquire a reddish tint."

Although some who suffer from lycanthropy seek medical or psychological treatment, Grant has never seen a doctor about what he prefers to call his "moon madness." Since his teenaged years when he began to develop considerable size and strength, he has family members simply lock him in his room during the six-day duration of his werewolfism. "I would never wish to injure anyone," he assured me. "But who knows what I might do when I am under the influence of the wolf within me? It is better that we take no chances."

Ira, 32, another who endures his monthly bouts of lycanthropy, prefers being outdoors during the full moon and said that he would probably become extremely violent if someone were to attempt to confine him. "Although I am aware of the blood of the wolf that flows in my veins each day of the month, I am truly seized—possessed, if you will—by the wolf mind-set only during the two nights when the moon is full. Since I am by my nature and occupation an outdoorsperson, I stay by myself in the woods until the mental transformation has run its course. And for me, those nights are glorious! When the weather permits, I strip naked and run freely upon the forest trails. Once, and I am certain this was no delusion, I actually ran with a pack of wolves until dawn."

Ira also avoided orthodox members of the medical profession. "They would only try to make me believe that I was mentally unbalanced," he laughed. "And I like myself this way just fine, thank you."

According to Ira's understanding, lycanthropy goes back to about 1848 in his family tree. "That was when an ancestor of mine, who had been out west in the Rockies somewhere fur trapping and such, came back to Boston and began behaving like a wolf whenever the moon was full."

Loretta, 33, said that she was proud to have wolf blood coursing through her body when the moon was full. "I have some Native American tribal heritage in my genes," she continued. "To the Native people, the wolf was the great teacher. Some shamans have told me that many centuries ago, all of humankind existed as wolves before we slowly evolved into humans. Therefore, I guess everyone has a little wolf in them. Some of us just acknowledge it more and feel it more, and allow ourselves to express the wolf within us."

Loretta said that her grandmother taught her the ways of the wolf in nature and when Loretta was a little girl she strongly suspected that Grandma could change into a wolf whenever she wished. "I feel the eyes of the wolf ever watching over me," Loretta said. "And during the full moon, I permit my wolf nature to take over. I generally go away by myself in the outdoors and camp somewhere quiet until the nights pass and I am once again half-human, instead of all wolf."

Loretta agreed with the other lycanthropes of my experience in one essential area. Although she had consulted a Medicine priest about her werewolfism, she would never consider for a moment confiding her situation to an orthodox medical doctor.

Certain medical professionals with whom I have spoken probably feel that they can also get along very well without any lycanthropes to look after.

Angela, a registered nurse who works in a facility where a number of men and women thus afflicted were confined, told me that the size of their staff of caregivers diminished appreciably during the nights of the full moon. "Sometimes it seemed as though nearly everyone called in sick whenever the moon was full," she said. "No one wanted to work on those nights, because most of the patients just went wild and became uncontrollable. We couldn't even call in volunteers, because the word was out that when the moon was full, nearly all of the patients believed that they were werewolves."

One night a female patient, snarling at her from all fours on the floor of her room, suddenly bared her canine teeth and bit her on the arm. "I couldn't help myself," she admitted. "I kept thinking of *An American Werewolf in London* when all it took was a bite from a werewolf on the moors and the two guys became werewolves themselves. I know it was silly, but for days afterward I worried that I might become as disturbed as the woman who bit me. I mean, I knew that she wasn't really a werewolf like in the movies. But what if the bite of someone who believes she is a werewolf can have the same effect on the victim? What if I would start thinking that I was a wolf! I really had to get a grip on myself there for a while."

In their paper "A Case of Lycanthropy," published in the *American Journal of Psychiatry* in 1977, psychiatrist Harvey Rosenstock and psychologist Kenneth Vincent discussed the case history of a forty-nine-year-old woman who received daily psychotherapy and antipsychotic drugs and who still perceived herself as a wolfwoman with claws, teeth, and fangs. Medical personnel would manage to get the woman under control until the next full moon—when she would snarl, howl, and resume her wolflike behavior. Rosenstock and Vincent stated that the woman was eventually discharged and provided with antipsychotic medication, but she declared that she would haunt graveyards until she had found the male werewolf of her dreams.

CHRONICLES OF THE WEREWOLF

The Middle Ages was a dark and dismal time when demons, disease, and terrible monsters haunted all of Europe. In order to offer some defense against the hideous creatures of darkness and the devil, clergymen, judges, and the tribunals of the Inquisition earnestly devoted themselves to arresting those evil witches, murderous werewolves, and other bloodthirsty shape-shifters who masqueraded as ordinary humans. Switzerland can lay claim to the first official execution of werewolves, when in 1407, individuals so accused were tortured and burned in Basel, but the Inquisitors in France have the dubious distinction of recording the most cases of werewolfism in all of Europe, beginning with the celebrated werewolf trial at Poligny in 1521. After enduring the torture chamber, three men admitted to consorting with she-wolves and demons in order to gain the power to transform themselves into wolves—then they confessed to having killed and devoured many small children over a nineteen-year period. They were summarily burned at the stake.

In 1584, a werewolf attacked a small girl in a village located in the Jura Mountains. When the child's sixteen-year-old brother came to her rescue, the creature turned on him and killed him. Enraged villagers, hearing the screams, attacked the werewolf and managed to club it to death. Amazed, they watched the grotesque body of the creature transform itself into the nude body of a young woman they recognized as Perrenette Gandillon.

An official investigation resulted in the imprisonment of the entire Gandillon family, who seemed deliberately to have encouraged their group transmutation into wolves by means of a strange sort of hypnotic ritual. When the eminent Henri Boguet, Judge of Saint-Claude, examined the family, he found that they walked on all fours and howled like wolves. In his book *Discours des Sorciers* (1610), Judge Boguet stated that the Gandillon family had surrendered all resemblance to humanity. Their eyes turned red and gleaming; their hair sprouted to great length; their teeth became long and sharp; their fingernails had turned thick and clawlike.

The famous case of Gilles Garnier, who was executed as a werewolf at Dole, France, in 1573, provides grim details of attacks on numerous children, in which Garnier used his hands and teeth to kill and to cannibalize his young victims. In view of the heinous crimes and Garnier's confession that he was a werewolf, the court was quick to decree that he should be executed and his body burned and reduced to ashes.

The infamous werewolf Peter Stubbe of Cologne revealed that he possessed a magic belt that could instantly transform him into a wolf. To return to human form, he had but to remove the belt and wipe the blood gore from his latest kill from his mouth. Although the authorities never found his bestial belt, they beheaded him for his crimes in 1589.

According to testimony in the case against Jacques Roulet in 1598, a group of hunters came upon two wolves devouring the body of a fifteen-year-old boy. Since they were well armed, the men pursued the wolves and were astonished to see the pawprints slowly becoming more humanlike. At last, they tracked down and apprehended a tall, gaunt, bearded man with long matted hair and barely clothed in filthy rags, his hands red with blood and his long nails clotted with human flesh.

The loathsome creature identified himself as a vagabond named Jacques Roulet, who with his brother and a cousin, possessed a salve that enabled them to assume the form of wolves. Together, the three werewolves had attacked, killed, and eaten many children in various parts of the countryside.

According to a number of ancient magical texts, one of the methods by which one might become a werewolf was to disrobe and to rub completely over one's naked body an ointment made of the fat of a freshly killed animal and a special mixture of herbs. The person who wished to accomplish the lupine transformation should also wear a belt made of human or wolf skin around the waist, then cover his or her body with the pelt of a wolf. To accelerate the process of shape-shifting, the apprentice werewolf should drink beer mixed with blood and recite an ancient magical incantation.

In 1610, Pierre de Lancre, a noted judge of Bordeaux, France, paid a personal visit to the Monastery of the Cordeliers to interview a werewolf who had been confined to a cloister cell for seven years. Jean Grenier, a youth who had boasted of a series of child-murders, had told the court in graphic detail how he changed into a werewolf and prowled about at night seeking to lure small children into his hungry clutches. With surprising insight for the seventeenth century, the court had judged Grenier to be insane even though numerous eyewitnesses testified to having seen him in the form of a wolf when he performed vicious attacks on several victims.

In his *L'inconstance*, published in 1612, Judge de Lancre described the accused werewolf as being possessed of glittering, deep-set eyes, long, black fingernails, and sharp, protruding teeth. Grenier appeared to walk on all fours with much greater ease than he could walk upright. He freely confessed to being a werewolf and told the startled judge that he still craved human flesh, especially the sweet meat of plump little children.

The Monstrous Werecreature of Le Gevaudon

During a three-year period, 1764 to 1767, a grisly epidemic of murders attributed to a werewolf or some kind of unknown beast occurred in the rugged mountain country of south central France known as Le Gevaudon. Two hundred and thirty-four years later, the stories of the beast still haunt the area and baffle those who have sought to solve the mystery of the true identity of the frightening creature.

Recent theories have nominated two possible candidates for the gory mantle of the Beast of Le Gevaudon—some kind of wandering leopard that managed to find its way into the mountainous region or a huge wild boar that had become predatory and developed a taste for human flesh. However, contemporary descriptions of the Beast don't seem to give either the educated guesses of an out-of-place leopard or a massive boar much credence, as eyewitnesses of the creature's depredations described it as walking upright on its hind legs, its body covered with a shaggy coat of dark hair. Its head bore a piglike or wolflike snout and the pointed ears of a small dog.

The traditional occupation of the children in Le Gevaudon was that of family herdsmen, so this made them the prime targets of the Beast. Its first appearance in the mountainous province was in July 1764. The monster claimed its first victim, a girl, near the village of Saint Étienne-de-Lugdares. Her little body was found with its heart ripped out.

In the following week, five more children from villages around Saint Étienne-de-Lugdares were found dead—all of them with their hearts torn from their bodies. At this time, no one had yet seen the thing that was killing their children, but the families pulled the herds and the children out of the summer grazing grounds.

In September, Jean-Pierre Pourcher, a farmer living near the village of Zulianges, saw a bizarre-looking creature shuffling along a road. As it approached him in the half-light of dusk, he became convinced that the strange thing was the murderer of the children. Pourcher fired his musket at the animal, which he later described as being as large as a donkey with reddish hair and powerful legs, but he missed in his nervousness and confusion.

As if seeking vengeance for the attempt on its life, the monster grew much braver and daily stalked the countryside, leaving terrible death in its trail. The monstrous creature grew bold enough to attack groups of people, and survivors described the same man-wolf-being each time.

A small child, Jean Panafieux from the village of Chana-leilles, was among a group of other children when the Beast snatched him from their midst. Andre Portefaix, a teenaged boy, attempted to rescue the terrified child by attacking the monster with a pitchfork. Inspired by Andre's example of courage, other boys began to join in the struggle for little Jean's body, grabbing up long sticks to beat at the werewolf. Although the boys succeeded in driving off the Beast, it was not without the deaths of Jean Panafieux and one of the older members of the group of rescuers.

On January 15, 1765, the father of fourteen-year-old Jean Chateauneuf found his son's body on the mountain slopes where he had been attending the family's goatherd. As with the other victims of the Beast, the boy's heart had been ripped from his chest, and the monster had drunk of his blood. With great sorrow, Chateauneuf carried his son's body home.

That night at sunset, Chateauneuf was shaken from his grief by the sound of something scratching at a window. He looked up from his prayers to see the hideous features of the Beast leering in at him. The grieving father cried out for help, but in the failing light of dusk, it was impossible to follow the monster's trail.

The situation in Le Gevaudon was becoming desperate. Some authorities estimated that the lives of well over one hundred victims had been claimed by the Beast. An emissary from the villagers, the brave teenager Andre Portefaix, was sent to the winter court at Versailles to entreat Louis XV to send soldiers to hunt down the werewolf. The King, who was a trifle bored with the winter season at court, gave young Portefaix a commission and dispatched a company of dragoons and light cavalry under a Captain Duhamel to hunt down the monster of the mountains.

The troops reached Le Gevaudon in February 1765 and began at once to hunt the Beast. On February 6, they discovered its large, humanlike tracks in the snow, and they followed the trail until they located the creature the next day in a dense thicket. Five shots were fired at the dark figure they saw moving within the heavy and twisted growth, and a great howl arose from the monster as at least one musket ball found its target. The men were distracted from pursuing the werewolf that day when they found within the creature's lair in the thicket the mutilated body of a young girl who had been missing for some time.

The killings abated after the encounter at the thicket, and Duhamel concluded that the monster had died of its wounds. Satisfied that his mission had been successfully completed, he returned with his troops to their station in the far south of France.

A month later, however, the ghastly killings resumed. If the Beast had been wounded, it had recovered from its injury. If it were truly a werewolf, the villagers argued, it would take more than a musket ball to kill it. More likely, it had just decided to lie low until the troops had left its hunting grounds.

The Beast of Le Gevaudon now prowled night and day, until the terrified farmers and villagers began to abandon their land and homes and flee to other districts and provinces, so they would not end up as a bloody meal for the monster. The countryfolk had grown so frightened of the Beast that they would not even fire their muskets at it—even though it had presented itself as a target within easy range many times.

Some said now that the death toll claimed by the monster had reached nearly 200. A second appeal to Versailles went

unheeded, and the Beast's reign of terror continued throughout the months of 1766 and into 1767.

After much delay, a second expedition was dispatched to
hunt the Beast of Le Gevaudon—this time headed by
Antoine, the King's personal gun bearer. Antoine shot a large
wolf while enroute to the mountains of Le Gevaudon, so he
returned at once to the comfort of the court to display the
animal as the dreaded monster that had killed so many of the
King's loyal subjects. Satisfied, Louis called an official end to
the werewolf hunt.

Undeterred by the King's official decree, the Beast went
on prowling and killing.

In June 1767, the Marquis d'Apcher, who lived on the
edge of the monster's killing grounds, organized a hunting
party of farmers and villagers whose members vowed not to
disband until the Beast had been destroyed. On the evening
of June 19, the werewolf hunters managed to track down the
creature and surround it in the open woods at Le Sogne
d'Auvert.

As a number of the men were attempting to flush the
monster out of the woods, an elderly farmer named Jean
Chastel had leaned his double-barreled fowling piece against
a tree and was reading a book of prayers, trying to find some
spiritual comfort in this time of great trial. As he glanced up
at the sound of bushes shaking, he saw the hideous thing
coming toward him. Chastel calmly pulled both triggers and
fired two barrels filled with specially molded silver pellets
into the Beast's chest—and the monster's terrible reign of
terror and bloody killings was over.

The murders ended, but to this day an aura of mystery
surrounds the true identity of the Beast. The carcass of a
huge wolf was paraded victoriously through the mountain
villages, but many scholars insist that the old records were
purposefully distorted. None of those who had survived the

attacks of the Beast had described an ordinary wolf, regardless of how large it might be. The carcass of the alleged monster was shipped to Versailles, but enroute, because of the summer's heat hastening its decomposition, the men assigned to the transport claimed to have buried it.

Some authorities on magic and the occult have speculated that the Beast had actually been the last of a line of sorcerers who had lived in the region and who had acquired the special satanic salve that could transform them into werewolves. Perhaps, these scholars suggest, the truth of the monster's identity was too terrible for the men who had killed it to reveal, so they substituted the carcass of an ordinary wolf.

The Loup-Garou *of Witch's Roost*

Kent C. sent a fascinating report of his encounter with a wolflike entity that occurred when he was a teenager living in a small town in northern Michigan.

"The community had been settled in the early 1800s by families who had immigrated from France," Kent said, "and there were a lot of old stories about witches, vampires, werewolves, and other creatures of the dark that were still circulating since those early days. Especially significant for us teenagers were the ruins of an old stone cottage in the woods outside of town that everyone called Witch's Roost. According to the local legend, the woman who had lived there in the late 1870s had been a witch who had given birth to a male son who turned out to be a 'loup-garou,' which is French for 'werewolf.' So, naturally, generations of teenagers from our small town tested their mettle by going out there during a full moon and howling for the spirit of the *loup-garou* to show itself."

Kent stated in his account that every so often someone would swear to have seen something dark and unearthly moving around near the ruins in the moonlight and the local legend of the ghostly *loup-garou* would be perpetuated.

"I was a senior in high school in 1986, and one night during the full moon in September, a bunch of us were hanging out at a friend's house and talk got around to the *loup-garou* at Witch's Roost," Kent said. "I admitted that I had never been out there after dark, and a couple of girls, Estelle and Kelly, said that they had always been too frightened to go. Estelle's friend Nancy had actually seen the spirit of the werewolf near the ruins and she had been scared half to death. In fact, she had spent the next three nights sitting in church, saying 'Hail Mary's,' and praying to every saint she could think of."

The prospect of taking two wide-eyed, highly suggestible, and apparently gullible girls out to Witch's Roost seemed irresistible to George and Jerry, each of whom claimed to have been out to the ruins "lots of nights during a full moon" and hadn't seen a thing. They began to coax Estelle and Kelly, promising to protect them from the werewolf, and they chided Kent for having neglected an important local ritual.

"I figured it was a rite of passage that I had to undergo sooner or later," Kent said, "so the five of us piled into Jerry's car and we drove as close as we could get to the ruins."

Cautiously following the flashlight beams that illumined the narrow trail that led to the ruins, the five high school students set out to walk the half-mile to the haunted site. "The movie *The Color of Money* was out that summer, and Warren Zevon's 'Werewolves of London' was on the soundtrack during the neat scene where Tom Cruise dances around the pool table, sinking one ball after another—so Jerry and George started singing the 'Ah-woooo, ah-wooo' howling part of the song," Kent said. "Naturally, this got Estelle and Kelly agitated, and they kept telling them to pipe down. In turn, the guys tell them to look up at the full moon and start howling."

When the group reached the old stone cottage, little more than a few piles of rocks, Jerry suddenly ceased his howling and called for absolute silence. "We should now be very quiet and call upon the spirit of the werewolf to show himself to us," he said in a mock serious tone. "George, please guide us in a summons to the spirit world."

Kent said that his friends had apparently cooked up some nonsense between them before they left town, because he was certain that neither of them had the slightest interest in the paranormal or the spirit world, other than attending an occasional horror movie. "George had hardly begun this phony mumbo-jumbo chant when we all heard a rustling in the bushes behind us," Kent said. "It had been an unusually warm September night, and the temperature all of a sudden seemed to drop thirty degrees."

Kent and George turned their flashlight beams in the direction of the eerie sounds and every one of the teenagers let go with a scream, shout, or gasp when they saw a large wolf or dog snarling at them from the bushes.

"I will never forget the downright hair-raising sight of that huge wolf that crouched growling at us from the nearby bushes," Kent said. "We've argued for years now whether it was a wolf or a German shepherd, but I stick with wolf, for there is still the occasional wolf sighting in upper Michigan."

What none of the friends ever debated was the fact that when Jerry picked up a stone from the rubble of the cottage and threw it at the snarling beast, it completely vanished.

"I don't mean it turned tail and ran away," Kent emphasized in his report of the strange encounter. "It just disappeared into nothingness. George and I still had our flashlight beams trained right on it, and it was as if someone had been showing a picture of a wolf on a screen and suddenly turned off the projector, leaving the screen blank where once there had been a clear image. And the rock that Jerry had thrown crashed into the bushes right where the wolf had been standing just seconds before, showing us his long, sharp teeth."

Fifteen years later, Kent is more convinced than ever that he and his high school friends encountered the spirit of a true *loup-garou*, a werewolf. "Kids still go out there to conduct this silly little rite of passage," he said, "and every now and then, some of them come back with some pretty scary stories about seeing a big black wolf out near the ruins of Witch's Roost."

WERECATS

In 1994, Ray Jones retired to an acreage outside of a medium-sized city in central Kansas and began a second career as a wood-carver, entering contests and winning prizes that increased the value of his work. Since he had always wanted to be self-sufficient and as free of society's encumbrances as possible, Jones worked a sizable vegetable garden and kept a few chickens, milk cows, and geese to provide most of his dietary needs.

"One night in June of 1998, when I was working late in the outbuilding I had converted into my wood-carving studio, I thought I heard Elsie and Esther, my two guernsey cows, making those kind of spooked sounds that cattle make when something strange is troubling them," Jones said. "Buster, my old Airedale, sat up and growled—and then the geese down by the pond cut loose, squawking and trumpeting like all Billy-hell. There are no 'watchdogs' as good as geese, 'cause they are so dang territorial."

Figuring it was time to investigate the reason for his livestock's restlessness, Jones put down his tools and stepped outside of his studio. "There was a really bright full moon overhead, and I could see pretty much everything around me," he recalled. "Then I heard the chickens squawking in the henhouse, and I figured that maybe some stray dog or cat was after them."

Jones stood in the henhouse door, waved a stick menacingly in the air, and bellowed his most frightening threats to any stray four-legged beast that might be troubling his hens. "Although it was almost completely dark in the henhouse," he said, "I felt the hair stand up on the back of my neck when I saw something dark stand up and growl back at me. I'm about five-eleven, and it was as tall as I am. Then it charged me, knocking me flat, placing its paws on my chest and looking down at me. I nearly had a heart attack when I found myself staring into the open jaws and pointed fangs of a black panther. I could feel and smell his fetid breath on my face as he sat on my chest, sizing me up for a meal."

At that point "good old Buster" came on the scene and began barking at the terrible beast that had his master pinned to the ground. "I started worrying more about Buster than me," Jones said. "One swipe of its claws could slice the old dog into hamburger."

Something seemed to startle the big cat or else it thought better of feasting on the man and his dog. "It rolled off me," Jones said, "and I swear that it stood upright on its hindlegs, before it dropped back down to all fours and ran off into the night."

Ray Jones called the sheriff's office to report the attack and to warn others that a big cat was on the prowl. "At first they thought I had been drinking," Jones said. "Then they told me what I already knew, that there were no black panthers in Kansas and that there hadn't been any cougars reported in the state for decades. A deputy finally did drive out to investigate the scene, but he just chuckled and said that sometimes in the dark a big old tomcat could seem mighty big and vicious and startle a fellow half to death."

Jones said that he will always know exactly what he saw: a black panther that was capable of bipedal movement on its hindlegs—a cat man. "Fortunately, there were no other reports of such a creature in the area, and I guess he just jumped back into whatever nightmare he had jumped out of."

Such panthers and lions and cat people occasionally leap out of some nightmarish dimension and create living nightmares for those humans who happen to encounter them. Our only natural enemies as a species are the big cats—the lions, tigers, leopards, cougars, and panthers. Of all the predators in the world of nature, the big cats are the only ones that hunt human beings—and they have done so since the sabertooth first caught our scent as we cowered in caves. Deep in our ancestral memory banks, we all nourish a fear of coming face to face with the snarling terror of a hungry lion or tiger.

But what about the bizarre reports of werecats and cat people? If silver bullets, crosses, and garlic won't deter werewolves, what can we possibly use against werecats? It's darn certain that catnip won't appease such creatures as those that prowl our forests, rural areas, and even our city streets.

In July 1964, two campers on Mt. Tamalpais in Marin County, California, complained to authorities that a pair of cat people had disturbed them on three different occasions during their stay in the area. They described the two werecats as tailless, standing five feet in height, and weighing a solid 200 pounds. The marauding entities had heads close to their bodies and were very muscular below the shoulders. For seven frightening hours one night, the campers had heard the two creatures "chittering" back and forth somewhere out in the darkness near their camp.

During several summers in the 1960s, the rural residents of Lorain County, Ohio, were terrorized by a giant catlike creature possessed of a large head, a massive light brown body, and an insatiable appetite for dogs, cats, and sheep.

In 1969, a Chicago motorist ran into his own nightmare on a road near Niles, Michigan. The werecat had red eyes, brown hair, and emitted an awful squealing sound. The man's car windows had been shattered in four places where the monster had punched them with huge, clawed fists.

In April 1970, a motorist who experienced engine trouble while driving on the edge of Shawnee National Forest in southern Illinois was jumped by a large catlike creature as he stepped out to investigate. The lights of an approaching diesel truck frightened the beast away. The dazed man was able to drive to Cairo, where he received medical treatment.

Mysterious catlike creatures seemed to descend upon unsuspecting humans all over the United States during October 2000. Windham County, Vermont, had so many sightings that the state Fish and Wildlife Department was forced to investigate. In Waupaca County, Wisconsin, residents reported the appearance of a large catlike beast that weighed in excess of 200 pounds. In Peoria, Illinois's historic Springdale Cemetery, people were sighting a very muscular and very large catlike creature haunting the graves and headstones.

Year after year, in nearly every section of the United States, sensible men and women file reports of large, catlike monsters marauding about the landscape. Since the 1950s, I have personally collected reports of these unidentified cat creatures that seem to have enormous appetites, eating large sections of pigs, sheep, and cattle before they disappear into the night. Occasionally, perhaps in self-defense or maybe just for sport, these beasts have broken the necks of a number of large dogs.

Strangely enough, these cat creatures are never shot or killed, but they do very often leave paw prints, which are seldom precisely identified, but which can be demonstrated beyond doubt not to belong to any known indigenous animal.

In 1968, a Connecticut bus driver swore that he had seen something that looked like a tiger walk across Valley Street in New Haven and disappear into the brush. He told police officers that he had made the sighting near West Rock. Although seven police cruisers were on the scene within minutes of the call, they could find no trace of anything that looked like a tiger in the area.

At about the same time in Branford, Connecticut, a large unidentified catlike creature was seen walking "in a most stately manner" near the driveway of Senator Lucy T. Hammer's 40-acre country estate. It was the senator's husband, Thorvald Hammer, an iron company executive, who sighted the bizarre intruder while he was eating. He had become so fascinated by the animal that he had gone outside and watched it until it entered the woods.

Later, the tracking dogs of game wardens and the police were able to find only the slashed remains of a squirrel to provide evidence that some kind of predator had been in the area.

Just as the full moon was rising over the sand dunes across the Annisquam River at Crane's Beach Reservation on March 17, 1984, David Myska of Allston, Massachusetts, saw a large catlike animal, possibly a mountain lion, on the cliffs above the dunes. Myska told the Ipswich police that it was too large to be a wolf or a coyote. The police explained that it had been 200 years since a cougar had been seen in eastern Massachusetts.

Writing of the incident in the December 1996 issue of *Fate* magazine, Charles A. Coulombe states, "Four nights later, one of the reservation's deer was found dead with a slashed throat and deep fang marks in its head and chest. Ipswich animal control officer Harry Leno declared that '[the deer] was horribly mutilated, yet no part of it had been eaten.' The deer's killer was 'an animal thirsting for blood.' "

Paranormal writer/research Tim Swartz sent me a report stating that in Michigan City and La Porte, Indiana, approximately forty people spotted a black panther in July and August 1985. On August 17, two employees of Indiana Public Service saw a strange catlike animal that they described as a cougar that "had rolled in coal."

During the winter of 1999–2000, several farmers in the Wabash area attributed the death of a number of boars to some mysterious catlike creature that was able to leap into high-fenced pens and attack the swine. The huge boars, many weighing several hundred pounds, had their throats chewed out and received long scratches down their sides.

In each of the incidents when large catlike creatures are seen on the prowl and livestock is found mutilated and partially devoured, there rises in the shadowy corners of the psyche a strong memory in the ancient belief that certain powerful shamans and sorcerers have the ability to transform themselves into wolves or panthers or some bizarre hybrid of monster somewhere between the two. A creepy, crawly superstition persists and suggests that the reason

these big cats are never found in spite of their leaving behind tracks and bloody remains of their kill is because they
transform themselves back into their human shapes and
blend once again unnoticed into the communities which
they periodically plunder for victims.

If we must reject such notions of human-to-animal transformation as beneath our contemporary standards of scientific enlightenment, then we are still left with the
uncomfortable evidence of mangled carcasses and the eerie
accounts of those frightened men and women—sensible, intelligent people such as you and I—who have encountered
such werecreatures and lived to tell about it. What was it that
they really saw? Did they really see ghosts, demons, bizarre
unknown creatures, or interlopers from other worlds or dimensions?

If there is another dimension somehow sharing this
planet, this universe, with our own defined borders of reality, then it may certainly be safe to assume that it is populated with an intelligent species or two who share their
world with their own assorted expressions of animals, birds,
reptiles, and so forth. If it is possible that from time to time
there appear "holes" or "doorways" in our dimension or
theirs which permit—or enforce—passage between the two
worlds, then it may be that all of the werecreatures of our
legends, myths, and nightmares are real and have their origin on this other plane of reality.

Six

THE WEE PEOPLE

Daniel Klemsrud was walking with a girlfriend in some wooded land near Boscobel, Wisconsin, in June 1995. They had been discussing politics and matters totally unrelated to any area of the paranormal when they suddenly felt as though they were turned around and lost.

"This was extremely inconvenient," he wrote in his account of the experience, "because I had been harboring very strong romantic feelings toward her, and I had hoped that an afternoon in the great outdoors would have expanded her feelings toward me and thereby encouraged me to express my love for her. I couldn't believe that I had somehow got turned around, because I had often gone hiking in this beautiful region and knew the area very well. My friend was becoming quite nervous and irritable, and she didn't seem at all pacified when I kept reassuring her that I simply could not have got us lost in the woods."

Although it had been a clear and sunny day, it now suddenly seemed as though the sky was dark and cloudy, and consequently, the wooded area in which they were walking became shadowy, murky, as if night were about to fall.

"As if things weren't confused and puzzling enough," Daniel said, "there now appeared a heavy mist that made it extremely difficult to stay on the trail."

His friend cried out that they were good and lost and she started shouting about how she never should have come on a walk with him, how she thought he was nothing but a jerk, and some other very unpleasant statements about his intelligence.

"Suddenly, from all around us, we could hear the sounds of giggling, like small children laughing at play," Daniel said. "The laughter was almost musical."

Thinking at first that they had come upon the children of some campers playing in the woods and that they would be able to lead them to their parents and a way out of the forest, Klemsrud walked toward a clump of bushes that were shaking as if they were sheltering some little eavesdroppers.

"I swear that as I pulled back the branches, I caught a glimpse of two smallish, yet perfectly proportioned, men in greenish jumpsuits scurrying into a hole," he said. "They were only about three feet in height and I saw a shiny buckle on the boot of one of them as he dove into what appeared to be a tunnel."

That was when he noticed that they were standing at the base of a rather large mound of earth that was completely barren of vegetation. "My friend asked if it were an old tribal burial mound, but I thought it looked like something quite different," Daniel said. "I think it is a fairy mound. You know, the Wee Folk, the nisse, elves, the forest folk."

Such a moment encouraged her to launch forth with another diatribe directed toward Daniel, this time questioning his sanity.

"But as I stood before the mound, I heard a message inside my head, '*Sometimes you must walk in a circle before you can ar-*

rive at the truth.' " he said. "I had sadly found out the truth about how my friend really felt about me. And fortunately we had gotten 'lost' and walked in a circle before I had blurted out my heart to her."

Responding to another inner message, Daniel reached in his pocket and found some loose change. The moment he tossed the coins into the opening of the mound, the sky became clear, the dark mist lifted, and he could easily see the path that he had missed just minutes before.

In his report accompanying the return of his questionnaire, Daniel Klemsrud admitted that this was not the first time he had encountered the Wee People. "I saw them often when I was a small child," he wrote. "Even when my parents and others told me that such creatures did not exist. I can remember once when I was very ill with chicken pox, one of them appeared by my bedside and gave me some elixir to drink from a little vial. My fever broke that night, and I soon had my strength back."

CLAP YOUR HANDS FOR TINKERBELL

Daniel Klemsrud is not alone in his childhood and adult encounters with the fairy folk. Among the 30,000 men and women who have returned *The Steiger Questionnaire of Mystical, Paranormal, and UFO Experiences*, a remarkable 19 percent claim to have seen elves, fairies, or some form of nature spirit.

In most traditions, especially in the British Isles and Scandinavia, the wee people, the fairy folk, were thought to be supernormal beings who inhabited magical kingdoms beneath the surface of the earth. Fairies have always been considered to be very much akin to humans, but they have also been known to be something more than mere mortals and to possess powers that humankind would consider to be magical.

Some theorists have suggested that the fairy folk may actually have been the surviving remnants of a past civilization populated by a species of early humans that were of diminutive stature compared to modern *Homo sapiens*. These little people may have been quite advanced and possessed a technology that seemed to be magical compared to the primitive tools of the migrating primitive hunter-gatherer humans who later became the established residents of the area. The little people may have died out, they may have been assimilated into the encroaching culture by interbreeding, or they may largely have gone underground, emerging topside often enough to be perpetuated in folklore and legend.

Other scholars and researchers of the considerable body of fairylore that exists worldwide maintain that fairies are entities that belong solely to the realm of spirit. Many of the ancient texts declare that the fairies are paraphysical beings, somehow of a "middle nature betwixt Man and Angel."

Some biblically inspired authorities have sought to cast fairies as an earthly incarnation assumed by the rebellious angels who were driven out of Heaven during the celestial uprising led by Lucifer. These fallen angels, cast from their heavenly abode, took up new residences in the forests, mountains, and lakes of Earth. As fallen angels, they now existed in a much-diminished capacity, but still possessed more than enough power to be deemed supernatural by the human inhabitants of the planet.

In a variation on that account of the fairies' origin, other scholars contend that after the war in Heaven, the dispossessed angels materialized on Earth and assumed physical bodies very much like those of humans—those beings declared "a little lower than the angels." Eventually, these para-physical beings took humans as mates, thereby breeding a hybrid species of entities "betwixt Man and Angel."

One factor has been consistent in fairy lore: The "middle folk" continually meddle in the affairs of humans—sometimes to work good, sometimes to do harm. Sometimes to elevate human consciousness, sometimes to seduce humans into following the ways of the darkside.

The fairies are said to be able to enchant humans and take advantage of them. It is often related that they can marry humans or—if they wish no lasting relationship—they can cast a spell on a likely lad or lass and have their way with them against the mortal's will. The Wee Folk seem too often intent on kidnapping human children and rearing them as their own. They also seem to delight in abducting adults and whisking them off to the underground kingdom to trifle with them. Those careless or disrespectful humans who trespass on forest glens, rivers, or lakes considered sacred to the fairy folk may suffer terrible consequences—even cruel deaths. Those entrepreneurs who wish to desecrate land whereon lie fairy circles or mounds in order to build a road or construct a commercial building may find themselves combating an unseen enemy who will accept only their unconditional surrender.

Don't Tread on Sacred Fairy Ground

In 1962, the new owners of a herring-processing plant in Iceland decided to enlarge their work area. According to Icelandic tradition, no landowner must fail to reserve a small plot of his property for the Hidden Folk, and a number of the rural residents earnestly pointed out to the new proprietors that any extension of the plant would encroach upon the plot of ground that the original owners had set aside for the little people who lived under the ground.

The businessmen laughed. For one thing, they didn't harbor those old folk superstitions. For another, they had employed a top-notch, highly qualified construction crew who possessed modern, unbreakable drill bits and plenty of explosives.

But the bits of the "unbreakable" drills began to shatter one after another. An old farmer came forward to repeat the warning that the crew was trespassing on land that belonged to the Hidden Folk. At first the workmen laughed at the old man and marveled that such primitive superstitions could still exist in modern Iceland.

But the drill bits kept breaking.

Finally, the manager of the plant, although professing disbelief in such nonsense, agreed to the old farmer's recommendation that he consult a local seer to establish contact with the Hidden Folk and attempt to make peace with them. After going into a brief trance state, the seer returned to waking consciousness to inform the manager that there was one particularly powerful member of the Hidden Folk who had selected this plot as his dwelling place. He was not an unreasonable being, however. If the processing plant really needed the plot for its expansion, he would agree to find another place to live. The Hidden One asked only for five days without any drilling, so that he could make his arrangements to move.

The manager felt a bit strange bargaining with a being that was invisible—and as far as he had previously been concerned, imaginary. But he looked over at the pile of broken drill bits and told the seer that the Hidden One had a deal. Work on the site would be shut down for five days to give him a chance to move.

After five days had passed and the workmen resumed drilling, the work went smoothly and efficiently until the addition to the plant was completed. There were no more shattered bits on the unbreakable drill.

The countryfolk of Ireland take their fairies seriously, and they know that to disturb the mounds or raths in which they dwell is to invite severe supernatural consequences upon oneself.

The trouble at the fairy mound outside the village of Wexford began on the morning when the workmen from the state electricity board began digging a hole for the erection of a light pole within the parameters of a rath. The villagers warned the workmen that the pole would never stay put, because no self-respecting community of fairy folk could abide a disturbance on their mound.

The big-city electrical workmen had a laugh at the expense of the villagers and said some uncomplimentary things about the level of intelligence of the townsfolk of Wexford. They finished digging the hole to the depth that experience had taught them was adequate, then they placed the post within the freshly dug opening and stamped the black earth firmly around its base. The satisfied foreman pronounced for all within earshot to hear that no fairy would move the pole from where it had been anchored.

However, the next morning the pole tilted unattractively in loose earth.

The villagers shrugged that the wee folk had done it, but the foreman of the crew voiced his suspicions that the fairies had received some help from some humans bent on mischief. Glaring his resentment at any villagers who would meet his narrowed, accusative eyes, the foreman ordered his men to reset the pole.

The next morning that one particular pole was once again

conspicuous in the long line of newly placed electrical posts by its weird tilt in the loose soil at its base. While the other poles in the line stood straight and proud like soldiers on parade inspection, that one woebegone post reeled like a trooper who had had one pint too many.

The foreman had endured enough of such rural humor at his expense. He ordered the crew to dig a hole six feet wide, place the pole precisely in the middle, and pack the earth so firmly around the base that nothing short of an atomic bomb could budge it.

Apparently fairies have their own brand of nuclear fission, for the next morning the intrusive pole had once again been pushed loose of the little people's rath.

The foreman and his crew from the electricity board finally knew when they were licked. Without another word to the grinning villagers, the workmen dug a second hole four feet outside of the fairy mound and dropped the pole in there. And that was where it stood as solid as the Emerald Isle for many years to come.

Favored by the Fairies

On the other side of the coin, throughout the long history of interaction between humans and fairies, there are those men and women who have somehow managed to win the favor of the fairies through a process beyond the ken of mortal men. On behalf of such humans, the wee ones can materialize to help a poor farmer harvest a crop and have it in the bins before a storm hits, or they can clean a kitchen in the twinkling of an eye to ease the stress of an exhausted housemaid. If they see fit to do so, the fairies can guide their favored humans with their ability to divine the future, and they will stand by to assist at the birth of a special couple's child, whom they will tutor and protect throughout his or her lifetime.

Betty Kirkland, who now lives in a suburb of Chicago, told in her questionnaire how she had acquired fairy helpers when she was just a child of three. "I am now thirty-three, married, with two little girls, eight and six—and I think they, too, have received fairy guardians, for I have seen little sparkles of light above their heads when they are sleeping."

Betty recalled how, when she was three years old, she first saw the Wee People on the farm in central Illinois where she spent her childhood. "I saw a little man and little woman picking apples that had fallen from the trees in our orchard. They were taller than I was at that age, so I thought at first they were just some very short people that my mother had allowed to enter our orchard. What really caught my attention is the way they were dressed. With their conical hats and bright green and red costumes, I thought they wore very strange clothing for farmers."

When Betty approached them, they just smiled at her and went on picking certain apples and placing them in colorful cloth bags. "But when in my childish curiosity and bluntness I asked them what their names were, they looked shocked, " she recalled. "The little man's mouth dropped, and the woman gasped in a shrill, tiny voice, 'Oh, no! She can see us! She's not supposed to be able to see us!' "

Then, Betty said, the man began to laugh in a high-pitched giggle. "Sure she can see us," he told his companion, "she's got the gift. See the glow around her wee head?"

Betty remembered that the woman asked the man if "the child is a changeling." Although that term meant nothing to her at the time, Betty later learned that a "changeling," according to fairy lore, is a hybrid fairy–human child that the fairies sometimes leave in place of a newborn infant that they "borrow" to take with them to their underworld kingdom.

The male fairy introduced themselves as fairies, himself as Acorn, his companion as Fluff. "She made a little curtsy when Acorn introduced her," Betty said. "I thought it was so cute when she did. I had never seen a woman do that before. Later that night, when my mother asked me to wash my hands and face for supper, I curtsied. Mom laughed and wondered where I had learned to do that. I told her that a fairy named Miss Fluff had shown me how, and Mom just laughed harder."

Betty enjoyed the company of Fluff and Acorn throughout her childhood. "They would usually just appear seemingly out of nowhere," she said, "so it didn't take me long to figure out that they were invisible to human eyes most of the time. Some evenings I would look out the window of my bedroom and see the 'fairy lights' of Acorn, Miss Fluff, and other fairies mixed in with the fireflies and dancing and swirling around in the darkness."

Once her two fairy guardians distracted an angry bull from butting eight-year-old Betty when she inadvertently crossed the pasture during a bovine mating ritual. Another time when she was ten, Acorn and Fluff chased off a stray dog that had invaded their farm and was likely rabid. It had approached Betty, growling, foaming at the mouth, about to charge, when sparkling lights swirled around its head and pulled it away by its floppy ears.

"Less than a year later, they saved me from drowning in the creek that ran near our farm," Betty said. "I had seen some older neighbor kids jumping off the banks into the water, and I had incorrectly assumed the depth as being much less than it truly was. And to make matters worse, I was alone that afternoon."

She was soon sputtering, thrashing about in the water, panicked that she could not touch the muddy bottom with her toes. "I would surely have drowned if Acorn and Fluff had not hovered over me and pulled me to the bank. There was no one else to help me, but my fairy guardians were there."

As she grew into her teenage years, Betty saw her fairy friends less and less. "But when I was ill or sad or depressed, I would first see sparkling lights swirling around me . . . and then I would hear their delightful laughter and know that everything would be all right," she said. "And so it has been throughout my adult years, as well."

For centuries now, hundreds of thousands of men and women have claimed to have seen the fairy folk—and many serious-minded scholars and researchers have felt that they have accumulated convincing proof that the Wee People truly do exist. Call the entities fairies, brownies, nisse, leprechauns, the good folk, the Hidden Folk, the gentry, or personify them as Puck, Robin Goodfellow, or Queen Mab, an incredible amount of folklore and anecdotal material has been built up around the accounts of the Wee Folk.

THE COTTINGLEY PHOTOGRAPHS

During World War I there occurred an event which transformed the English village of Cottingley into the Roswell of its day. Only in Cottingley, the tourists—believers and disbelievers alike—tramped over field and stream, hoping to catch a glimpse of fairies, rather than alien beings from UFOs.

In the December 1920 issue of *Strand Magazine*, published in London, there appeared several allegedly authentic photographs of real fairies. The pictures had been taken with an inexpensive camera by two young girls, Elsie Wright and her cousin Frances Griffiths, in a little valley through which ran a narrow stream near the village of Cottingley. One snapshot taken by Elsie in the summer of 1917, when she was sixteen, captures her ten-year-old cousin seated on the grass surrounded by four dancing fairies. Another, taken a few months later, shows Elsie with a tiny gnome.

Sir Arthur Conan Doyle, the famous author of the Sherlock Holmes mysteries, had managed to obtain the negatives and brought them to one of England's most eminent photographic analysts. At first the expert had laughed at the very notion of fairy photographs, but he ended up staking his professional reputation that not only were the pictures all single exposures, but he could detect that the fairies had actually moved while having their images snapped by the girls' inexpensive little camera. Furthermore, he declared, he could not detect the slightest evidence of fakery in the photographs.

Sir Arthur took the negatives to the Kodak Company's offices in Kingsway. These experts declined to go on record that the photographs truly depicted fairies, but they did issue a statement that they could find no flaws in the negatives or any evidence of trick photography or any tampering with the film.

Yet a third analyst observed that while such effects might be duplicated by employing some exceedingly clever studio effects, in his opinion the most significant factor in the Cottingley photographs was that the fairy figures seemed clearly to have been caught in motion as they hovered over flowers or the girls themselves.

As the British press spread the charming story of the Cottingley fairy photographs around the world, numerous reputable individuals came forward to testify that they, too, as children had played with the Little People. More elaborate and more expensive cameras were sent to Elsie and Frances in the hope that they might snap some additional photographs. According to the girls and to other witnesses, images of fairies did indeed show up on the plates of the more sophisticated cameras.

Sir Arthur acquired the services of one of England's most gifted clairvoyants to see if he might be able psychically to verify the girls' accounts of the fairies near Cottingley. The psychic-sensitive sat down with Elsie and Frances in the little valley and found that he was able to see even more of the fairy realm because of his mediumistic abilities. According to his heightened sensitivity, the entire glen was alive with many divergent forms of elementals. He saw wood elves, gnomes, fairies, goblins, and undines, graceful water sprites, around the valley and stream.

But try as he might, the clairvoyant told Sir Arthur that he was unable to transmit to the fairies the amount of psychic energy necessary to allow them to materialize. It appeared that only the two girls had the unique ability, coupled with their innocence and sense of wonder, that could somehow "feed" the elementals the requisite energy to permit them to attain a material presence.

Sir Arthur Conan Doyle issued a summation of his investigation of Elsie and Frances and their fairy photographs, along with his interpretation of the phenomena, in which he stated that while the proof offered by the Cottingley experience was not as "overwhelming" as in case of spiritualistic phenomena, "there is enough already convincing evidence [for the authenticity of fairies] available."

Although in the 1980s it was revealed that the two girls had quite likely faked the photographs of the fairies, in 1997 a motion picture entitled *Fairy Tale: A True Story* chose to emphasize the magical qualities of the Cottingley incident. Charles Sturridge, the director, was quoted in *Premiere*, November 1997, as saying that he didn't want to make a film about whether or not the two young girls had faked the fairy photographs. "I tried to do what the girls did—create an image that was perfectly believable." Sturridge emphasized that his film was really all about "the need to believe beyond what you can see."

Interestingly, yet another film about the Cottingley fairies, *Photographing Fairies*, appeared in 1998, and chose to depict the elemental beings primarily as spirits. Director Nick Willing described his feature film as "an Edwardian *X-Files*, dealing with faith, bereavement, and death."

Sighting a Sprite Outside of Little Rock

James Neff, a talented artist and the very able webmaster for popular radio talkshow host Jeff Rense's website, told of sighting a mysterious luminous object on an old country road north of Little Rock, Arkansas, on December 4, 1997. It was a very dark night with overcast skies, and his wife, who was driving at the time, his stepdaughter, and Neff were all leaning forward to watch for deer in the road.

Suddenly, about 100 feet in front of them, a strange sphere of light seemed to jump out of the thick yellow weeds and reeds along the roadside. Neff recalled that the object was self-luminous and resembled "a large dandelion head . . . composed of light or energy of some kind." The object did not roll across the road, but rather seemed to glide.

"Inside this slightly luminous shell were very defined, lighted spires or veins, only very straight, radiating in all directions from a very bright point of light at its core," Neff wrote in his report of the mysterious encounter. "It seemed that where these veins or spires touched the outer edge of the translucent shell there was a slight 'burst' of light."

Neff estimated the dimensions of the luminous object to be about six to eight inches in diameter. Strangely enough, it "scurried like an animal" across the road, speeding up as their automobile approached it. The object "jumped" into the weeds and high grass on the right side of the road and disappeared from their sight.

Neff said that all three of them had shouted in amazement the very moment that the glowing orb had first appeared on the left side of the road. "We definitely all three saw and described precisely the same thing," he stated. "This object was truly material and crystalline in quality and was not a trick of reflected light."

It impressed all of them that it was alive. Its movement as it scurried across the road, Neff said, "was typical of any nocturnal creature that we often see darting across the road in our headlights."

Later, Neff came to realize that what they had seen was a classic fairy or sprite: "What the Irish called 'luminaries,' the little people or beings that glow and scamper around in the deep forests. My stepdaughter commented that it looked very much like 'Tinkerbell.' "

James Neff concludes his report by affirming that he had never believed in fairies, goblins, leprechauns, or sprites, but "Now I think I do," he mused. "At least I may have seen what thousands of others have seen and described in much the same way we did: self-luminating, alive, animal-like, seemingly conscious of us—a fairy!"

WOODLAND ELVES

Their Peaceful Cabin Became a Place of Horror

In July 1997, when the Bredlow family took occupancy of the quaint little cabin on the cliffs high above the Pacific Ocean on the rugged Oregon coast, they looked forward to a peaceful two weeks that would allow the stresses of their teaching jobs to fade away into distant memories of recalcitrant students, indifferent parents, and clueless administrators. Yes, that was what they wanted most of all—a restful fourteen days that would strengthen them to meet the storms and trials of a new school year.

"Almost from the very first moment I set foot in the cabin, I felt a strange vibe coming from one of the storerooms in the back," Margie Bredlow, 47, stated in the lengthy account she attached to her questionnaire. "I think Violet, our little one, who just turned eight that May, felt it as well. She held Muggins, her stuffed kitty doll, up to her mouth and whispered into its torn cloth ear, 'I hope we don't have to sleep back there. I hope we get the bedroom by the kitchen.' "

Lloyd, 48, Margie's husband, and her older daughter DeAnne, 13, helped with the unpacking so they could all go on a hike through the woods before dark. "Lloyd, who teaches American literature, had brought along some recreational reading, the current bestsellers that he didn't have time to read during the school year," Margie said. "I'm a music teacher, so I am never without my guitar for family sing-alongs and my flute for some serious practicing of my own."

Margie said that *whatever* had taken offense by their very presence at the cabin started harassing them within hours of their arrival by arranging a peculiar kind of ambush during their walk.

"We had been walking cautiously along a narrow path that

would take us to a waterfall that cascaded down jutting rocks to the shoreline far below," Margie said. "We had all been laughing and joking about us city slickers having to get into shape, when all of a sudden a strange kind of mist settled around us. It was very frightening. We couldn't see a thing—or each other. The girls had been walking ahead of us, and we called out for them to answer us and walk back toward us at once."

DeAnne was soon at their sides, clasping her father's hand for security. Tears warped her voice as she asked what was going on.

"Some kind of freak fog," Lloyd offered as a plausible explanation, the best he could manage since he had no idea what had brought the thick, dark clouds down around them.

Margie said that they called for several minutes for Violet without receiving any response. "We were moving beyond panic. We tried not to think about her having fallen to the rocks below. We called and called, but she didn't answer us."

At last the peculiar fog bank dissipated, and they set out on the path, hoping to find Violet just ahead, perhaps sitting on a log, clutching Muggins.

"And then to our astonishment, we heard her voice coming from *behind* us," Margie said. "We all turned around with our mouths open in wonder. There she was, walking up the trail right behind us. We all knew that it was impossible for her to have walked by us as we were clustered together on the narrow path, shouting out our lungs for her. How, we wanted to know, did she get behind us?"

"They carried me through the air and set me down again," Violet answered quietly. "It was pretty scary, but they promised they wouldn't hurt me."

Margie and Lloyd tried their best to remain calm. Obviously some good-hearted folks had been on the path ahead of them and knew of another trail that ran parallel to the one

they were on. They must have assumed little Violet was separated from her family and picked her up and carried her
back with them on the alternate path.

"Why didn't you answer us, twerp?" De Anne demanded.
"We were yelling and yelling for you."

Violet shrugged. "I didn't hear you. Why were you yelling
for me?"

"Because we were worried about you, honey," Lloyd told
her. "We thought you had gotten lost in the fog."

Violet looked perplexed. "What fog?"

Margie wrote that she should have told everyone to pack
up the car at that very moment and ordered them to leave the
place at once. "Something was very strange. I felt it, but I
couldn't define it—so I told myself not to allow my imagination to run away with my reason."

That night after they had enjoyed a cookout on the stone
patio of the cabin, Margie was puzzled to see Violet dishing
up two plates from the leftovers. When she asked what she
was doing, Violet told her very seriously that "they" must be
fed twice a day or they would become angry with them and
make them leave.

When Margie wanted to know who *they* were, Violet
looked up at her with her big blue-green eyes and answered
without hesitation, "The two little people who carried me in
the air above the trail and who live in the storage room."

Margie felt a shiver in her solar plexus. The back storage
room had given her that strange feeling as she was unpacking, but Violet was probably just playing "pretend," the way
she did when she and Muggins and her other dolls had tea.
"All right," she said to Violet, "bring your guests their
plates."

Margie stood just a few feet behind her daughter as Violet
set the plates in front of the storage room, opened the door,
and knelt down to await their guests.

"We stood watching in silence, waiting for the little people who lived in the storage room to dine on our leftovers," Margie said. "Then Violet tugged my hand and whispered, 'They say they won't eat while we're watching.' "

Violet got to her feet, still holding Margie's hand, and the two of them had walked no more than a foot or two when they heard the door to the storage room slam shut behind them.

"I couldn't help jumping and letting out a shriek," Margie said. "Maybe there really were two elves—or *something*—in the storage room. I told myself that the wind had slammed the door shut, but my scream had brought good old Lloyd, ever my protector, on the run."

In answer to her father's demands to know what was going on, Violet explained with the forthrightness of an innocent eight-year-old that she was feeding the two little people in the storage shed. Lloyd made the logical assumption that she was referring to two chipmunks, rats, or whatever, and he became very angry. "My lord, child, you can't feed the wood rats or any other 'cute little critters' up here in the woods or we'll have a cabin full of vermin! Do you want mice or rats crawling around in your suitcase and chewing on your clothes?"

He swung open the door, then recoiled in disgust. "Where's a broom?" he wanted to know.

DeAnne peeked in and shuddered. "Yeeew, gross! There are two big rats in there eating some of our leftovers!"

Margie stepped to the open door and saw for herself the two rather plump wood rats stuffing themselves on gobs of her leftover potato salad and baked beans. "Oh, oh," she heard Violet say, "Please, Daddy, don't hit them with the broom! You're going to make them very, very mad!"

Lloyd scowled at his daughter. "I'm going to make them very, very scarce around here. We can't be feeding rats or our entire cabin will be overrun with them."

"Just as Lloyd reached the doorway and was about to step inside, the door slammed shut," Margie said. "And try as he might, tugging and pulling, it would not open. After about five minutes, he gave up, mumbled something about how it must somehow have locked from the inside and that was that. He set the broom aside and walked back outside to sit in the porch swing."

As soon as Lloyd was out of sight, the door swung open and the two paper plates, licked clean, sailed out on the floor. "They liked your potato salad and the Jell-O, Mommy," Violet said. "But they really wanted more of the baked beans. Oh, and they really don't like to be called rats, but they can look like anything we want them to."

Margie asked Violet how she knew what they were saying, and she said that she could hear them speaking "inside her head." That was how they talked to her when they had met her on the trail.

When they weren't appearing as rodents, Margie wanted to know, what did they look like?

"Like little people," Violet answered. "But weird little people with funny, crinkly faces."

Margie felt as though they had entered a strange kind of never-never land. "As a child, I had loved fairy tales and stories about woodland elves," she recalled. "But as I grew older, I had put away such childish beliefs. Or maybe I only thought I had. I had maintained an interest in the paranormal and loved books about angels. I really believed that angels were real, so, I asked myself, why not the woodland elves?"

The next few days were idyllic. Margie and Violet secretly brought the little people their plates of food, and all seemed well. In the evenings, the family would sing songs around an open fire as Margie accompanied them on her guitar. In the afternoons, after they had gone hiking or shopping for groceries in the nearby village, Margie would work on her own compositions for the flute while Lloyd read a novel and the girls would either read or work puzzles. It did seem magical. Two weeks away from telephones, television, and computer games.

Then in their fifth afternoon at the cabin, just before sunset, Margie heard the harsh snap of metal striking wood and the terrible scream that accompanied it.

"Aha!" Lloyd shouted victoriously. "No damn rat outsmarts me. Got him!"

Margie had been completely unaware that Lloyd had bought a rat trap at the small grocery store in the village. Then she realized that the awful scream that she had heard was coming from Violet, pressing against her forehead with both hands. The telepathic link that had been established between the little people and her daughter was apparently causing Violet to feel the pain of the "rat" that Lloyd had caught in the trap.

Margie ran to the storage room and flung open the door. "There, to my everlasting astonishment, was a smallish man dressed all in green doing his best to free another elfin creature from the metal bar of the trap that had slammed down across his foot," she said. "The injured elf, obviously in excruciating pain, was opening his mouth in a silent scream that was issuing in full volume from my daughter's mouth."

Summoning all of her strength, Margie managed to get her fingers under the spring bar and lift it high enough so the little man could free himself. In a flash, both elves disappeared, but Margie heard a tiny voice proclaim with an angry finality, "If it's rats he wants, it's rats he gets!"

Violet had ceased her emphatic screaming, but now De-Anne was shouting from within the cabin: "Rats, Mommy! Rats everywhere. In my suitcase, my clothes. They're all over the cabin. Dozens and dozens of them."

"It was true," Margie concluded her account. "The cabin

was completely overrun with rats. And there was no way I
was going to play Pied Piper with my flute and attempt to
lure them away. We just salvaged what we could of our belongings and got out of there as quickly as possible."

Whatever the two little elfin men represented and whatever they truly were, Margie now feels that there exist many
powers and principalities between Heaven and Earth.
"There may be all kinds of entities that exist throughout our
natural and our supernatural worlds. I know that my daughter Violet and I experienced direct contact with one form
that the unexplained can assume to communicate with us humans on many levels of consciousness and being."

THE NATIVE AMERICANS' LITTLE
VANISHING PEOPLE

When the Miami and Delaware tribes settled in the terri-
tory that is now the state of Indiana, they soon discovered
that they were sharing the forests with some very peculiar
neighbors. These people were only about two feet tall, with
white skin and light brown hair. Their clothing was woven
together from long grasses and bark, with tufts of fur and
feathers. Some of the little tribespeople built small huts out
of grass and tree branches, but most of them lived in caves
along the riverbanks. But the strangest thing about these little men and women was that they could vanish right before
one's eyes, as if they were somehow beings between humans
and spirits.

The Miami called them *Pa-i-sa-ki*, and the Delaware re-
ferred to them as *Puk-wud-jies*. Both names translate as "little
wild people of the forest."

Researcher/writer Tim Swartz passed along an old
Indiana story that tells of the Methodist minister who, in the
early 1800s, decided to put an end to the pagan tales about

the Puk-wud-jies that had enthralled a good many of his congregation and set out with ax in hand to chop down the tree that, according to local tradition, sheltered the entrance to the little people's underground kingdom. The minister had struck the huge tree only a couple of whacks when a hole opened in its base and he suddenly found himself surrounded by a large group of small, angry men. Although the Puk-wud-jies threw him to the ground and cut his throat with a flint blade, the minister managed to survive the terrifying ordeal—but he never again scoffed at the tales of the little forest people.

Not long ago, on *Across Indiana*, a television program seen on WFYI, Paul Startzman of Anderson, Indiana, told of a personal encounter with the Pa-i-sa-ki in 1927 when he was ten years old. According to Startzman, he had been hiking along an overgrown gravel pit when he came within ten yards of a little man no more than two feet in height. The unusual stranger had thick, dark blond hair capping a face that was round and pinkish in color. He was barefooted and wore a long, light-blue gown that came down to his ankles.

Before Startzman would speak or move, the little man turned and quickly disappeared into the underbrush. But later, he said, he and a friend from school sighted another Pa-i-sa-ki following them as they walked near the same old gravel pit.

It is interesting to note at this point that the Algonquin dialect, which was in extensive use throughout many of the northeastern tribes, called the wee inhabitants in their forests *Puck-wud-jinies*, which translates as "little vanishing people." These tribes, as well, spoke of the entities as being able to disappear, as if they were of a substance somewhere between human and spirit.

One begins to wonder if the elves' name for themselves

might well be something very similar to "Puck" or "Puke" or "Pooka." In Shakespeare's *A Midsummer Night's Dream*, Puck is the very personification of the woodland elf, the merry wanderer who declares what fools we humans are. We must also consider the similarity between Puck and the old gothic *Puke*, a generic name for minor spirits in all the Teutonic and Scandinavian dialects. Puck/Puke is cognate with the German *Spuk*, a goblin, and the Dutch *Spook*, a ghost. Then there is the Irish *Pooka*. So now we have Puck, Puk, Puke, Spuk, Spook, and Pooka—names from the forests of England, Ireland, Scandinavia, Holland, Germany, and the northeastern and central United States, all describing a little vanishing person, an entity somewhere between human and spirit.

TROLLS

There's No Trespassing in Sorenson's Woods

When he was seventeen, Richard O'Donnell learned that Trolls are not those cute little bug-eyed, benevolently grinning creatures with the tufts of bright red hair that became omnipresent as dolls, keychain decorations, nightlights, and a host of other paraphernalia some years back. "Trolls are ugly, mean and far from benevolent," Richard, who is now thirty-five, wrote in his report of his personal encounter with the monster so popular in Scandinavian folklore.

Richard said that his family was one of a few "token Irish" in a small town in northern Minnesota that had been settled predominantly by immigrants of Norwegian, Swedish, and Danish stock. "Although we had our corned beef and cabbage on St. Pat's Day," Richard noted, "we joined our friends and neighbors at their lutefisk suppers, and I never turned down any of those rich Scandinavian cookies and cakes."

Ever since he could remember, he had heard stories about the family of Trolls that lived in a cave on Ulmer Sorenson's property north of town. "A lot of kids would go out there to test their mettle by throwing rocks into the mouth of the cave and daring the Trolls to come out and chase them. Some of the braver guys even walked a few feet inside the cave and shouted their challenges. Later, they told everyone how badly it smelled inside the cave, 'worse than skunks or civet cats,' they claimed."

Every now and then, some friend of his would breathlessly describe having seen one or more of the Trolls moving around in the woods after dark, and it was common knowledge among the kids that those nocturnal raids on farmers' chicken coops that carried away hens and eggs were the work of hungry Trolls, not wily foxes.

Richard's father told him that the stories about the Trolls had probably been kept current by Ulmer Sorenson himself, to discourage kids from plundering apples from his orchard. "Dad said that the Scandinavian folks had their stories about the wee people and other dark creatures of the forest just as did the Irish with their leprechauns and gentry," Richard said. "Dad thought old man Sorenson was smart to keep the legends alive and keep the lads away from the apples during harvest."

Richard had always found his father to be knowledgeable and wise in so many practical areas of life that he thoroughly accepted his explanation of the Troll stories that the townspeople and kids were always repeating.

"Late one afternoon on a warm July day, I decided to ignore the 'no trespassing' sign on Sorenson's fence and cut across his woods to make a shortcut to my girlfriend's farmhouse," Richard said. "I was walking on a worn deer path when up ahead I could see a short, stocky guy coming toward me. As he drew nearer, I saw that he was one ugly dude. He had coarse black hair that literally jutted from his skull, deepset black eyes, and an enormous honker. I could not believe the size of his nose. And when he grinned at me, I saw yellowish, jagged teeth that seemed badly in need of dentistry."

Living in a small Minnesota village, Richard was perplexed that he had never before seen the stranger anywhere in town or in school. "He was about five-four or so and built like a fire hydrant. He was dressed in a worn bib overall a couple of sizes too large; a torn, dirty work shirt; and his bare feet—at least size thirteens—were covered with thick, black hair."

As they stood facing one another, it became clear from the stranger's frank stare that he was greatly covetous of Richard's new jeans and boots. Without speaking a word, but uttering an animal-like grunt, the brutish fellow suddenly tackled Richard around his waist and hurled him to the ground.

Richard stated in his description of the encounter that at that time he was five-foot-nine and 180 pounds of solid muscle, captain of the high school wrestling squad, and never one to turn down a tussle. "The ugly little guy was incredibly powerful, and he seemed very surprised when I did a reversal, escaped from his takedown, and flipped him over on his back," Richard said. "I was maneuvering his hairy arm behind him when this most incredible thing happened: I swear to all the saints that he started to grow larger."

Before Richard's amazed eyes, his opponent stretched about eight inches upward and gained about 50 pounds, to outweigh him and to tower over him at about six-foot-two. "And the smell of him became almost overpowering," Richard said. "He stank bad enough when he was a short little bugger, but now he could win a fall by his smell alone. Of course, not being an idiot, I realized that I was up against something beyond my powers of reasoning. This was no ordinary farm boy. Deep in the pit of my stomach, I knew that I would now be fighting for more than my pants and my boots."

The coarse-haired, foul-smelling stranger now filled out his bib overalls to the ripping point and the already torn shirt he wore split at the shoulders. His black eyes were turning red in color and from deep within the creature's chest came a low, steady growl.

"Then I knew for certain that the legends about the Trolls in Sorenson's woods were true," Richard said. "I had wrestled guys a lot taller and heavier than I was, but this was totally ridiculous. This thing was some kind of supernatural monster. In the old Scandinavian legends, Trolls could tower over small trees if they wanted to! I turned tail and ran like hell, leaving the thing roaring and screaming behind me. Twice I glanced over my shoulder to see if it was following me, but I didn't stop running until I got back into town."

Richard concluded his report by stating that he managed to convince a couple of his friends that he had not gone crazy and they returned with him to Sorenson's woodland. "Of course we found nothing but some flattened grass where we had wrestled," he said. "Since one of the guys had brought his rifle, we went down to the cave and yelled some old silly schoolboy challenges to the Trolls. None of us wanted to go inside, though, especially with that terrible stink that was making us all gag. We just went home with another story to tell—and I, for one, decided never again to take a shortcut across Sorenson's woods."

When Richard told his family of his encounter with the Troll over dinner that night, his father laughed and said that Ulmer Sorenson often hired temporary fieldhands from a pool of unemployed lumbermen from up north. "A lot of those men are pretty rough and tough and a bit short on manners," his father said. "And they might take a fancy to your new boots and jeans and decide to 'borrow' them without your permission. You best not tangle with any of them."

Richard did not press the issue with his father. "Nor have I ever done so with anyone else," he said, "but I will always know that there are many kinds of creatures and spirits that exist in the shadows all around us. Maybe they normally live in some other dimension and only occasionally pop into ours. Whoever they may be and whatever their names and ranks, I know that Trolls are among them."

In the next chapter we shall meet some truly evil entities who both dwell in the shadows and serve the Darkness.

Seven

CREATURES WHO SERVE THE DARKNESS

Susan Koebler, a young attorney from the Fort Worth, Texas, area, stated in her report that it is her habit to take a hot bath after concluding the day's work schedule. She lights a number of aromatic candles and places them around the tub to add to the therapeutic fragrance emitted by the powders and oils that she sprinkles into the steaming water.

"I stretch out in the tub, adjusting the water until it is as hot as I can comfortably stand it, then I sip a glass of white wine and listen to some New Age–type music," Susan said. "This ritual not only completely relaxes me, but I sometimes slip into a meditative state and really clear my consciousness of all the uglies and nasties that might have beset me at the office that day."

On this particular evening in late October 1997, Susan found herself entering a very strange "mental place." She began to feel herself drifting into an altered state of consciousness in which she saw herself with a group of other young women in a forest. "I had on this Grecian kind of gown, and I was linking arms with other girls and dancing under a full moon," she recalled. "It was so real, so detailed.

Honestly, it really felt like a past life memory when I might have been a member of one of the ancient Greek mystery schools."

After at least half an hour relaxing in this visionary experience, Susan emerged reluctantly from the tub, dried herself, and draped a robe loosely about her body. "I was still feeling extremely relaxed," she said, "so I walked into the bedroom and lay down on my stomach across the bed, my feet sticking out over the sides. I had lain there, nearly asleep, when I felt someone grab my ankles and start to turn me over on my back!"

Susan screamed her surprise, shock, and rage, feeling certain that someone had forced his way into her apartment and was now attempting to force himself upon her. Her scream became a stunned kind of gasp of horror when she saw that there was no one there.

"Yet someone, *something*, invisible, but of tremendous strength, was trying to spread my legs apart," Susan stated. "I fought against the thing with all my will. The struggle must have continued for several minutes. Every muscle in my thighs and lower back was burning with the pain of the constant tension—yet I would not yield and permit my genitals to be exposed in such a vulnerable manner."

At last the pressure ceased, and Susan lay gasping on the bed. Although she was still unable to see anyone, she was astonished to see the edge of the mattress depressed, as if someone were sitting there beside her.

"Then, suddenly, he was there—solid, visible, repulsive," Susan said. "His eyes were cat or snakelike with the pupils thin slits against yellow-gold retinas. His skin appeared smooth, kind of grayish-green in color. And his teeth! They were rotted, brownish stumps in what almost appeared to be set in double rows in purplish jaws. And this thing was very large and very muscular."

Susan stated that she could never be certain if the grotesque creature actually spoke aloud or if she perceived his thoughts telepathically. However the communication was accomplished, the effect was the same. *"You will want me. You will desire me,"* the monster told her.

Susan lay on the bed before the creature, sprawled out as if she were some kind of sacrificial offering to the dragonlike beast.

"And then the ugly thing smiled and reached out a hand with long fingernails to caress my hair, still soaked from the tub," Susan said. "The monstrous gargoyle was changing its tactics. It was moving away from attempted rape to seduction. But those putrid brown teeth jutting from its jaws in its pathetic attempt at a smile made a travesty of gentleness and compassion. It was only after one thing from me—and by now it was very apparent that the creature was very definitely male."

And then, Susan wrote, there was something about the monster's eyes that had suddenly become very compelling, very hypnotic.

"There was something in those reptilian eyes that wanted to make me stop resisting its sexual advances," Susan said. "I found myself staring into their depths, and it suddenly seemed as though I had been mistaken. My uninvited guest was really not so bad. In fact, he was really quite handsome and virile."

Susan will forever be thankful that she realized what the creature was doing to her, that it was seducing her with an almost irresistible hypnotic power.

"I cried out for my guardian angel to help me," she said. "I started to pray the Lord's Prayer and cry out for all things holy and of the Light to drive away this creature of darkness."

Susan concluded her report by stating that she is thankful

to her guardian angel and all benevolent entities who rallied around her that terrible evening to drive away whatever the grotesque monster was that materialized in her apartment and tried to force itself upon her.

Quite likely the entity that appeared to Susan Koebler was a type of demon that has sought to sexually molest human beings ever since our species became "fair" and appeared capable of providing a warm, fleshly body for a spirit being to possess for minutes, weeks, months—or permanently. There are essentially two types of such demonic entities: the "incubi," who pester mortal women, and the "succubi," who take great delight in seducing human men.

In my nearly fifty years of researching the strange, the unusual, and the unexplained, I have come to understand that as much as our materialistic and scientific age might wish it could relegate such supernatural sexual molesters to a much less sophisticated past—somewhere around the Dark or the Middle Ages—these demons have not relinquished their grip on the human psyche. According to a good many men and women, who swear that they have encountered such sexual offenders from the spirit world, the incubi and the succubi are as much a nasty nuisance in the shadow world of our supermarket and space-age culture as they were in the superstition-saturated and sexually tortured Middle Ages.

INCUBUS

Some years ago, Sofia, a very gifted medium/occultist, told me that an incubus could appear in many different forms—as an invisible entity; as an image of a loved one, either living or in spirit; as an image of an idealized love partner; or as a hideous, gargoylelike beast.

"The incubus attacks the more vulnerable—the lonely, the frustrated, the unloved, the young who are uncertain of their sex appeal," Sofia said. "A young woman who lies in her bed at night, tossing, turning, longing for a lover in her arms, sends out vibrations that bring these entities from every dark corner in the etheric worlds."

Continuing with her thoughts about the incubi, Sofia told me that perhaps the majority of women who have experiences with the demon only report having some invisible thing make love to them or try to make love to them.

"I'm not talking about witches, mediums, or occultists now," she said. "I'm referring to the high school girls, the college girls, the career gals, the young housewives, who maybe suffer one or two assaults from an incubus. Sexual frustration seems to attract these creatures, and although they may *feel* like a human male to these girls, if they could view these things— which, thank Goddess, they usually cannot—they would see the most grotesque kind of animal-like entities right out of some medieval painting of demons."

The Ouija Board Summoned an Incubus

Indiscriminate use of the Ouija board seems to be an almost surefire method of producing, if not a lusty incubus, then at the very least a foul-talking, sex-obsessed entity that makes a passion of obscenity. Ardith L. included the following encounter with an incubus with her *Steiger Questionnaire of Mystical, Paranormal, and UFO Experiences.*

"In 1988, when I was a college senior, my roommate that first semester was obsessed with working the Ouija board," Ardith wrote in her report dated May 1997. "Marty had been using the board ever since she was eleven years old, and she would take out the board and run the planchette over the letters and numbers anytime she needed advice on what seemed to me to be the simplest of matters, like what dress she should wear to the dance or what television show she should watch that night after studies. I told her more than once that she had better learn to think for herself, not to rely on some old spook called Scotty."

"Scotty" was Marty's nickname for the entity that claimed to be the spirit that advised her through the board. The being had told Marty long ago that his name was Alexander Angus MacGregor, so she had soon begun calling him "Scotty."

Friday or Saturday nights on the weekend, Ardith's and Marty's room would be packed with coeds, all seeking sage counsel from Scotty.

"Sometimes Scotty would be really sweet in his answers to the girls," Ardith said. "In matters of love, which was what the girls asked about 90 percent of the time, he could be sensitive and thoughtful. Then, suddenly, he would erupt into profanities and really dirty language, graphically describing just what it was that he would like to do to the girl who was asking the question."

Throughout the months that Marty and she roomed together, there were times when Ardith was amazed at the accuracy of Scotty's insight and predictions. "Then I would be appalled at the foul talk that would come through and I would wonder if it was really just Marty moving the planchette and being really catty and nasty toward some of the other girls who gathered around the board. I just didn't know what to think about Scotty."

Ardith was able to make up her mind about the true nature of the spirit entity one night when Marty had gone home for the weekend to visit her parents.

"I couldn't believe that she had left her Ouija board behind," Ardith said. "This was her security blanket. I laughed to myself, thinking that poor Marty might have withdrawal symptoms until she got back to the dorm."

Ardith sat down at Marty's desk and picked up the planchette. "I just meant to play around with it a little, but I suddenly felt a shock, almost like electricity had passed through my fingers, so I dropped the planchette and moved away from the desk. I told Scotty that was enough for me—and to just leave me alone."

Ardith emphasized in her written account of the experience that she had been joking around when she "spoke" to Scotty. She didn't really believe that there was any spirit in the board or anywhere else for that matter. All those opinions would soon change dramatically.

"I was just falling asleep later that night when I heard a weird kind of vibration coming from Marty's desk," Ardith said. "I was astonished to see a kind of greenish glow emanating from the Ouija board. Then I was totally frightened when that glow assumed a human shape and began to move toward me."

What happened next altered Ardith's entire view of the universe: "The glowing form sat down on my bed and I felt the pressure of a body press against me. My blanket and sheet were tossed aside, and my pajamas were torn from my body. I wanted to scream, but I couldn't. I couldn't even move as the thing got on top of me—and I knew as only a woman can know that whatever it was, it was male."

When Ardith awakened the next morning, she sat up abruptly, telling herself with the first moment of clear consciousness that it had all been a terrible nightmare. "But I lay on top of the bed naked," she said. "My covers and pajamas were scattered across the floor. I still couldn't believe what had happened to me until I saw the scratches on my shoulders and back. I took a long hot shower and got dressed to go to chapel services on campus."

When Marty returned from her weekend visit, Ardith confronted her with the details of Scotty's sexual assault. "What really freaked me out," Ardith said, "was the kind of knowing smile and look that she gave me. That was when I knew that Marty had been having a sexual relationship with Scotty—whatever the hell he really was—and that it had probably begun when she was just a child. And I got a real sense that she had deliberately left the Ouija board behind that weekend to give me some kind of initiation into her little cult. I really believe that she had set me up with her horny spirit lover."

Fortunately, Ardith was able to move in with two other girls in another room, citing irreconcilable differences with Marty. "For a time, I thought I might have to seek psychological counseling, because I was having terrible nightmares about the ordeal. But then I wondered who would believe me when I told them that a spirit from a Ouija board had raped me. And then I worried that if I found a counselor who claimed to believe my account, he might have me committed to an asylum."

Ardith went on to explain that she began a program of reading the Bible and other inspirational works on a daily basis. "I worked out my own therapy, absorbing sacred texts that focused on the Light. And speaking of the Light, it is now eleven years later and I still sleep with a nightlight on and never forget to say my prayers for protection before going to bed."

In concluding her account of an attack by an incubus, Ardith stated that she never said a word to anyone else on campus about what had happened to her that night, and Marty's weekend seances with the Ouija board continued to be a popular diversion among certain coeds who were interested in the occult and spirit contact.

"But I never attended another session with Scotty," she

said, "and I did everything I could to discourage others from becoming involved with Marty and her obscene spook until the day I graduated."

THERE ARE ALWAYS ENTITIES WAITING TO EXPLOIT HUMANS

Cybele, an experienced metaphysician who teaches a class in psychic development, told me that she always warns her students that their initial attempts at opening higher levels of consciousness could make them easy targets for possession by such negative entities as the incubus and the succubus.

"Too many of them have no idea what they're getting into when they undertake psychic development classes," she told me, "so I must keep emphasizing that unless they remember always to surround themselves with Light and to apply a disciplined approach to their metaphysical studies, they are easy prey for a sexual molester from the lower planes. Until they develop enough psychic strength and knowledge, their wide-open psyches can attract sexually aggressive entities like hounds to a female in heat."

Cybele said that most of her students would be horrified if an entity jumped into bed with them. "Others would like it too damn much," she acknowledged with a wry chuckle. "I feel a great responsibility to teach my students to exercise control over such encounters, or their chances to enjoy a normal relationship with a fellow human would disappear. There's always an entity hovering about who is all too willing to take care of anyone's sexual frustration."

Beware the Demon Lover

Some years ago, I was quite shocked when an elderly female medium whom I had known for many years told me in the strictest confidence that she had had a spirit lover when she was a young woman.

"I wish that I had never allowed it to come into me," she said in a hushed voice. "You see, after I had my spirit lover, I could no longer be satisfied by a mortal man. Sexual intercourse with my spirit lover was beyond description. When I got married, I was disappointed. I tried not to blame my husband, but he just couldn't compare."

Her strict advice to any young female medium or occultist was not to get started sexually with any spirit. "It'll ruin your chances for happiness with any mortal man," she said. "A spirit lover might be able to make love like Pan the goat god himself, but he can't keep you warm on cold nights or buy your groceries. It's a terrible thing to judge a man while he's making love to you, but that's what will happen if you've taken up with a spirit lover. And your man will be able to tell by the way you respond that he's way behind in the comparison. So I repeat: Don't start with a spirit lover, or you might find yourself awfully lonely in your old age."

SUCCUBUS

If a number of female occultists and mediums have confessed to both forced and reciprocal sexual liaisons with incubi, certain of their male counterparts have admitted physical dalliance with succubi. However, some years ago, when I gently broached the subject with a male medium named Stewart, I found myself being threatened with a punch in the nose.

"In addition to being my spirit guide, Serena is my soul mate," he growled. "Don't you dare even think of comparing her to a succubus. We were once man and wife in a past life, and our love bond has remained firm—even though I am presently on the earth plane and she resides in spirit. There is absolutely nothing sexual or immoral about our relationship. We express love of the highest vibration to one another."

A medium in his seventies informed me without the slightest hesitation that he and his spirit guide, Bright Star, had moved their relationship from the ethereal to the erotic many years ago. "You remember that old television series about the astronaut and the pretty genie in the jug?" Howard explained. "Well, that's like my relationship with Bright Star—only we kept going into areas where the television folks cleaned it up for the kiddies."

Howard went on to state that their union had been legitimatized by marriage. "Bright Star became my spirit guide when I was a young man in my late twenties," he continued. "Not only was she a marvelous guide, but she seemed to epitomize everything that I desired in a woman. And she was so beautiful. Whenever I entered the trance state, I saw her lovely face, her long black hair twisted into braids, the colorful Native American costumes she wore. I found myself wanting to stay in trance forever, but I did have to earn a living."

Becoming quite emotional in describing his interaction with the spirit guide, Howard told how the two had gradually fallen in love over the years. "When I was in my early thirties, we were married by a minister who was in spirit—and I have never been unfaithful to Bright Star with a woman of the earth plane since the day we were wed. And immediately I discovered that my complete physical and spiritual union with her accelerated my powers as a medium."

While it is difficult to know exactly how to assess Howard's claim of a blissful sexual union with an other worldly spirit—psychopathology, wish fulfillment, delusion, or a remarkable alternate reality—the following story about a young occultist's concerted effort to conjure a succubus to satisfy his erotic needs contains a powerful moral that we humans should never underestimate the power of a demon to insult, humiliate, and abuse us.

He Deliberately Conjured a Succubus to Serve Him

Jude, a bright young scholar, well versed in occult studies, told me how he had deliberately set about summoning a succubus. "All the ancient texts warned about the appearance of these beautiful, voluptuous creatures of the night that would straddle men in their beds and make love to them until their so-called victims were spent, drained, exhausted," Jude said. "I thought, man, how bad can that be? I mean, wouldn't that be an answer to prayer, rather than a nightmare, for a randy twenty-four-year-old like me?"

An older occultist, under whom Jude had served a two-year apprenticeship, tried his best to dissuade his young student from such a reckless pursuit. But Jude was determined: "I thought how fabulous it would be to have a luscious spirit lover whenever I wanted her. No fuss, no muss, no tears, no long talks about commitment."

He entered into an exhaustive regimen of incantations, rites, rituals, and conjurations—and he claims that he succeeded in summoning a succubus that looked like his ultimate fantasy of a sensual lover.

"She would come some nights when I completed the rituals and conjurations, and we would make love like I never thought possible," Jude said. "She said that her name was Lillith. Of course I didn't believe that she was *that* Lillith, you know, Adam's first wife, the demon he married before Eve, according to ancient tradition. Rather, I figured that her name was symbolic of what she was—a red hot, lusty demon."

Lillith claimed to be nearly fifteen hundred Earth-years old, and Jude said that her skin was actually rather cold to the touch. "But she had learned nearly every trick in the book during her centuries of seduction," he added, "and things soon got as hot as molten lava."

The ill-fated affair ended rather badly for the young occultist and his cosmic concubine. Jude decided to go a bit kinky and set up some mirrors so that he could have the added sensual pleasure of watching their myriad positions of lovemaking reflected again and again. What he saw in the mirrors nearly caused him to lose his mind.

"I still nearly vomit and hurl whenever I think of it," he said, clenching his teeth and moaning at the memory. "I saw myself making out with the most god-awful kind of reptilian creature I could ever have imagined. And I saw that repulsive image of that snake woman wrapped around me reflected in the mirrors again and again and again."

Jude concluded his cautionary tale with the sobering comment: "And if it took me a long time of study and effort to summon the succubus, you will never guess what I went through getting rid of that serpent woman!"

HEEDING DEMONIC VOICES THAT CRY MURDER

While those demons that seek to possess and enjoy sexually the physical bodies of mortals are terrible and demeaning enough, even worse are those fiends who invade the psyches of men and women and command them to maim, mutilate, or murder their victims. Perhaps the most monstrous of all the frightening creatures that issue forth out of the dark are those tortured individuals who heed fiendish commands to kill. These monsters are not werewolves or vampires or cat people—they are real men and women who could be friends, relatives, the neighbor down the street—any one of us who hears demon voices that demand unquestioning obedience.

Those possessed by demons are truly human monsters, willful agents of death, who practice ritual slayings, human sacrifice, and large-scale slaughter of innocent victims. The media proclaim in each day's newspaper headlines and news-broadcasts that these disciples of murder and mayhem are very real. And so are the demons who scream at them relentlessly to do their awful bidding and kill without mercy.

Here is what Dr. Morton Kelsey, an Episcopal priest, a noted Notre Dame professor of theology, has to say to those who protest that demon possession is a superstititous throwback to the Middle Ages: "Most people in the modern world consider themselves too sophisticated and too intelligent to be concerned with demons. But in thirty years of study, I have seen the effect of demons upon humans."

Dr. Kelsey maintains that demons are real and can invade the minds of humans. Demons are not figments of the imagination, but are negative, destructive spiritual forces that seek to destroy the possessed host body and everyone with whom that person comes into contact.

The Reverend James LeBar, an exorcist for the Archdiocese of New York, commented in September 2000 that there had been a "large explosion" of exorcisms in recent years. In New York alone, he said, the number had accelerated from none in 1990 to a total of 300 in the last ten years. Reverend LeBar said that as men and women have diminished self-respect for themselves and decreased reverence for spirituality, for other human beings, and for life in general, one of Satan's demons can move in and "attack them by possessing them and rendering them helpless."

All right, you say, but Reverend LeBar is a priest, an exorcist. His theological training has conditioned him to believe in demons. Then take into serious consideration the comments of Dr. Ralph Allison, senior psychiatrist at the California State Prison in San Luis Obispo: "My conclusion after thirty years of observing over one thousand disturbed patients is that some of them act in a bizarre fashion due to possession by spirits. The spirit may be that of a human being who died. Or it may be a spirit entity that has never been a human being and sometimes identifies itself as a demon, an agent of evil."

Dr. Wilson Van Dusen, a university professor who has served as chief psychologist at Mendocino State Hospital, is another health care professional who has boldly stated his opinion that many patients in mental hospitals are possessed by demons.

"I am totally convinced that there are entities that can possess our minds and our bodies," he said. "I have even been able to speak directly to demons. I have heard their own guttural, other-world voices."

All too often, those hellish guttural voices have commanded their possessed hosts to kill, to offer human sacrifice to Satan.

In a recent report released by the American Psychological Evaluation Corporation, Dr. Andrew Blankley, a sociologist, issued alarming statements about the rise in contemporary sacrificial cults, warning that society at large might expect a "serious menace" to come. According to Dr. Blankley, human sacrifice constitutes an alarming trend in new religious cults: "Desperate people are seeking dramatic revelation and simplistic answers to complex social problems. They are attracted to fringe groups who provide the ritualistic irrationality that they crave. In the last ten years, fringe rituals often include the sacrifice of a human being."

Need more proof than a sociologist's alarming report?

Dr. Al Carlisle of the Utah State Prison System has estimated that between 40,000 and 60,000 humans are killed through ritual homicides in the United States every year. In the Las Vegas area alone, Dr. Carlisle asserts, as many as 600 people may die in demon-inspired ceremonies each year.

Mutilated bodies of hitchhikers and transients are being found in forested regions, beside lonely desert roads, and alongside riverbanks—their hearts and lungs removed, strips of flesh slashed from their bodies.

Devil-worshipping rites are being held in our state and national parks. Human blood is mixed with beer and drunk by all participants. Human bone fragments, teeth, and pieces of flesh are discovered in the ashes of campfires.

Bikers, arrested on other charges, confess to being part of a nationwide kidnapping ring that captures viriginal young men and women for sale to satanic cults both here and in Europe. The youthful victims are marked for human sacrifice.

The terrible power which drives and compels those obsessed with sacrificial murders is something so much more insidiously evil and complex than can be created by the distortion of creeds, ecclesiasticisms, or belief structures. The monstrous voices that command men and women to kill others are not those of mortals. Those who have fallen under the deadly spell of the possessing entities claim to have been controlled by something outside of themselves—usually personified as Satan or one of his demons. Those demon voices—whether you prefer to identify them as symbolical of some strain of psychopathology or as literal perverse and evil entities—can utter the command to kill to a quiet, conventionally reared individual just as readily as to a disheveled disciple of the iconoclastic.

However one wishes to identify these Parasites of the Spirit, they have the ability to sense and to seize the moments of vulnerability in the strongest of men and women. They possess the uncanny power of knowing the precise moments when even the most righteous can be tempted, when even the most devout can be led astray, when the most disciplined moralist may be seduced.

Perhaps these demonic entities are the archetypal shape-shifting monsters that have inspired countless generations of mortals to protest that grotesque reptilian creatures or hideous half-human, animal-like monsters have forced them to commit horrible crimes.

Here is only a sampler of recent cases of men and women who were possessed by demons and commanded to kill:

Sacrificed for a Magical Golden Sword

On January 5, 1990, authorities searching an Ohio farm commune found the slain bodies of a family of five—all victims of human sacrifice. Jeffrey Lunden, a self-declared prophet of a new religion, had decreed the sacrifices necessary to persuade the "forces" to present the cult with a magical golden sword.

Satan's New ID is 966

Daniel Rakowitz couldn't quite understand whether or not the voices said that he was actually Jesus reborn, but he knew that they were insistent that he was a messiah. The voices also told him to form a new satanic religion to be named the Church of 966, thereby discarding the old and familiar 666 label. To ensure his messiahship, he sacrificed his girlfriend in September 1989.

Theresa Was Sacrificed on an Altar of Evil

Once they had accepted Satan as their savior, heavy metal, grass, and sex parties just weren't enough. Soon the demon voices ordered Terry Belcher, the young high priest of the cult, to sacrifice Theresa, one of his followers, in January 1988.

The "Night Stalker" Was Proud That Lucifer Dwelt Within Him

When the jury passed sentence on Richard Ramirez in 1985, he was convicted of twelve first-degree murders and thirty other major offenses of rape and burglary. Throughout his trial, the infamous "Night Stalker" flashed the devil's pentagram scratched into his hand or placed his fingers to the side of his head to fashion demon's horns. Defiantly, he declared his worship of Satan.

Demons Gave Him Power Over Many Things

On June 11, 1998, taking the stand against his lawyers' advice to make statements concerning the killing of two students and the wounding of seventeen in Hattiesburg, Mississippi, in October 1997, Luke Woodham told the astonished courtroom that his involvement in satanism had given him power over many things. Woodham went on to declare how he had been able to cast spells and send out demons to accomplish various tasks for him.

"I've seen demons," he said. "I know what I was dealing with. I felt like I had complete control, complete power over things. . . . It's real in spite of what people think."

He Sacrificed Thirteen to Save California from Destruction

The voices told Herbert Mullin that California was about to be destroyed by a cataclysmic earthquake and a giant tidal wave unless he immediately began sacrificing human life to Satan. The voices nullified Mullin's squeamishness by declaring that the sacrificial victims would actually be grateful for being given the opportunity to serve the greater good of California. Before he was stopped on Feburary 13, 1972, Mullins had sacrificed thirteen victims and, in his mind, become the Savior of California.

Warriors on a Mission to Kill Witches

In May 1983, Michael and Suzan Carlson went on trial in San Francisco for obeying their demonic visions and hunting down and killing three victims that the voices identified as witches that must be slain to set California right.

Demon Voices Told Him He Would Never Die

While other households in Queens, New York, watched the Thanksgiving Day parade on November 22, 1990, Joseph Bergamini honored the satanic promise that he was immortal by stabbing and killing his mother and wounding his father.

From Jesus Freak to Slayer of an International Icon

As a teenager, Mark David Chapman had experienced a vision of Jesus which led him to become an advocate for the common man. When a vision later revealed that the popular idol John Lennon was no longer a working-class hero, but a prosperous businessman, his inner voices decreed that the former Beatle must die on the night of December 8, 1980.

Their Homicidal Home Movie Betrayed Them

In June 1988, Jason Rose and John Jones were indicted for the ritual sacrifice of nineteen-year-old Melissa Ann Meyer. The two satanists had cast their own fate in the form of life imprisonment when it was revealed that they videotaped their human sacrifice.

The list of demon-possessed killers goes on and on:

- January 1986, satanic priest Harold Smith and four disciples were jailed following a series of murders in Houston.

- February 1986, Dana Jones, admitted member of a sex magic cult founded by Aleister Crowley in 1907, was arrested for the ritual mutilation-slaying of a man in Denver.

- Inspired by the vampire movie *Lost Boys*, Tim Erickson and other Minnesota teenagers decided to form a vampire cult in March 1987. They murdered a drifter and drank his blood.

- July 1991, Jaime Rodriguez was convicted and sentenced to life for beheading a teenage runaway as a sacrifice to Satan. He also severed one of her fingers to wear as a charm around his neck. Augustin Pena, a fellow satanist, kept the girl's head in his refrigerator.

- April 1994, Carey Grayson and three others murdered a female hitchhiker in Birmingham, Alabama. Police stated that the victim was mutilated in an apparent ritual that involved cannibalism.

- May 1996, three satanists in San Luis Obispo tortured and murdered a fifteen-year-old girl. The demon-possessed trio told arresting officers that they hoped the sacrifice of a virgin would put them in good with Satan.

- December 2000, prosecutors charged a man in Great Falls, Montana, with killing a ten-year-old boy, butchering him, eating his flesh in specially prepared dishes, then feeding the remains to his unsuspecting neighbors. A psychiatric evaluation indicated such demonic fantasies about cannibalism and the taste of human flesh. Encrypted writings found in the suspect's home revealed a list of recipes involving the bodies of small children.

DEMONS VERSUS THE U.S. PRESIDENCY

The Demonic Dossier on the U.S. Presidency is a frightening one:

- When John Wilkes Booth, the assassin of Abraham Lincoln, was but an infant in his crib, Asia Booth had a horrid vision of her son being one day transformed into a monster with a grotesque hand that would commit a terrible deed.

- On the morning of July 2, 1881, Charles Guiteau could no longer resist the demon voices that commanded him to kill President James Garfield. The President clung to life through the agony of a long summer before yielding to the assassin's bullet in his back. Guiteau was relieved that he had fulfilled his mission. He went to the gallows confident that the demon he hailed as "Lordy" would take care of him in the afterlife.

- Lee Harvey Oswald was obsessed with his fears that "devilmen" would usurp all earthly governments. The death of JFK would serve as a kind of sacrifice to keep them at bay.

- Sirhan Sirhan's legal defense in his trial for the murder of Robert Kennedy strongly considered arguing that he had been possessed by the fanatical spirit of a dead Arab nationalist.

- Squeaky Fromme, one of Charles Manson's family, received mental instructions from her imprisoned master to murder President Gerald Ford on August 5, 1975.

- On January 11, 1990, the Secret Service arrested John S. Daughetee, a medical school dropout, who was acting under the orders of his "voices" when he robbed eight banks to finance his assassination attempts on Presidents Reagan and Bush.

THE CLERGY DECLARE A HOLY WAR ON DEMONS

In January 1999, the Vatican issued a revised Catholic rite of exorcism for the first time since 1614, essentially reaffirming the existence of Satan and his unholy legions of demons and advising those priests conducting exorcisms to deal with evil as a force "lurking within all individuals," instead of one that threatens people from without.

In September 2000, headlines around the world announced, SATAN DEFEATS THE POPE IN VATICAN EXORCISM STRUGGLE, and the account that followed such an attention-grabbing declaration told of a demon-possessed teenaged girl who screamed insults in a "cavernous voice," displayed superhuman strength in pushing away Vatican guards, and "sneeringly laughed" at the efforts of the Holy Father and Father Gabriele Amorth to exorcise her. Later, papal spokesmen insisted that the Pope had been able to calm the girl during her outburst, but that he had not attempted an exorcism. That task had been assigned to Father Amorth and Father Giancarlo Gramolazzo, who lamented that the nineteen-year-old had been a splendid and pure girl until her terrible case of possession.

On September 19, 2000, the *Chicago Sun-Times* reported that the Archdiocese of Chicago had appointed a full-time exorcist for the first time in its 160-year history.

In the November 28, 2000, issue of the *New York Times*, an article by John W. Fountain ("Exorcists and Exorcisms Proliferate Across U.S.") quoted Reverend Bob Larson, an evangelical preacher and author who heads an exorcism ministry in Denver, as saying that he had forty "exorcism teams" across the nation. "Our goal is that no one should ever be more than a day's drive from a city where you can find an exorcist," said Reverend Larson.

The evangelist questioned why anyone should be "freaked out" by the existence of demons and those of faith who would seek to drive them out of the victims of demonic possession. "It's in the Bible," he said.

If, as some theologians and scholars predict, there is soon to take place a major conflict between the Forces of Light and the Forces of Darkness, one would be well advised to be wary of those seductive creatures of the shadows who have for centuries sought to confuse us humans into believing that their counterfeit illumination is truly a Guiding Light.

Eight

INNER EARTH EMPIRE OF EVIL

Norma Hall is often required to travel away from home for her job with the state board of health. One night as she lay in a motel room in Missouri, dozing contentedly, she suddenly felt as though she was not alone.

"I felt a chill and the very uncomfortable feeling that someone was watching me," she stated in her account of the harrowing experience. "When I nervously looked over my shoulder, I saw a dark figure in the corner of the room. I shouted out, 'Who's there?' and the interloper began to move toward me."

Norma was startled to see what appeared to be a very short, hooded man in a dark robe approach her. "I switched on the lamp on the night stand," she said, "and he put up his hand to shield his eyes from the bright light. I could see that his palm and fingers were very gray in color and that he had extremely long fingernails."

Summoning all her courage, she demanded to know what the intruder was doing in her room. "I am a tall woman, five-ten in my barefeet," she said, "so when I got out of bed and stood to face my bedroom invader, I towered over him. I was amazed that he seemed even shorter when I stood before him. He was scarcely five feet tall."

But the voice that rumbled from his stocky, robed body seemed as though it had been amplified by some mechanical device: "We want you, woman! We need you. Come with me."

The "we" in the bizarre hooded stranger's declaration frightened Norma, and she looked desperately around the motel room to be certain there were not any more of his weird kind in the shadows.

"He lowered his hand from his eyes to reach out for me, and I was repulsed by the gray complexion and the shriveled facial features that he exposed," she said. "He looked like an animated corpse . . . or like someone who had never seen the sun. And he smelled dank, damp, like he had just pushed aside the earth that had covered his grave. Only his very large eyes with their black pupils seemed alive—his eyes and his little twitching nose and lips. He reminded me of a large, gray rat standing there, and I still shudder every time I think of him."

The grotesque, hooded, rodentlike man continued to intone his invitation that Norma come with him. "His voice had somehow become quite soothing," she stated. "It was almost as if he were crooning a lullaby of some sort in this singsong hypnotic voice. I stood, nearly mesmerized, as he 'sang' about how wonderful life was down in the caves and how I could be a great mother figure among those who dwelt there. I don't know how long I stood there listening to this eerie kind of chant, but my mind finally shook itself free of the ugly little man's spell, and I screamed at him to get the hell out of my room. I must have screamed and yelled more than once, because all of sudden there were people pounding on the walls for me to pipe down."

Norma said that when she began screaming and the

neighbors began rapping the walls with their fists, the monstrous little man seemed at first confused, then saddened by his failure to lure her to accompany him.

"And then, as incredible as it may seem," she concluded in her report, "he walked back to the corner of the room where I had first sighted him—and he just seemed to disappear right into the wall."

Norma ran to the wall to press against its surface to see if she could discover any hidden door or camouflaged opening of any kind. "It was a solid wall," she said. "Yet the grotesque little man had completely disappeared without a trace."

Sleep was impossible for Norma Hall that night. She checked out of the motel at dawn and drove to her next appointment, still wide awake. "I don't think I slept a full night through for weeks afterward," she said. "Have you ever heard of any creature like the one that I encountered in that Missouri motel room? Was it a ghost, an alien, a troll? What the heck was it?"

Yes, I have most certainly heard of such strange nocturnal visitors often during the fifty years that I have been actively investigating weird encounters with creatures from the darkside. However, it is still no easy task to determine with any finality if such entities are visitors from another dimension, spirit beings from other planes of existence, or if they truly are who they themselves claim to be—the Old Ones, an elder race that occupies the caverns and caves of Inner Earth. According to ancient traditions, these mysterious inhabitants of our planet's interior possess a technology that has always been—and remains—superior to that of our topside scientists, thus allowing them to appear to vanish into walls or into thin air. Some say these same Old Ones employ remarkable communication devices which can telepathically influence the thoughts and actions of us surface folk, sometimes for our good, other times for our detriment, depending, it seems, on which of the elder race are in control of the machines—the ones who despise us or the ones who feel benevolent toward us.

One constant that might be said about the Old Ones from underground is their everlasting quest for new blood from us topsiders, oftentimes attempting to seduce our adult men and women or kidnapping our infants from their cribs and our children from the city streets and forest lanes. In this regard, they are very much like the fairy folk. In fact, they might have given rise to the fairy legends—or vice versa. On the other hand, what appear to be fairies or Old Ones might be, in reality, demonic entities manifesting from some other dimension with an aggressive agenda of seduction, deceit, and destruction. When we embark upon a serious study of those entities from out of the dark who seek to molest humankind in various and sundry ways, we soon discover that there may well be a great deal of overlapping among the categories into which we, with our finite human minds, attempt to place these shadowy manifestations. In the final analysis, we may be dealing only with the forces of good and evil and viewing them through their reflections in the myriad mirrors of human consciousness.

Terrible Screams from a Deserted Mine

Returning to an examination of those monsters from out of the dark who reveal themselves as the Old Ones or those inhabitants of Inner Earth, the following report from two young men in Arizona is quite representative of such encounters.

In November 1997, twenty-two-year-old Duane Berger said that he and his friend Mark, 20, had decided to camp near an old deserted copper mine and soak up some of

Arizona's pioneer history. That afternoon, they took a lot of pictures both in and out of the tunnel, and they walked into the mine as far as they felt it was safe to do so.

Later, as daylight was fading, they built a campfire and fixed some steaks, beans, and Texas toast. "By the time it was dark, we had each downed a couple of long-necked beers, and we were just sitting around the fire, feeling pretty good about life in general, when we began to hear these terrible screams that seemed to be coming from the old mine."

At first, neither of them knew what to say or how to respond. "Just imagine that you and a buddy are alone out in the desert hills, that as far as you know there is no one else around for miles and miles, and then, suddenly, you start hearing these godawful female screams coming from an old deserted mine." Duane asked rhetorically, "what would you do? I think both of us just tried to ignore those pitiful screams for as long as we could."

"So what is that?" Mark finally asked, carefully placing the longneck he had just opened back in the cooler. "And where is it coming from?"

According to Duane's report of the incident, prior to that time the two friends had never really discussed the supernatural or the possible existence of ghosts or creatures of the dark. "But I don't think either of us thought for a moment that those screams could somehow be the product of spirits," Duane said. "The cries and moans sounded just too real, like a whole bunch of women were being tortured or something."

After a few moments of nervous discussion and assessment of the very eerie situation, the two young men were forced to conclude that the screams were definitely coming from somewhere within the mine. They knew that no one other than they had been in the vicinity all that day and there had been no signs of human visitation immediately prior to their arrival that they could discern.

"There were no fresh tire tracks or evidence of campfires to indicate that anyone other than the two of us had visited the old mine for a long, long time," Duane said. "We hadn't gone very far into the mine during our exploration, so the only theory we could devise is that someone was living deeper within the mine and that someone—whoever it might be— was terribly mistreating whatever women were with them."

Although neither of them had ever visualized himself as a hero, neither could they imagine that they could remain detached from a scene in which women might be being held and tortured by some cruel captors. "The only weapons we had were the steak knives and a tire iron," Duane said, "but we knew that we couldn't just sit there and listen to those poor women being so horribly mistreated."

The two friends mustered their courage and entered the mine shaft. "We had barely walked a dozen yards when we saw a greenish glow ahead of us," Duane stated. "As we got closer, we could make out the dark figures of two men in hooded robes. It was clear that they intended to block our going any farther into the mine."

As soon as they saw the two hooded figures, Duane and Mark were convinced that they had stumbled upon a cult of some sort that might even be practicing human sacrifice. "We whispered to each other that we had really done it now," Duane said. "Now the cultists would probably come after us to keep us from telling the authorities about their satanic practices in the old mine."

But as the frightened young men drew nearer to the light, they saw that their adversaries were barely five feet in height. With growing confidence that the two of them—both muscular men over six feet tall—could physically defend themselves against a bunch of "midget cultists," Duane and Mark boldly demanded that the hooded figures release the women they were hurting.

That was when a deep, mechanical voice boomed out of the cowled figures in unison and told them: *"The women are beyond your help! Leave at once or perish! Leave at once—or you shall join them in the caves."*

Duane put the beam of his flashlight beam directly into the face of one of their robed opponents, and he was astonished to see what appeared to be some kind of red harlequin-type mask covering the being's upper facial features. "The rest of his face seemed to be a really sickly gray color," Duane said. "He didn't appreciate the light in his eyes, and he yelled what I assumed was a curse in some strange language."

Next, complains Duane, "comes the part that no one ever believes." The robed figures produced some type of wandlike instrument and directed a yellow light at the two young men that held them both immobile. Next, they aimed a greenish beam against a wall of the mine shaft. The wall of solid rock seemed to melt away, allowing them to walk into the wall and disappear. Within seconds, the wall was once again nothing but hard rock.

Duane said that the effects of the yellow light dissipated in less than a minute, leaving their bodies feeling "tingling, like the sensation you get when you bump your 'crazy bone' in your elbow."

After the effects of the ray had worn off, Duane and Mark spent no more than ten or twelve seconds deciding what they should do next. "We realized that we were up against something and *someone* totally beyond our experience, our imagination. We knew that we had encountered some incredible supernatural beings or aliens from another world or demons from hell—so we just kicked out the campfire, grabbed up our gear, and got the hell out of there as fast as we could possibly move."

In the years since their frightening encounter with the mysterious cave beings, Duane said that he often reflects on the fate of the women that they heard screaming from within the mine. "I know that there was nothing that we could have done to help them," he said. "A couple of steak knives couldn't compare to rayguns that could momentarily paralyze you, then open and close holes in stone walls. Some nights when I can hear those awful screams again in my mind, it seems to me as though we were hearing tormented souls crying out straight from hell. And I really wonder if Mark and I didn't stumble on some ungodly, cursed opening that actually went from Hell directly up to Earth."

"Mr. X" and the Haunted Mine That Stole His Friend

The bizarre experience of Duane and Mark reminded me of the story that UFO researcher John Robinson told about the man who had contacted him after he had related the account of Steve Brodie during Long John Nebel's radio show in March 1957. Brodie had been a prospector in a Western state who claimed to have been held captive for two years by mysterious black-cowled entities in an underground cavern. Whenever Brodie had sought to escape, he was frozen into immobility by a rod wielded by his captors; and during his imprisonment, he said that he had seen other captives burned horribly by an application of similar rods. When the underpeople released him for reasons only they could comprehend, Brodie claimed to have awakened walking down Broadway toward Times Square, dressed in the same prospector's gear that he was wearing when he had been taken prisoner.

The day after Robinson had related the strange tale on the radio, he was surprised when a business associate confided in him that the Brodie story might explain an experience of his own that had occurred when he was seventeen.

According to the man, whom Robinson identified only as "Mr. X," he had been visiting a friend named Fred when the two of them set out to explore a "haunted mine" in the area. According to local legends, the mine had been abandoned when the miners had opened some sort of cave. From that time on, ill fortune had plagued them. Portions of the mine tunnel had caved in, crushing several miners. A couple of the investors had died as a result of a series of strange accidents, and a numer of the miners had simply disappeared without a trace.

The two teenagers passed the deserted buildings of the mining camp and climbed over a large pile of debris located at one side of the mine entrance. It was there, standing as if on guard at the mine opening, that the boys saw a grotesque monster.

About four and a half feet tall, but very thick in bulk, the being let out an unearthly scream and started around the edge of the mine toward the boys. The teenagers fled back to town in terror.

Mr. X remembered seeking refuge in a movie theater, only to have dark figures walk up and down the aisle, seemingly searching for the row in which he was sitting. Later that night, before he pulled the blinds of his bedroom window, he felt certain that he could see a dark form squatting in the crotch of a high limb in the tree nearest the house.

The next day, he left on the bus to return to his home in Los Angeles. A few days later, when he tried to telephone Fred, he was informed by Fred's distraught parents that he had disappeared. The only clue the authorities had to work on was the discovery of his bicycle near the entrance of the haunted mine.

"To this day, fifteen years later," Mr. X told Robinson, "I am afraid that whoever or whatever it was that got Fred will find me."

THE QUEST FOR SUBTERRANEAN SUPERHUMANS

Those readers who wish to pursue the subject of a subterranean world with any diligence will soon discover a vast collection of books documenting the fact that virtually every culture in the world has several legends which take the ancient inhabitants of Inner Earth into account. These legends either incorporate the underground visitors into their religions as deities or consider them as superior humans because of their wisdom and/or superior technology.

Buddhists have incorporated *Agharta*, a subterranean empire into their cosmology, believing fervently both in its existence and in the reality of the underworld superhumans who occasionally come to the surface to oversee the development of *Homo sapiens*. Western occultists interpret *Agharta* to be a continuation of the great civilization of Atlantis, whose present-day inhabitants are content to remain in their network of subterranean cities and embark on only occasional excursions to the surface world.

Certain metaphysicians and researchers have combined the two interpretations of Inner Earth summarized above and believe that they have discovered proof of such periodic visitations from the subsurface masters and teachers in manuscripts of great antiquity. The Indian epic *Ramayana* is frequently mentioned in this regard, for the ancient text frequently describes Rama as an emissary from *Agharta*, who arrived among the people on an aerial vehicle. It is remarkable to note that the *Ramayana* contains a description of a "flying saucer" as detailed as any provided by contemporary UFO contactees.

In the secular world of adventurers, explorers, and scientists, there have always been those bold-thinking individuals who embrace the concept that there is a vast underground empire beneath our feet.

In 1823, Captain John Cleve Symmes, a dour, humorless retired war hero, petitioned the U.S. Congress for funds to conduct an expedition to explore the interior of the Earth. Captain Symmes and his small band of followers felt somewhat annointed for the task because the great American clergyman of the Colonial period, Cotton Mather had defended the theory of a hollow earth in his book *The Christian Philosopher*. Mather, in turn, had developed his thesis after reading a little-known essay that had been penned in 1692 by the English astronomer Edmund Halley.

The theory that there was a vast uncharted world inside our own captured the imagination of Edgar Allan Poe, who in 1835, published his longest tale, "The Narrative of Arthur Gordon Pym," which told of a fantastic land located in the center of our planet, entered by a hole at the South Pole. So convincingly did Poe weave the pseudoscientific beginning of his narrative that the great educator Horace Greeley soberly endorsed the Pym adventure as a true account. He obviously did not complete the story and encounter its later sections of very evident fantasy. It is likely, however, that young Jules Verne, who would have been nine at that time, did finish reading the story and many years later may have been inspired to base one of his classic novels, *A Journey to the Center of the Earth*, on a similar theme.

While it is unlikely that even a fervent pulpit-pounding evangelist such as Cotton Mather could persuade a scientist to launch a serious expedition to explore the hollow earth theory in 2001, such was not the case as recently as 1942 when Nazi Germany sent out a group of its most visionary scientists to seek a military vantage point within the Earth's interior. Although this expedition set out at a time when the Third Reich was applying maximum effort in their drive against the Allies and could hardly spare any military resources, Hitler enthusiastically endorsed the project.

As a member of numerous occult societies, such as the Thule and the Vril, the Fuhrer believed that the ancient Masters may have retreated to the Inner Earth and created a New Atlantis in subterranean caves. Subscribing to another popular psuedoscientific theory, Hitler had long believed that Earth was concave and that humankind lived on the *inside* of the globe. According to the theory advanced by a number of the Fuhrer's like-minded scientists, if the Nazis were to station their most accomplished radar experts in the correct geometric position they would be able to determine the precise position of the British Fleet and the Allied bomber squadrons, because the concave curvature of the globe would enable infared rays to accomplish long-distance monitoring.

When Hitler, Goering, Himmler and their fellow exponents of the Hollow Earth belief sent the expedition to the island of Rugen in the Baltic Sea to establish the radar base, they had complete confidence in their application of the ancient vision of the concave planet. At the same time, there were certain very old traditions that insisted that the Knights Templar had hidden the Holy Grail and the Ark of the Covenant somewhere on one of the Baltic islands. Far from a fanciful plot device created for the *Indiana Jones* motion picture series, Hitler really did send out expeditions to acquire as many holy relics as possible. The Fuhrer and his inner circle believed that such a grand accomplishment as possessing legendary artifacts of power and majesty, as well as discovering an entrance to the Inner Empire, would convince the ancient Masters who lived there that the Nazis were truly worthy of mixing their blood with them in the hybridization of a master race.

An important element in the Nazi mythos was the belief that representatives of a powerful, underground secret race of beings emerged from time to time to walk among humankind. Hitler's frenzied desire to breed a master race of Nordic types was inspired by his obsessive hope that it would be the Germanic peoples who would be chosen above all other humans to interact with the subterranean supermen in the mutation of a new species of heroes, demigods, and godmen.

In their *Morning of the Magicians*, authors Louis Pauwels and Jacques Bergier quote one of the Fuhrer's confidantes, Hermann Rauschning, governor of Danzing during the Third Reich, who repeated a conversation that he had once had with Hitler concerning his desperate plan to be worthy of uniting with the new human mutations that were being created by the masters who resided in their underground kingdom: "The new man is living amongst us now!" Hitler said, speaking the words in what Rauschning recalled as a kind of ecstasy. "He is here! Isn't that enough for you? I will tell you a secret. I have seen the new man. He is intrepid and cruel. I was afraid of him."

Rauschning went on to state that he was told by a person very close to Hitler that the Fuhrer often awoke in the night screaming and in convulsions. Always the frightened dictator would shout that *he* had come for him. That *he* stood there in the corner of the room. That *he* had emerged from his underworld kingdom to invade the Fuhrer's bedroom.

If, as Rauschning recalled, Hitler appeared to relate his encounters with the representative of the emergent mutant species in a kind of ecstasy or trancelike state, we can wonder if there is credence to the many rumors and theories that the Fuhrer was mediumistic. In addition to his membership in several occult societies, Hitler's birthplace, the little village of Branau-on-the-Inn, was for many years a center of spiritualism in Europe. It has often been said that the infant Adolf shared the same wet-nurse with Willy Schneider, who along with his brother Rudi, became a world-famous medium.

WARNINGS AND COUNSEL FROM MYSTERIOUS GRAY AND RED MEN

Adolf Hitler was not the only world leader who claimed to have received visitations from otherworldly counselors. However, instead of these entities being new mutations of humans, we might suggest that these mysterious advisors were representatives from a very old race that had sought refuge under the surface of our planet.

According to numerous accounts, a mysterious Red Man first appeared to the great Napoleon during his ambitious campaign in Egypt. The strange visitor who materialized in the French military genius's bedchamber claimed that he had given sage counsel to the rulers of France in years past and that he had now come to warn him of certain errors in his planning.

"You have become far too ambitious," the Red Man admonished Napoleon. "The French people are growing to be wary of your overwhelming lust for power."

When Napoleon objected to such an analysis of his motives, the mysterious entity smiled and shook his head. "I have been at your side since you were a schoolboy," he chided him. "I know you better than you know yourself!"

Once he had the military man's attention, the Red Man

told him that his orders to the French fleet had not been obeyed. Even though the Egyptian campaign had begun on a note of triumph after the bloody battle of the Pyramids, the invasion would fail—and Napoleon would return to France to find her closed in by England, Russia, Turkey, and an allied Europe. Domestically, the Red Man warned, Napoleon would be confronted by angry mobs in Paris. True to the Red Man's prediction, the Egyptian campaign failed.

In 1809, after the Battle of Wagram, Napoleon made his headquarters at Schonbrunn where, one lonely midnight, he again received his mysterious nocturnal adviser.

The Red Man made his third and final appearance to Napoleon on the morning of January 1, 1814, shortly before the Emperor was forced to abdicate. On this occasion, the arrival of the Red Man was witnessed, for he appeared first to Counsellor of State Mole and demanded that he be allowed to see the Emperor on matters of great importance. Mole had been given strict orders that the Emperor was not to be disturbed, but when he yielded to the stranger's demands and informed Napoleon of his arrival, the Red Man was granted immediate entrance.

It is said in many accounts that Napoleon beseeched the Red Man for more time to complete the execution of certain proposals, but the visitor explained that he was neither deity nor prophet. "I am but a messenger," he said to Napoleon. "I am to inform you that you have three months to achieve a general peace or it will be all over for you."

In a futile effort to gain more time, Napoleon desperately attempted to launch a new eastern campaign. However, such a move left Paris to fall into the hands of the forces allied against him. On April 1, three months after the Red Man's final midnight visit, Talleyrand and the Senate called for Napoleon's abdication.

* * *

King Charles XII of Sweden, hailed as the Alexander of the North, went into the winter woods to seek the counsel of a little Gray Man with a ruddy complexion, who presented him with a ring that would not vanish until the day of the ruler's death.

Charles cut a mighty swath across Europe, Russia, and Turkey, and his feats became legendary. But he, too, resisted the repeated appearances of the little Gray Man and his entreaties to make peace with his enemies. In 1718, as the Swedish army was besieging Fredrikshald, one of the King's officers noticed that his "magic ring" was no longer on his finger. Moments later, Charles fell dead from a head wound.

In the year 1777, a despairing George Washington sat in his rude hut at Valley Forge. A movement in a corner of the room caused him to turn to see a rising, curling vapor surrounding a long-robed, long-haired, reddish-faced entity, whom he first took for a native tribesman, but later decreed that it must have been an angel. Washington told Anthony Sherman, a close friend, that the dark-complexioned angel had shown him a vision of the birth, progress, and destiny of the American colonies, and had thus given him the courage to continue the struggle for independence.

A WARNING TO FUTURE HUMANS

While it may be said that the mysterious counselors who manifested themselves to great world leaders such as Napoleon, Charles XII, and Washington were magnanimous in intent as long as their advice was perfectly obeyed, by far more accounts of the underpeople deal with those who are quite unpleasant and openly hostile to those of us who live on the surface of the planet. In 1945, a bizarre tale published in the

March issue of *Amazing Stories* firmly established the agenda of the evil Inner Earth empire in the collective consciousness.

According to Ray Palmer, who was fiction editor of the Ziff-Davis stable of magazines from February 1938 to September 1949, in September 1944 a letter from a Richard S. Shaver came to his attention. In what at first appeared to be a claim by some crackpot about an ancient language that "should not be lost to the world," Palmer, more or less on a whim, decided to print the letter, complete with specimens of the alleged language, in the next issue of *Amazing Stories*.

The publication of the strange letter brought an avalanche of mail to Palmer's desk. All of the intrigued letters to the editor wanted to know where Shaver had acquired the alphabet displayed in his correspondence. Smelling a good story in the making, Palmer relayed the curiosity of the magazine's readers to Shaver and received a 10,000-word manuscript in reply. Impressed with the sincerity of the crude manuscript, which Shaver had ominously entitled, "A Warning to Future Man," Palmer retitled the piece, "I Remember Lemuria," added a few trimmings and polish, and published it in the March 1945 issue of *Amazing Stories*, thereby setting off what *Life* magazine six years later would declare "the celebrated rumpus that racked the science-fiction world."

Shaver and Palmer had created a "rumpus," because the stories claimed to be true accounts of human interaction with a race of malformed subhuman creatures called "deros" who inhabited a vast system of underground cities all over the world. The ancestors of the dero were a race of people called the Abandondero, descendents of those who were unable to leave the planet when the "Titans" or "Atlans" from Lemuria discovered that the sun's radiations were radioactive and thereby limiting to life. While those who left Earth in a mass exodus sought a planet with an uncontaminated sun, the

Abandondero planned to escape the radioactive poisoning by abandoning the surface and creating cities in vast underground caverns.

Although the sun does hasten the aging process, it also has many health-giving rays which the Inner Earth dwellers had then denied themselves. Vast numbers of the underpeople began to degenerate into physically stunted near-idiots, no longer capable of constructive reasoning. According to Richard Shaver, these were the "dero," the detrimental or degenerate robots. "Robot," as Shaver uses the word, doesn't mean a mechanical representation of human, but is rather a designation for those who are governed by degenerative, negative forces.

Standing between the viciousness of the degenerate dero and the surface civilization are the "tero" ("T" was the Atlans' symbol of deity in their religion; therefore the "t" in tero represents good). The tero have learned methods of staving off much of the mental degenerative effects of their subterranean way of life by the use of certain machines, chemicals, and beneficial rays. They have not been successful in discovering a means whereby they are able to prevent premature aging, however, and they die at an average age of fifty.

Shaver's "warning" to future humankind is that the dero are becoming more numerous and have scattered the benign tero with their constant attacks. The greatest threat to us lies in the grim fact that the dero have access to all the machines of the Atlan technology, but they don't have the intelligence or the highly developed moral sense of the ancients to use these machines responsibly.

The dero have possession of "vision ray machines" that can penetrate solid rock and pick up scenes all over Earth. In order to accomplish instant transport from one point to another, they have access to the Atlans' teleportation units. Frighteningly, the dero long ago gained control of the mental machinery that can induce "solid" illusions, dreams, and compulsions in topsiders. In addition to the aerial craft that we call UFOs, the dero possess death rays that can wreak terrible havoc.

According to Shaver, the dero are notorious for their sexual orgies, and they apply "stim" machines that revitalize sexual virility and "ben" rays that heal and restore the physical body. These mechanisms were created by the ancient Atlans thousands of years ago and are still in perfect working order, due to the high degree of technical perfection with which they were constructed.

We surface dwellers are the descendants of the Abandondero who were unable to gain access to the caves at the time of the great exodus of the Titans from Earth. Most of our early ancestors died off; some degenerated into lumbering hominids such as the Neanderthals; others, the hardy ones, survived, and through the centuries our species has developed a greater tolerance for the sun, which allows us to live even longer than the subsurface tero with their machines of rejuvenation. At the same time, the beneficient rays of the sun have prevented in our kind the mental and physical deterioration that perverts the dero and weakens the tero.

Although we have a common heritage with the tero and the dero, the passage of time has prevented the great mass of surface dwellers from possessing more than dim memories of the glory days of Atlantis, Lemuria, Mu, and the epochs when there were "giants in the Earth." However, Shaver cautions us, by no means have the dero forgotten us. These sadistic monsters take enormous delight in creating terrible accidents, confusing the goals of our political leaders, provoking surface wars between nations, and even in causing nightmares by focusing "dream mech" on us while we sleep.

In later years, Ray Palmer left the pressures of working for Ziff-Davis and their string of magazines and chose to establish a publishing company in his native Wisconsin. When I met with him in the late 1960s, Ray lived on a heavily wooded, 124-acre farm near Amherst, Wisconsin, just a few miles from the converted school building that housed his Amherst Press and from where he issued magazines such as *Flying Saucers, Space World, Rocket Exchange, Forum,* and *Search.*

Those UFO buffs and faithful readers of Palmer's publications who met him for the first time were often taken aback when they saw that he stood only four feet eight inches in height. "They just can't help saying something like, 'Aha! You really are a man from Mars!' " Ray laughed.

Actually, his diminutive stature was due to a crippling childhood disease and not to environmental conditions on Mars. Regardless of his lack of height, for decades Ray Palmer cast a giant shadow over the publishing world of the occult, the paranormal, UFOs, and the Hollow Earth mystery.

Since controversy raged about how much of the Shaver Mystery was Shaver and how much was Palmer, I could not resist asking Ray directly one day when I drove over to visit with him.

Palmer admitted that he had enlarged Shaver's original 10,000-word manuscript to a 31,000-word story for *Amazing Stories.* "Although I added the trimmings, I did not alter the factual basis of Shaver's manuscript except in one instance," he said. "I could not bring myself to believe that Shaver had actually gotten his alphabet and his 'warning to future man,' and all the 'science' he propounded, from actual underground people. Perhaps I made a grave mistake, but I altered what he stated were his 'thought-records' into 'racial memory.' I felt certain that the concept of racial memory would be far more believable to the readers, and offer a reasonable and perhaps actual explanation of what was really going on in

Shaver's mind—which is where I felt it really was going on, and not in any caves or via any 'telaug rays' or 'telesolidograph' projections of illusions from the cavern ray operators."

After the publication of "I Remember Lemuria" in March 1945, *Amazing Stories* received 50,000 letters from readers who had been intrigued, enthralled, or frightened by Richard S. Shaver's "true" story of the cave people. For a magazine whose usual mail response was somewhere around 45 letters a month, such a deluge of mail indicative of overwhelming reader interest in the Shaver Mystery was beyond phenomenal. Palmer had no difficulty convincing the circulation director that they should increase their usual print run by 50,000 for the follow-up Shaver piece, and the magazine maintained that print figure for the next four years while he ran the series to its conclusion.

Ray Palmer had definitely achieved a mighty *coup* in the magazine world—though many readers did protest the inclusion of supposed nonfiction in a publication that was devoted to fiction. From his perspective, he only cared that he had prompted lively debates among his readers and he had upped circulation beyond the wildest dreams of his employers. As for the validity of the cave people, he remained quite skeptical until he visited Richard Shaver's home in Pennsylvania. After he had spent a couple of nights there, some very strange occurrences led him to wonder whether Shaver was relying on "racial memory" or direct dero contact to write his stories.

The first night of his visit, Palmer prepared for sleep, convinced after an evening of serious discussion that Shaver was truly sincere in his beliefs and that he was not "consciously perpetrating a hoax." Shaver had retired to his own bedroom, while his wife remained downstairs to tidy up after the late-night talk session.

Then, Palmer said, he began to hear strange voices issuing

from Shaver's bedroom. "There were five voices," Palmer recalled. "There was a woman's voice, a child's voice, a gruff
man's voice, and two other male voices of varying pitch and
timbre."

What the voices were discussing, Palmer said, startled him
beyond all imagination. The five "persons" were describing
their having witnessed a woman being drawn and quartered
that afternoon.

Horrified at hearing such a graphic and gory description
of such an evil and barbaric act, Palmer shouted at the voices,
"What's this all about?"

The childish voice told the others to pay no attention to
Palmer: "He's a dope!" Then the voices switched to an unknown language that Palmer was unable to identify. Since
very often all five voices were speaking at once, "excitedly
and volubly," Palmer knew that the vocal bedlam that issued
from Shaver's bedroom could not have come from the man's
lips—he could not have been imitating five distinct voices at
the same time. When, finally, Mrs. Shaver entered the bedroom, the voices ceased at once.

The next day, when he was left alone in the Shaver home
for a brief period, Palmer said that he searched the rooms for
some kind of recording device, wires, microphones—any evidence at all that Shaver had somehow tricked him with the
remarkable verbal production number of the previous night.
He was unable to discover any kind of mechanical device or
any evidence of a hoax. "Those voices that I had heard
weren't in my mind and they couldn't all have come from
Shaver's lips at the same time," he concluded. "That would
have been humanly impossible."

Once I pointedly asked Ray Palmer what he had meant
when he wrote in an issue of his *Search* magazine that the
dero had nearly killed him and that he lived a life of "perpet-

ual and terrible pain" that never subsided for a second. He had also once written, "I know the dero are real, and I know what they can do!"

Palmer's answer was a direct and decidedly uncomfortable one:

> My experience with the dero took place when I was still editing *Fate* magazine in Evanston, Illinois. One night we had a very hard rainstorm and the drain in the basement plugged up. I was wading around in the water, trying to unstop the drain, when I suddenly felt myself being lifted high into the air. Helpless, I hung suspended for just a moment, then I was slammed down to the basement floor with great force. I was paralyzed as a result of this attack— and I most certainly do bear the effects of this paralysis to this day. I am not certain *what* attacked me, but I am certain that it was no accident.

Tommyknockers

For generations, those hardy gentlemen who descend into the earth to mine coal, tin, copper, silver, or other minerals have told weird tales of encountering strange little men, commonly called "Tommyknockers." While some mining folklore maintains that these entities are the ghosts of men who have lost their lives in the tunnels beneath the earth, other traditions believe the Tommyknockers to be akin to elves or dwarves (or dero?). Those who have seen the beings state they stand around three feet tall and have very large, oversized heads for their smallish bodies. Their features are wrinkled, very often framed by long beards, and their arms are disproportionately long, nearly reaching to the tops of their little miner's boots.

Tough Irish laborers insisted that it was no trick of the senses that appeared before them when they were digging in a stretch of tunnel that was cut under the Thames River in London in the fall of 1968.

Big Lou Chalmers felt something brush his neck. When he turned around, he saw "something" in the shape of a man with his arms stretched out. Chalmers said he didn't stop to study the details of the Tommyknocker, he just made a run for it.

Another laborer who saw the figure came up from the tunnel as white as a sheet and headed off to get a stiff drink.

Men who have spent a lot of time in the mines state that they hear the Tommyknockers more than they see them. They most often first become aware of the wee creatures because they hear them knocking, tapping, on the other side of the walls. And when the miners knock on the tunnel walls, the Tommyknockers working unseen within the wall itself knock right back.

There are tales of the Tommyknockers saving the lives of miners, and there are other accounts of the mischief that the little people enjoyed playing on their human counterparts. Sometimes the tricks of the Tommyknockers could get pretty rough, such as causing small cave-ins or stealing valuable tools. To keep the peace between them, many a miner would leave a portion of his lunch for the Tommyknockers in a gesture of good will.

Alfred Scadding was the sole survivor of the famous 1936 Moose River Mine disaster. Just minutes before the mines caved in, he was on his way to join other workers. But then, as he later told the story: "I came to a cross cut, a tunnel running across the one I was in, and as I passed I looked left. I saw a small light, like a flashlight, about two feet from the ground and swinging as if in someone's hand, moving away from me. Two minutes after I saw the light, the mine came in on us."

After his rescue, Scadding was told that there were no human beings down in the mine at that time other than the two miners who were trapped with him. Yet he said that after the three of them had been trapped for some time, they clearly heard the sounds of shouting and laughter. Scadding insisted that they were all clearheaded and conscious, and at first they thought they were somehow hearing children playing and that there must be a vent somewhere to the surface. For twenty-four hours, Scadding said, they heard the bizarre sounds of people laughing and shouting and having fun.

Who could find the plight of miners trapped in a cave-in to be the source of amusement? Ray Palmer would quickly have nominated Richard Shaver's dero for such a dubious distinction.

Rather than the Tommyknockers being the ghosts of departed human miners or representatives of the fairy or elf clans, these smallish entities working the mines and "knocking" on the walls in underground tunnels throughout the world may truly be the members of an ancient hidden world—call them The Old Ones, the Altans, the Elder Race, or the dero. If they should be spirits, then they may be the ethereal guardians of mines that were once worked many thousands of years ago by a long-forgotten prehistoric species of humanoids.

WHO OCCUPIED THE CAVES MILLIONS OF YEARS AGO?

In Pershing County, Nevada, a shoe print was found in Triassic limestone, strata indicative of 400 million years, in which the fossilized evidence clearly revealed finely wrought double-stitching in the seams.

Early in 1975 Dr. Stanley Rhine of the University of New Mexico announced his discovery of humanlike footprints in strata indicative of 40 million years old.

Fossilized tracks of both bare and shod feet of decidedly humanlike impression have been found in rocks from the Carboniferous to the Cambrian period in geological sites ranging from Virginia and Pennsylvania, through Kentucky, Illinois, Missouri, Utah, Oklahoma, and Texas. The prints give every evidence of having been made by some unknown bipedal creatures with humanlike feet about 250 to 500 million years ago.

We cannot say "human feet" when we discuss such impossible discoveries as these remarkable footprints being discovered in the stones of time because we humans, *Homo sapiens*, are officially less than 150,000 years old, and we became the dominant species roughly 45,000 years ago. Although there is far from a scientific consensus regarding our various "cousins" on the *Homo sapiens'* family tree, as well as the dates of their "births" and "deaths," many paleoanthropologists recognize "Lucy," a 3.18-million-year-old *Australopithecus afraensis*, as the "mother of humankind."

We will leave the scientists to engage in their sometimes heated debate over exactly when the genus *Homo* replaced the apelike *Australopithecus*. The mystery on which we shall focus our attention is this: If our species' oldest ancestor is but 3.18 million years old, and the triumphant exodus of our evolving species out of Africa took place only around 150,000 years ago, then how could these geologic strata throughout the United States and scattered around the world be revealing so many "human" footprints, tools, and other artifacts roughly 250–500 million years old?

In 1953, miners of the Lion coal mine of Wattis, Utah,

broke into a network of tunnels between five and six feet in height and width, which contained piles of coal of such vast antiquity that it had become weathered to a state of uselessness for any kind of burning or heat. A search outside the mountain in direct line with the tunnels revealed no sign of any entrance. Since the tunnels were discovered when the miners were working an eight-foot coal seam at 8,500 feet, the evidence is irrefutable that an undetermined someone had conducted an extremely ambitious mining project so far back in time that all exterior traces had been eroded away.

According to Professor John E. Wilson of the Department of Engineering, University of Utah, the tunnels "without a doubt" were man-made: "Though no evidence was found at the outcrop, the tunnels apparently were driven some 450 feet from the outside to the point where the present workings broke into them . . . There is no visible basis for dating the tunnels . . ." (*Coal Age*, February 1954.)

Jesse D. Jennings, professor of anthropology at the University of Utah, could offer no opinion as to the identity of the mysterious ancient miners, but he denied that such vast tunnels and coal mining rooms could have been the work of any Native American tribes.

In addition to deep-driven tunnels with coal so ancient that it is no longer able to burn, there are an incredible number of unexplained finds in mines that indicate some intelligent workers who thrived in those epochs we consider prehistoric. To list only a very few, I will mention the following:

A strange, imprinted slab was found in a coal mine. The artifact was decorated with diamond-shaped squares with the face of an old man in each box.

In another coal mine discovery, miners found smooth, polished concrete blocks which formed a solid wall. According to one miner's testimony, he chipped one block open only to discover the standard mixture of sand and cement that makes up most typical building blocks of today.

An iron spike was discovered in a silver mine in Peru.

An iron implement was found in a Scottish coalbed, estimated to be millions of years older than humans are believed to have existed.

A metal, bell-shaped vessel, inlaid with a silver floral design, was blasted out of solid rock near Dorchester, Massachusetts.

In 1912, two employees of the Municipal Electric Plant, Thomas, Oklahoma, used a sledge to break open a chunk of coal too large for the furnace. An iron pot toppled from the center of the chunk, leaving an impression in the coal.

Carved bones, chalk, stones, together with what would appear to be greatly ornamented coins, have been brought up from great depths during well-drilling operations.

Two hypotheses come immediately to mind which may explain the presence of such perplexing evidence of a human or humanoid presence in a vast antiquity: (1) such artifacts as those listed above were manufactured by an advanced civilization on Earth which, due either to natural or technological catastrophe, was destroyed and their survivors retreated to build an underground place of refuge; (2) they are vestiges of a highly technological civilization of extraterrestrial origin, which visited this planet millions of years ago, leaving behind colonists who retreated beneath the earth's surface, but who still maintain contact with their home planet.

In our final chapter, dealing with those entities who dwell apart from us in the darkened corridors of reality, we shall meet the monsters that appear to visit us from other worlds in the universe—the aliens.

Nine

MONSTERS FROM OUTER SPACE

In his recently published memoirs, *Leap of Faith: An Astronaut's Journey into the Unknown*, retired United States Air Force Colonel L. Gordon Cooper provides his readers with the astonishing revelation that he once chased UFOs over Germany in his F-86.

As if that were not enough red meat for the flying saucer buffs, Cooper also claims that when he was a captain stationed at Edwards Air Force Base on May 3, 1957, he learned of a metallic saucer-shaped object that had landed at 8:00 A.M. The incredible contact was even filmed by an astonished technical film crew that had been on assignment some 50 yards away. Although the UFO had zoomed out of sight when the startled photographers attempted to move closer for a better camera angle, Cooper was ordered by Pentagon officials to have all the film developed—but not printed—and to ship it off to the appropriate officials at once. Cooper writes that he obeyed orders, but he also admits that he peeked at some of the negatives and confirmed that the film crew had most certainly captured a flying saucer on celluloid.

Cooper's mind-blowing revelations follow those of a fellow astronaut, Dr. Edgar Mitchell, who shook up both UFO buffs and skeptics alike when he proclaimed, "Make no mistake, Roswell [the alleged crash site of an alien craft in July 1947] happened. I've seen secret files which show the government knew about it, but decided not to tell the public" (*The People* [London], October 25, 1998).

Cooper goes on to tell of an Air Force master sergeant friend of his who was assigned to a recovery team to retrieve a crashed UFO in a canyon in the Pacific Southwest. According to his friend, they found two very human-looking fellows sitting atop a metallic, disk-shaped wreckage, smiling at them. The alien pilots were hustled away, and Cooper's friend told him that he never found out what happened to them.

There have been some UFOnauts described as human in appearance, but most, although "humanoid," would more aptly fit the monster category.

Three Strange Men at the Side of the Road

Robert, a short-order cook at an all-night diner, was getting off work about four o'clock one morning when he thought he saw three men praying at the side of the road. Because he was extremely tired and didn't want the glare of oncoming traffic in his eyes, he had taken a little-traveled country road. Although he was tired to the bone after a grueling night's work, his curiosity got the better of him and he stopped the car to see what was up with the three men kneeling beside the road.

In retrospect, he may have been a bit foolish when he decided to open his car door and step out on the gravel—for that was when he discovered his mistake. The three beings weren't men at all. He didn't know what they were.

The figures he saw that night were short and stood in a triangular pattern, facing the opposite side of the road. The entity at the point of the triangle suddenly raised its arms above its head, and it appeared to be holding some kind of rod in its hands. Robert was startled when he saw blue and white sparks jumping from one of the creature's hands to the other, just above and below the rod.

Robert was now becoming extremely anxious about his safety. He had parked beside the strange trio in a rather remote stretch of country road next to a heavily wooded area just west of the main highway. Their strange ritual with the sparkling rod completed, they turned to face him.

The headlights of his car illuminated the three beings so he was able to get a good look at them. They were all about three and a half feet tall with grayish complexions and skin-tight uniforms about the same shade of gray as their faces. They had large, straight mouths without lips, and indistinct noses. Their eyes seemed basically normal in human terms, but they had no eyebrows. The upper portion of their heads was bald, with what appeared to be a roll of fat or a ridge of bone running across the top.

Their bodies were, in Robert's opinion, a bit lopsided. Their chests appeared to swell to an unusual bulge on their right sides, and their arms were of uneven length, the right one longer than the left. Their clothing above the waist—if indeed it was clothing—was skin-tight and gave no evidence of any line separating it from the skin portion of the creatures, which was the same grayish color.

Although he had felt some understandable anxiety at being alone in a remote area with such an eerie trio, Robert said that he felt no real fear of the humanoids until he started walking toward them to meet their advance. Then, suddenly, he strongly sensed that he should stop, turn, and run for his car, and get the hell out of there. As he accelerated past the three creatures, he was nearly overcome by a powerful, nauseating odor that seemed to be directed at him by the dark figures, who stood watching him drive away.

A Bigfoot-Type Creature in a Mysterious Bubble of Light

When Mrs. R.H. awoke about 2:30 A.M. and got out of bed to get a drink of water, she noticed a light coming through the drawn curtains—and when she pulled the curtains apart, she was startled to see a row of individual lights forming an arc not more than two yards from her window.

The lights, six in number, were about four feet above the ground and alternated in color, from vivid blue to silver, and appeared as beautiful to Mrs. R.H. as if they were Christmas lights. Somehow, they seemed to be internally illuminated, casting no radiance to the ground or on a nearby shed.

While the "Christmas lights" hovered outside her window, her attention was drawn to a stronger light farther away. Near this light source stood a tall, grotesque, apelike creature. The monster moved to a spot about ten or so yards from her house and now appeared to be standing within the bright light, as if it were some kind of bubble or shield which enveloped it.

The massive apelike beast appeared to have some kind of snout, but she could make out few other features. Its body was gray in color and without any distinguishing characteristics.

Mrs. R.H. estimated the strange bubble of light to be about seven feet in diameter. Although she could see no valves or levers inside the large glasslike bubble, the creature's arms began to move in such a manner as to suggest the operation of some kind of controls. While she was trying to call the police, the mysterious bubble and its Bigfoot-type humanoid disappeared.

"More Frightening than the Frankenstein Monster!"

Kathleen May described the alien being that she and seven other Flatwoods, West Virginia, residents saw on September 12, 1952, as looking more frightening than the Frankenstein monster. Mrs. May had her attention called to the saucer by a group of excited boys, including her sons, Eddie, 13, and Fred, 12, who had been at a nearby playground when they sighted a flying saucer emitting an exhaust that looked like red balls of fire. According to the boys, the UFO had landed on a hilltop in back of the May house.

Mrs. May later told reporters that she kept telling the boys that it was just their imagination, but they continued to insist that they had seen a flying saucer land behind the hill. Finally, Gene Lemon, a husky seventeen-year-old, found a flashlight and said that he was going to investigate. At the urging of her son, Mrs. May agreed to accompany him, and the other boys fell in behind them. About halfway up the hill, she began to change her mind about whatever the boys had seen being in their imaginations, for she could see a strange, reddish glow emanating from somewhere near the top.

After about half an hour of tramping through the brush that covered the narrow, seldom-used, uphill trail, Gene Lemon directed the beam of his flashlight on what he believed to be the green, glowing eyes of an animal. Instead, the beam spotlighted an immense, humanlike figure with blood-red face and greenish eyes that blinked out from under a pointed hood. Behind the monster was a "glowing ball of fire as big as a house" that grew dimmer and brighter at intervals. The 17-year-old's courage left him in a long scream of terror, and the intrepid band of flying saucer hunters fled in panic from the sight that Lemon's flashlight had illuminated.

Later, Mrs. May described the monster as having "terrible claws." Some of the boys, however, had not noticed any arms at all, and some said that when it had moved toward them, it had not really walked on legs, but "just moved." Most of the witnesses agreed that the being had worn dark clothing, probably dark green. Estimates of the monster's height ranged from seven to ten feet, but everyone agreed about one characteristic of the alien—it had emitted a sickening odor, "like sulphur," Mrs. May said, yet unlike anything she had ever encountered.

Lee Steward, Jr., of the *Braxton Democrat*, arrived on the scene only moments ahead of Sheriff Robert Carr, but the reporter found most of the witnesses too frightened to speak coherently and some were receiving first aid for cuts and bruises received in their pell-mell flight down the hill. A while later, he persuaded Gene Lemon to accompany him to the spot where they had seen the monster.

Stewart saw no sign of the giant alien or of the pulsating red globe of light that ostensibly served as its spacecraft, but he did inhale enough of the unusual odor to declare it "sickening and irritating." In his report of his investigation, he stated that he had developed a familiarity with a wide variety of gases while serving in the Air Force, but he had never been confronted by any gas with a similar odor.

Each of the witnesses later swore that the monster had definitely been moving toward them, but they also agreed that this apparent aggressive movement could have been due to the fact that they were between the alien and the large, glowing globular object that was quite likely his spacecraft.

EXTRATERRESTRIAL INVADERS

On January 7, 2000, the *Christian Science Monitor* reported that China was "curiously entering the new century by trying to build bridges of communication with extraterrestrials." Sun Shili, head of the Chinese UFO Research Organization, reported more than 3,000 sightings of unidentified flying objects across China in 1999 and emphasized that such a rash of UFOs was being taken very seriously.

According to *Agence France Presse*, on January 27, 2001, an airport in southern Siberia was closed down for 90 minutes when a UFO hovered above its runway, preventing conventional aircraft from flying. The crew of an I1-76 cargo aircraft refused to take-off when they sighted a large glowing object hovering above the runway of Siberia's Barnaul airport, and the crew of another cargo plane refused to land when they spotted the same luminescent UFO above the runway, choosing to take their jet to another airport. After the mysterious object had performed whatever unknown mission constituted its unknown agenda, it left the airport and disappeared.

In June 1998, a CNN/Time poll found that 27 percent of all Americans believe that aliens have already visited Earth, but an amazing 80 percent maintain that the government is conducting a cover-up to keep the truth of extraterrestrial visitation from the general population.

On June 8, 1999, a National Institute of Science/Roper Poll asked a nationwide sample of men and women a number of questions regarding their responses to a sudden confirmation of extraterrestrial life. When first asked what they thought UFOs were, 25 percent assumed that they were alien spaceships; 19 percent opined that they were misinterpretation of normal phenomena; 12 percent believed they were secret government vehicles; 9 percent suggested they were hallucinations; and 7 percent theorized they might be visitors from other dimensions.

When the poll respondents were queried concerning how they felt the general public would deal with the confirmation that extraterrestrial life was visiting Earth, 25 percent felt that the majority of people would become greatly disturbed and panic; 10 percent feared that their fellow citizens would behave irrationally and become dangerous; 14 percent guessed that the public at large would begin to behave in strange ways; 36 percent assumed that vast numbers of people would be very concerned about alien invasion; 13 percent expected most U.S. citizens to handle the confirmation of alien visitation in a calm and rational manner.

In the late 1960s, Harold D. Lasswell, professor of law and political science at Yale University, offered his speculations on what would happen when our human civilization is confronted by extraterrestrial aliens. If that alien culture were technologically superior to ours—which it would be if it had successfully conquered space to land on Earth—then ". . . we would be in the same relationship to another planet that folk societies have often occupied in reference to an industrialized nation of Western Europe or an empire of advanced weaponry."

Lasswell went on to conjecture that our "religions, arts, and sciences would suffer by comparison with whatever doctrines and formulas are imputed to the ruling group." In such an event, there would be the grim possibility that the superior culture might select the brightest, healthiest, and most promising earth children and separate them from their families so they might be reared in the aliens' greater intellectual and technological environment. Hopefully, such a culture might also be somewhat benign and paternal and force humans to abandon all aggressive pursuits and devote their time to aesthetic endeavors.

If the alien culture should be generally comparable to our own in scientific advancement and technological development, perhaps superior only in the area of space flight, for example, then Lasswell sees us ". . . in the midst of a greatly expanded, though familiar situation" which could bring about a kind of return to a cold war rivalry, as East and West seek to win the favor of the new civilization on the scene.

If the extraterrestrial invaders are "unified and strong," Lasswell concluded, "Earth will be at a disadvantage."

In a classic encounter with "extraterrestrial invaders," some earthlings in Kentucky found themselves at a definite disadvantage in fighting off their alien foes. No matter how many times they got shot, the doggone little critters just wouldn't stay down.

The Aliens in Their Nickel-Plated Bulletproof Vests

On the evening of August 21, 1955, a UFO touched down in a rural area outside of Kelly-Hopkinsville, Kentucky, and set loose a bizarre group of alien invaders on eight adults and three children who had gathered at the Gaither McGehe farm for some Sunday evening fellowship. Representatives of the Air Force, local police, and area newspapers conducted an extensive and well-documented investigation of what has become a classic encounter in the annals of UFO research. The adults involved in the incident were found to be rather staid, reserved individuals, the kind of people unlikely to have invented such a wild and incredible adventure for the sake of sensational publicity. Some even went so far as to leave town when the curiosity seekers and flying saucer cultists began to arrive in the community, and they remained consistently reluctant to discuss the ordeal with Air Force personnel or other investigators.

According to the Sutton family, who were renting the Gaither McGehe farm, their teenaged son, Billy Ray, had left the farmhouse that Sunday evening to get a drink from the well. As he drank the cool water from the chipped cup that was set by the well, he was startled to see a bright object land about a city block away from the farmhouse.

According to all those assembled there that evening, Billy Ray's observation of the strange aerial phenomenon was met with a pronounced lack of interest until they saw little men, less than four feet tall with long arms and large, round heads, approaching the farmhouse. The smallish invaders looked like monsters with their nickel-plated jumpsuits, their glowing, yellow eyes, and their general otherworldly appearance.

Fearing for their lives, the farmers picked up the Suttons' rifles and shotguns and began to fire upon the alien creatures. They told investigators that such a counterattack on the monsters was to no avail. The bullets just seemed to bounce off the little beings' nickel-plated armor.

Although the Suttons and their neighbors were positive that they made direct hits on the creatures, they just jumped right up and disappeared into the darkness, only to regroup for another charge toward the farmers in the house. According to the farmers' observations to various investigators of the shootout, the alien beings' extremely large eyes appeared to be very sensitive to light. In retrospect, they all felt that it had been the farmhouse's outside lights, rather than the farmers' bullets, that had truly prevented the invaders from advancing into the home.

The Suttons and their neighbors battled the seemingly invulnerable little monsters for nearly four hours before they managed to get into their motor vehicles and drive in panic to the Hopkinsville police station to get reinforcements. Chief Greenwell was convinced by the hysteria of the three children and the obvious fear of the eight adults that they had definitely been battling *something* out there on the old McGehe place. Everyone in those parts knew that the Suttons were not a drinking family or prone to exaggerations.

With Chief Greenwell in the lead, more than a dozen state, country, and city law enforcement officers arrived to investigate the farmers' claims and, if necessary, do battle with the alien invaders. On the way to the farm scene, the officers noticed what appeared to be a peculiar shower of meteors coming from the direction of the Sutton farmhouse. One officer later said that the meteors had made a "swishing sound" as they passed overhead.

Although the small army of investigators found no traces of extraterrestrial aliens or their spaceship, they found several "peculiar signs and indications" that something mighty strange had taken place that evening on the Suttons' farm. For one thing, the teetotaling, conservative Suttons and their neighbors had thought whatever they perceived real enough and threat enough to put bullet holes in the walls of every barn and outbuilding on the place.

Sutton claimed that he had blasted one of the beings point-blank with his shotgun, only to have the creature simply do a somersault and roll off into the darkness. Taylor, one of the men at the Sutton place that night, told investigators that he had knocked one of the little men off a barrel with a .22. "I heard the bullet hit the critter and ricochet off," he said. "The little man floated to the ground and rolled up like a ball. I used up four boxes of shells on the little men."

THE ABDUCTORS

Martha was abducted while she was driving home from working late at the restaurant where she is employed as a waitress. She remains very bitter that her close encounter with beings from a UFO left her with awful memories of physical abuse at the hands of "little people who cooed and chippered like birds."

Likening her abduction experience to having been sexually molested, Martha said, "Those *things* touched me in places where I don't invite the fingers of just anyone—especially total and completely weird strangers. At first, I really felt that they intended to torture me. When they started taking blood samples, I thought they were going to bleed me to death."

Betty said that a smallish entity of a "gray, lifeless color" took blood from the back of her hand after she had been taken aboard a craft of some kind. At the time of her communication to our office, there was still a faint scar on her hand.

"The puncture mark was sore for three weeks," she said. "It is located on the back of my right hand, on the vein that leads to the ring finger. I have Rh-negative type O blood. I am also certain that the gray entity also punctured my navel with a needle before I passed out."

Charles is haunted by the memory of lying naked on a table in a small, metallic room in some kind of vehicle. He felt sedated, calm, and trusting. Shadowy figures moved around him, poking and probing his flesh. He is convinced that sometime during that experience some kind of device was implanted in his brain.

"Ever since then, I sometimes hear a crackling sound in my head, like some kind of integration process is trying to occur. On occasion, I feel heat and pain in my head. My perceptions have changed dramatically. I know *them* now, deep inside. I feel them. I sense them. I feel the need to broaden and sharpen my senses."

What is the true meaning of the UFO abduction experience? Can it truly be that Earth men and women are being taken aboard alien vehicles and given bizarre medical examinations? Does the intelligence behind the phenomenon of the UFO abductions only wish to examine our physical bodies out of curiosity regarding another species? Or are they attempting somehow to use their advanced technology to transmute us into a more advanced version of *Homo sapiens?* Are those men and women who are being examined by these smallish alien entities being evaluated as possible citizens of a brave new world? Or are they being assessed as participants in some intergalactic experiment in species crossbreeding?

Did Her "UFO Dreams" Make Her Pregnant?

Twenty-six-year-old Mary B. is convinced that she has a special mission here on Earth, but she is very confused as to what it might be. In a report attached to her questionnaire, she stated that she had begun having dreams about "UFO people" when she was only five. In her dreams, she would see a large spaceship hovering over her parents' home, and then on a beam of light, smallish alien beings, very elflike in appearance, would come into her room and look at her.

Mary said that they seemed to be examining her, as if they were doctors of some kind. They never spoke to her, and their tiny mouths seemed fixed in a permanent kind of half-quizzical smile. She was fascinated, rather than alarmed, by their presence in her bedroom.

As she grew older, the examinations continued. Mary remembers having her dramatic "UFO dreams" at least every few months. Shortly after she turned ten, the entities came to her, took her by the hand, and seemed to lift her out of her body and take her to some kind of astral realm.

During that strange visit to another world, Mary recalls being taken to a lovely pink room where everything was soft, gentle, and loving. She remembers very pleasant music playing in the background. She couldn't identify the melody as any familiar tune, but it relaxed her and made her feel very comfortable. She felt somehow as though she had been taken to a nursery.

Her most dramatic interaction with the aliens occurred when she was thirteen. She was visited in her room by the smallish entities who stood back in the corner while a much more human-appearing man approached her. Although Mary swore in her written account of the incident that she had not had any kind of physical experience with any boy her own age or any older man, she was aware that the stranger was engaging in sexual intercourse with her. The man caressed her, but did not speak or make sounds of any kind.

Within two months, Mary said that she knew she was pregnant. She was only thirteen years old, and she was very frightened. She could not work up the nerve to tell her parents because of the bizarre circumstances. She considered telling her school counselor, but she could not bear the shame and humiliation. How could anyone believe that she got pregnant through a dream? How could she make anyone believe that her only sexual experience came from the strange man who entered her room on a beam of light, the man who was accompanied by the same elflike entities who had been visiting her since she was five years old?

Then, she reports, she had another dream in which the familiar entities came to her room and seemed once again to examine her. This time she felt a bit of pain, and she clearly remembers lying as if she were paralyzed while the little people performed some kind of operation on her.

"A short time after this dream," Mary said, "my periods resumed. I knew with all my being and my inner conviction that I was no longer pregnant.

"Several months later, I had the last of my UFO dreams. The smallish people took me aboard this spacecraft. Once again I was in that beautiful pink room, and this time I was looking at a baby—a beautiful baby boy. The entities smiled and indicated that I could pick up the baby. I did so, and I had the strongest feeling that I was holding my own child. I caressed him and said, 'I love you.' "

Then, Mary said, everything became hazy: "The pink room seemed to get smaller and smaller, and I seemed to be covered with a pink mist. I awakened back in my room. That was years ago now, and I have never had another UFO dream of that type."

THE REPTILIAN GRAYS

I first participated as an observer in the hypnotic regression of men and women who claimed to have been abducted by crew members from UFOs in 1967 and recorded hundreds of hours of remarkable data. Later, from 1972 to 1994, I myself conducted dozens of hypnotic regression sessions with UFO contactees or abductees who recalled having been given some kind of medical examination by alien beings. In some instances, the experiencers still bore peculiar punctures and markings in their flesh.

Among the hundreds of abductees, contactees, and other witnesses of alleged extraterrestrial activity whom I have interviewed, there has been a general consensus among the percipients:

The UFOnauts stood between four and half to five feet tall and were dressed in one-piece, very tight-fitting clothing, usually gray or greenish-gray in color.

Their skin color was most often reported as being gray or greenish-gray, and they seemed devoid of body hair of any kind.

Their heads were round, large, disproportionately over-sized by our human standards. In a few reports, pointed ears were mentioned, but usually the witnesses commented that the aliens had no external ears of any kind.

Their facial features were dominated by large, lidless, star-ing eyes, very often with slit catlike or reptilian pupils. They had no discernible lips, and where one might expect to see a nose, the witnesses cited only nostrils, nearly flush against the smooth texture of the face. On a few occasions, witnesses reported very flat noses, or in some cases, tiny "stubs."

Since my early investigation into the UFO enigma in the late 1960s, it has seemed apparent to me that if humankind is indeed interacting with an extraterrestrial species, then those UFOnauts, the "Grays" as they are nicknamed, are represen-tatives of technologically superior reptilian or amphibian humanoids. Furthermore, it also seems evident that these Serpent People have been interacting with Earth for millions of years—either appearing in cycles of programmed visita-tions or steadily monitoring our species' technological and society development from underground or undersea bases.

When we wondered in Chapter 8 who had been inhabit-ing the underground caverns and leaving bipedal humanlike footprints in the sands of time over 250 million years ago, one speculative answer was that these impressions had been made by extraterrestrial visitors. Now let us theorize that these visitors may have been members of a reptilian hu-manoid culture that evolved into the dominant species on their planet millions of years ago—and who for at least 250 million years has interacted in Earth's evolution as colonizers, observers, or perhaps even the genetic engineers who helped to design *Homo sapiens* and greatly accelerate our species' physical and intellectual evolution.

Nearly every ancient culture has its legends of wise Serpent Kings who came from the sky to advance the benevolent and civilizing rule of the Sons of Heaven upon Earth. To name only a few, there is Quetzalcoatl, the feathered serpent of the Aztecs, who descended from heaven in a silver egg; Oannes, half-human, half-fish, who surfaced from the Persian Gulf to instruct the early inhabitants of Mesopotamia in the arts of civilization; the Nagas, the handsome, semidivine Serpent People with supernatural powers who figure in the Hindu and Buddhist traditions. The awe and respect that our ancestors had for these wise serpentlike humanoids has very likely been retained in our collective unconscious today.

Let us suppose that after this highly advanced extraterrestrial reptilian species had been observing the evolution of Earth for millions of years, they made a decision to interfere with the slow, gradual evolutionary process of *Homo sapiens* and initiated a program of genetic engineering whereby they accelerated the physical and intellectual development of one of humankind's early bipedal ancestors. Exceedingly detached and patient in its approach to such scientific projects, the reptilians experimented with skin pigmentation, facial and body hair, height, weight, and intelligence in their efforts to improve developing humankind.

At the same time, of course, the planet's natural process of selection and survival was taking place, so that by the time the serpentine scientists had created cities of rather sophisticated inhabitants about 200,000 years ago, Neanderthal was just beginning to huddle together in caves.

By 100,000 years ago, the genetic engineers from beyond

the stars looked with pride upon a flourishing culture that had spread its influence throughout every section of the planet. These extraterrestrially accelerated humans, known today as the Titans, the inhabitants of Atlantis, Lemuria, and Mu, structured a technology that was beginning to rival that of the Serpent Gods from the stars. The Atlans also learned how to manipulate and to control the natural energies of Earth. Sadly, most of these forces and technologies were developed for purposes of exploitation and destruction. Tragically, little thought had been given by the reptilian genetic engineers to teaching humankind about the individual sovereignty of others. To complicate matters even further, the humans had turned out to be a prolific species, which seemed to take special delight in reproducing. What had begun as an earthly paradise engineered by the Serpent People had deteriorated into a civilization of civil strife and internal warfare.

A great catastrophe is supposed to have submerged the great island kingdoms beneath the seas. Nearly all the Atlans and the Lemurians died in the splintering of their world or in its sinking beneath the ocean. Those who did survive the destruction of their lost continent spread the accounts of the death of a great civilization in prehistory, and the tales have been passed to our time through the many variations of the Great Deluge legends.

A discomforting element in this hypothesis is the very strong possibility that the reptilian genetic engineers who helped program early humankind may have been the very same ones who were responsible for the great cataclysms that destroyed what they coldly assessed as an experiment that got out of control. The Serpent People may have come to the conclusion that they had acted inappropriately when they decided to interfere with the natural evolutionary process of Earth, and they resolved to "correct" their error and to pass an edict that their kind would never again interact with us in an overt manner. After the world before our own that we remember in our species' collective unconscious was destroyed, colonies of the Serpent People then retreated into underground caves and caverns and great numbers of their reptilian race elected to return to the stars.

Rumors of such rich underground kingdoms as that of the Naga, the proud and attractive Serpent People of Indian tradition, have been kept alive for centuries with certain heroes and leaders from many different cultures even claiming that they themselves may be the result of a mating between reptilian and human parents. From time to time the wise ones leave the caves to tutor select earthlings and to assist the intellectual and technological, rather than the physical, evolution of the surface dwellers.

Then, in the late 1940s, when a series of violent detonations demonstrated that humans have developed nuclear power and may become a threat to other worlds as well as their own, the subterranean Serpent People send their saucer-shaped aerial vehicles into the skies to monitor the potentially dangerous activities of the human topsiders.

After the crash of one of their craft in Roswell, New Mexico, in July 1947, the reptilian Grays begin cautiously to reveal themselves and allow certain of their underground bases to be toured by select members of the U.S. military and government. An alliance is made between the Grays, who considered themselves to be native Terrans, the descendents of the Serpent People, and representatives of a secret government that operated in the shadows of those who had been elected by the democratic political system. Unfortunately, the more benevolent and loyal of the Grays are very soon supplanted by mercenary agents of the Draco, an extraterrestrial race of reptilians that is in the process of reclaiming Earth. The devious Draco-Grays envision ways to dupe the shadow government, whose representatives seem to be motivated primarily by greed, personal aggrandizement, and the desire for military superiority over other topside nations.

Around 1954, the shadow group makes a secret deal with the Grays that permits mutilation of cattle and the abduction of humans in exchange for their advanced extraterrestrial technology. The Grays offer assurances that the human abductions would merely be ongoing examinations designed to enable them to monitor a developing civilization; but by 1982, there are steadily increasing reports of women who claim unusual and unwanted pregnancies after their abduction experience aboard alien spacecraft, which are now steadily arriving from the Draco's home planet. In certain instances these pregnancies are terminated by the extraterrestrials, who remove the fetuses in subsequent abductions. In other cases, the earthwomen are monitored during the pregnancy and the birth of their hybrid star children.

After receiving a large number of such reports, including those in which male abductees claim semen was taken from them, the shadow agencies of the terrestrial governments are forced to conclude that the alien visitors are performing unauthorized crossbreeding experiments with unwilling human subjects—and there is nothing they can do to stop them.

Hypothesis or frightening truth?

Proponents of underground alien bases remain adamant that certain areas of the United States, particularly the southwestern states, are crisscrossed by an intricate tunnel system that lead to massive UFO hangars and scientific laboratories. The Archuleta Mesa, near Dulce, New Mexico, is the place most often mentioned by UFO enthusiasts, many of whom camp there for days at a time, performing self-imposed surveillance duty. The mysterious Area 51 in the Nevada desert also ranks high as a hiding place for underground extraterrestrials, allegedly sharing alien technology with aereonautical engineers. Some UFO researchers maintain that there is even an underground alien base beneath the Denver Airport.

THE TERROR ON THE GROUND:
THE MEN IN BLACK

The Men in Black, the notorious MIB, are a phenomenon within a phenomenon. In many instances, those witnesses who have been percipients of UFO activity—or such related manifestations as Bigfoot-type creatures, monsters, and phantom entities—have suffered a peculiar kind of personal harassment. At first, there are often sinister voices that whisper threats on the telephone and warn researchers and witnesses of unusual phenomena to terminate specific investigations or to forget entirely what they have seen. Those who have taken photographs or videos of UFOs or obtained any kind of physical evidence of paranormal phenomena have been called upon by rather mysterious men dressed in black who confiscate the pictures, the negatives, the video film, or whatever proof the witnesses may have had of their sighting—very often by claiming government affiliation.

In the majority of such instances, those who received such an unwelcome visit from the MIB described their inquisitors as rather short men, very often five foot six or less, with dark complexions and somewhat Asian features. When pressed for more complete descriptions and details, the witnesses have stated that the MIB usually wore dark glasses, but if the "shades" were ever removed, they had very large eyes that were noticeably slanted, but slanted in a manner somehow different from Asians. Some witnesses have mentioned peculiarly misshapen ears. Other percipients have taken notice that the MIB seem to have difficulty speaking because of their short-windedness, often suggestive of severely afflicted asthmatics.

In certain instances, the MIB behaved in a manner assessed by witnesses as more silly than threatening. Some who have received a visit by such strange individuals have said that they felt as though they were being interrogated by comedians, Three Stooges–type characters, who were only pretending to be tough and authoritative Air Force or government investigators.

Many researchers have noted that the MIB seem obsessed with time when they are questioning witnesses of UFO or paranormal activity. Very often they will begin an interrogation by asking the time, as if they are somehow uncertain of the process of measuring time. Others have commented that the MIB are often dressed in outdated styles and often use slang expressions that have long been out of vogue.

After witnesses of UFO or paranormal phenomena have received a visit from the MIB and surrendered whatever evidence the alleged agents of the government demanded, the harassment is by no means over. Telephones ring at all hours with threatening or nonsensical mechanical voices. Television and radio programs are interrupted by weird signals, claiming to be of alien origin. Network video and audio are blotted out to be replaced by images of robed, sometimes cowled, figures, who instruct the witnesses to continue to cooperate and to keep all UFO information confidential. In exchange for this silence and cooperation, the mysterious entities sometimes promise the witnesses key roles in marvelous projects that will benefit all humankind.

Beginning in 1947, shortly after the alleged UFO crash outside of Roswell, New Mexico, and continuing to 2001, thousands of UFO and paranormal witnesses, investigators, abductees, contactees, and even chance percipients of UFO overflights claim to have been visited by ominous strangers dressed in black who made it frighteningly clear that they represented a powerful and everywhere-present *someone* who would violently enforce their orders to discontinue research or to surrender all artifacts, video films, and photographs. Often such threats have been punctuated with the allegation that such cooperation was essential for "the good of your family, your country, and your world."

My friend the late author-researcher Michael Talbot once pointed out that Eastern mysticism has an interesting analog for the MIB phenomenon, known as the Brothers of the Shadow. Talbot said that according to Eastern adepts, the Brothers of the Shadow are cunning and evil, intent upon keeping a student of the occult from finding out the proverbial answer to the true nature of reality.

"In mystical jargon, this answer is the 'Veil of Isis,' " Talbot said, "and is synonymous with the 'Great Secret' of Maeterlink. In occultism, as in the UFO mystery, there is recorded a constant barrage of psychic hoaxes. The Brothers of the Shadow, like the MIB, are known for threatening students of the occult whenever they get too close to lifting the Veil of Isis. As Madame Blavatsky said when referring to the Brothers of the Shadow, they are 'the leading "stars" on the great spiritual stage of materialization.' "

Paranoia may become highly contagious, but I have become convinced through personal investigation—and personal experience—from 1966 to the present day that the phenomenon known euphemistically as the Men in Black is very real and that its victims are not simply suffering from particularly eerie delusions. There have been cases in which clumsy, amateurish researchers with few social graces and absolutely no skills in interviewing witnesses of UFO activity have unwittingly—or dimwittedly—assumed the role of the MIB. In a few other instances, actual government agencies with careless and indifferent personnel may have inadvertently intimidated percipients of UFO phenomena and unknowingly fit the descriptions of the menacing Men in Black. But in my opinion, 98 percent of true MIB visitations have been from paraphysical entities from a Great Phenomenon that exists in the dimension of the unknown that we as yet can view only "through a glass darkly."

The best way to deal with visitations from such entities is to refuse to play their game—and especially do not cast them in the role of bad guys. It is this dualism that comes so quickly to humans that sets up an atmosphere of conflict with the aliens that approach us from out of the dark. If you permit or encourage hostility, then that is what you will receive.

I believe that the manner in which the so-called MIB conduct themselves depends to a large part on the nature and attitude of the percipient with whom they have chosen to interact. They provide immediate feedback, as if they were malign echoes. Cry out in fear, and they will give you good reason to fear them. Threaten them, and they will prove how threatening they can truly become—and how quickly they can carry out their maledictions.

I have become convinced that such aspects of the Greater Phenomenon as the MIB are constructed primarily as teaching mechanisms. The important thing for those who find themselves victims of the negative aspects of the phenomenon is to begin at once to structure their reality to exclude such entities of darkness as the MIB, thereby breaking their hold on their conscious and unconscious thought processes. Refuse to play their game—and you will soon deprive them of the energy that they need to exist in our physical dimension. They will then be forced to return to the shadows whence they came.

NIGHTMARES UNLIMITED

By now the attentive reader will have noticed that the monsters from Outer Space are beginning to sound very much like all the scary creatures from Earth that we have glimpsed peering at us from out of the dark wherever we have sought the Beings from Beyond. The apelike monsters seen lumbering near UFOs seem very much like Bigfoot and Sasquatch. The Grays conducting their hybrid breeding experiments between their kind and abducted humans seem very much like the wee people . . . or the dero. And are the Men in Black really the agents of a secret government agency or shapeshifting demons serving his Satanic Majesty in his eternal mischief of sowing seeds of confusion and distrust?

Could all these seemingly disparate phenomena be nothing more than programmed illusions beamed at us by extraterrestrials who are psychologically probing our reactions and responses to things that go bump in the night? Or are there truly wicked dero directing their telepathic rays at us while we sleep, tormenting our dreams and frightening our waking hours, just for their own sadistic satisfaction?

Perhaps all of these varied eerie manifestations issue from an unseen world of spirits that is as close to us as the unwelcome sound of *something* scratching on our pillow at night as we lie in our beds, attempting fitful sleep. Vampires and werewolves that must subsist on the blood of others might really be grotesque spirits, true members of the undead, who seek our life force to sustain their shadowy existence in a dimension whose borders overlap with our own. Maybe our entire planet is haunted with the ghosts of yesterdays and unrealized tomorrows.

One thing is certain: For reasons yet undetermined by the psychologists who seek to chart the hidden corridors of the mind, there is something within the human psyche that craves monsters. Philosophers may write that all we see or seem is but a dream within a dream, but it may be our nightmares that truly inspire us to get out of bed and accomplish something meaningful to hold back the greater terrors of hatred, distrust, and fear of our brothers and sisters.

Do we love monsters because they make the adrenaline surge in an otherwise structured and humdrum workaday world? Or does the very thought of creatures that defy science, reason, and logic thriving very well, thank you, in our caves, lakes, seas, and skies stretch the elastic of the imagination and pump up the creative juices?

Well, be assured, my friend, the monsters are out there. Whatever the well-intentioned rationalists and materialists in your world might try to tell you, monsters are real. Somewhere in the darkness, there is a monster who knows your name. And it may be as near to you as your next nervous glance over your shoulder.

Acknowledgments

A special thanks for the use of their remarkable photographs of paranormal phenomena must go to:

Timothy Green Beckley
Global Communications
11 E. 30th Street #4R
New York, NY 10016

Jose Escamilla
Escamilla Filmworks
14100 Calvert St. #2
Van Nuys, CA 91401

Clarisa Bernhardt
P.O. Box 669 Station Main
Winnipeg, Manitoba R3C
2K3 Canada

Frank "Nick" Nocerino
P.O. Box 302
Pinole, CA 94564

Paul B. Bartholomew
203 Broadway
Whitehall, NY 12887

Chuck Pelton
Pelton Publications
1371 Kilrush Court
Pinole, CA 94564

Barry A. Conrad
Barcon Video Productions
3653 Mesa Lila Lane
Glendale, CA 91208

Index